THE
EVERYTHING
ASTROLOGY
BOOK

The Everything Series:

THE
EVERYTHING
ASTROLOGY
BOOK

Discover your true self among the stars!

Trish MacGregor

Adams Media Corporation
Holbrook, Massachusetts

Dedication

With much love to Rob and Megan,
the Taurus and Virgo who ground me;
to Mom and Dad, the best of Capricorn and Libra;
and to Barbara Jaynes, Scorpio and kindred soul

Acknowledgments

Special thanks to Al Zuckerman and Pamela Liflander,
the Virgo and Libra who got the ball rolling,
and to Renie Wiley and Phyllis Vega for their expertise.

An Everything Series Book. The Everything Series
is a trademark of Adams Media Corporation.

Published by Adams Media Corporation
260 Center Street, Holbrook, MA 02343

ISBN: 1-58062-062-0

Printed in the United States of America.

J I H G F E D C

Library of Congress Cataloging-in-Publication Data
The everything astrology book / Trish MacGregor.
          p.   cm.
        ISBN 1-58062-062-0
       1. Astrology. II. Title.
       BF1708.1.M29   1998
       133.5—dc21   98-17890
                          CIP

Illustrations by Barry Littmann

*This book is available at quantity discounts for bulk purchases.
For information, call 1-800-872-5627 (in Massachusetts, call 781-767-8100).*

The author can be reached at mac111@ix.netcom.com

Visit our home page at http://www.adamsmedia.com

CONTENTS

Part Two: The Houses

Part Three: Aspects

CONTENTS

Introduction

In November 1981, I was teaching English to Cuban refugees through a federally funded program at Florida International University in Miami. A reporter from a local newspaper came to the Fort Lauderdale center where I taught to do a story on the program.

He was a Taurus; I'm a Gemini. Earth to air, fixed to mutable. On the surface, that combination didn't thrill me. But the chemistry was there and I'm an optimist, so I asked for his birth data and drew up his birth chart.

Back then the computations were done the old fashioned way, without the convenience of computer software. It took awhile. But as soon as I looked at the man's natal chart and compared it to my own, I understood the pattern. It struck me at a visceral level. It felt right. It resonated.

Taurus rules my seventh house of marriage and partnerships. My Venus and Mars occupy that house, each exerting its sphere of influence. In terms of romance, it meant I had an instinctive understanding of Taurus. A lot of energy would go into the relationship, which might spill over into a business partnership as well.

In the man's chart, his Mercury was in my sun sign of Gemini in the first house of self. Since Mercury is the "mental" planet, this indicated he would be intellectually attracted to a Gemini. Also, Gemini ruled his second house of finances and material possessions, with Uranus deposited firmly in that house. This indicated he would gain suddenly and unexpectedly in financial areas through a Gemini and/or Gemini-related pursuits. I recognized enough similarities in our horoscope patterns to move ahead, with sufficient differences to keep things interesting.

Eighteen months later, the man and I got married. We've been married fourteen years now. Both of us are full-time writers, and act as each other's first editors.

This is just one instance in which astrology proves valuable. The prevalent patterns seized my attention, but what I chose to do with those patterns was entirely up to me—and to him.

None of us is the sum total of our sun signs, our moons, our rising signs, our aspects. Nothing is cast in stone. Astrology is merely a tool that illuminates our passage through life; it's the pattern the soul chose to come in with. It indicates propensities, talents,

challenges, hints, and clues. Free will remains the wild card that makes even identical twins very different.

This book focuses on natal or birth astrology, which is based on the time, date, and place of your birth. Computer software programs that sell for as little as ten dollars can compute the complex math in fifteen or twenty seconds. Most New Age bookstores charge five or six dollars for a computerized natal chart.

It will be helpful if you have your chart handy as you read through the chapters. But even if you don't, the section on sun signs provides a broad spectrum of information about work, romance, and finances. Do NOT base your life on astrological generalities. Use the inherent patterns in your birth chart in conjunction with your own intuition. Then bring your free will to bear against the patterns in your chart that disturb you. After all, *you* create your destiny.

The advantages of an astrological viewpoint begin with living in tune with nature rather than in alienation from it.

—THOMAS MOORE
The Re-Enchantment of Everyday Life

What Is Astrology?

CHAPTER 1

A Few Basics

Astrology describes our potential, not our fate. It's an organic system rather than a mechanistic device, something that grows and deepens as we learn its symbols and begin to understand its language. It deals with *patterns* that prevail in our lives; it's one way of interpreting our individual realities. It increases our awareness and knowledge of ourselves and the people around us. It empowers us.

In natal astrology, the patterns in a chart are created by the date, time, and place of birth. These three elements individualize the chart and place the planets within particular signs and within the twelve houses of the horoscope.

In addition to the Sun and the Moon, a chart includes the sign and placement of the planets: Mercury, Venus, Mars, Jupiter, Saturn, Uranus, Neptune, and Pluto. Many astrologers also include the North and South Nodes of the Moon, the Part of Fortune, some of the asteroids, the Vertex, and Midpoints.

The Birth Chart

I was seventeen when I first became interested in astrology. In retrospect, I suspect the interest was triggered by a drastic change in my family life—not a divorce or the death of a parent or sibling, nothing that tragic. The event was a move.

For sixteen years, I had enjoyed an idyllic life as the child of American parents living abroad. I was born and raised in Caracas, Venezuela. My roots were there. I knew nothing else. But the political situation had deteriorated to the point where many American families were pulling out and my parents decided to leave as well.

Suddenly, I was deposited in a country where everyone was supposed to be equal and life was supposed to be great. This was in late 1963, early 1964, and I quickly discovered that equality for women hadn't yet arrived on this democratic shore. I didn't fit in. I didn't understand American life. So I began to look for answers in the most unlikely places.

Other than learning the language of astrology so I could draw up charts, my main concern was philosophical. Were the specifics of

my birth—date, time, and place—as random as they appeared to be?
If so, then the tendencies in my birth chart were merely coinci-
dental, the product of a physical act that produced a child nine
months later.

This idea pointed at a universe that was purely random and
went against what I sensed intuitively. Over the years, as I delved
into astrology and other facets of metaphysics, I came to regard the
birth chart as a blueprint of the soul's intent. I began to view my life
as an opportunity to achieve those intentions. I discovered that certain aspects (geometrical angles formed between planets) in my
birth chart coincided with certain tensions and stresses in my life. I
realized that some of these aspects also matched areas of ease and
pleasure in what I experienced.

From this point on, any time I did a birth chart, I interpreted
it as an organic whole, a living pattern of who the individual
was and might be. A birth chart became a kind of hologram
encoded with information that could be used for self-awareness.
It didn't matter whether I or anyone else was the random
product of a sexual union; I recognized the practical value of
astrology. The question of who or what had set the whole thing
in motion mattered less than the fact that I had found a tool
that worked for me.

Eventually, I came to believe that my original intuition was correct, that we really are masters of our own destiny. I came to believe
that we choose it all, that before birth our souls select the circumstances into which we are born—and the optimal astrological conditions that will allow us the opportunity to develop and evolve
spiritually. These conditions are outward expressions of internal
needs and help create the reality we experience. Within these patterns, our free will reigns supreme.

This concept seems deceptively easy to grasp at first. But as you
work with it, peeling back the layers, you realize that everything
which happens to you—from the grand to the mundane—is the result
of a belief that you hold. And if it's your belief, you can change it. If
you change the core belief, your experience also changes. This is
what empowers you.

The next three tables show the various symbols you'll be using
in this book.

Table 1-1: Signs and Symbols

There are twelve signs and each has a symbol, an astrological shorthand.

Aries	♈	Libra	♎
Taurus	♉	Scorpio	♏
Gemini	♊	Sagittarius	♐
Cancer	♋	Capricorn	♑
Leo	♌	Aquarius	♒
Virgo	♍	Pisces	♓

Table 1-2: Planets and Symbols

Besides the Sun and the Moon, we'll be using eight planets, two nodes, and the Part of Fortune in birth charts.

Sun	☉	Uranus	♅
Moon	☽	Neptune	♆
Mercury	☿	Pluto	♀
Venus	♀	North Node	☊
Mars	♂	South Node	☋
Jupiter	♃	Part of Fortune	PF/⊕
Saturn	♄		

Table 1-3: Aspects and Symbols

Due to the placement of planets in the houses, geometric angles are created between the planets and between the planets and the angles of the houses. These angles are called aspects. Each aspect has a particular function, meaning, and symbol. In this book, the following aspects are used:

Conjunction ☌: A separation of 0 degrees between two or more planets

Sextile ✶: A separation of 60 degrees between two or more planets

Square □: A separation of 90 degrees between two or more planets

Trine △: A separation of 120 degrees between two or more planets

Opposition ☍: A separation of 180 degrees between two or more planets

Other symbols used in a birth chart are:

Ascendant or rising sign, **AS**: The sign and degree of the zodiac rising at the time of birth

Descendant, **DS:** Opposite the Ascendant, cusp of the seventh house.

Midheaven or Medium Coeli, **MC**: The highest point of the zodiac at the time of birth

Imum Coeli or Nadir, **IC**: The zodiac point opposite the midheaven

Other symbols you'll see in the charts but which we won't discuss are:

Equatorial Ascendant **Eq:** The ascendant of the chart if you'd been born at the equator. Symbolizes who you think you are.

Vertex **Vtx:** A point of fate or destiny.

What a Birth Chart Looks Like

A birth chart is circular, with 360 degrees. The ascendant, represented by a horizontal line through the middle of the chart in Figure 1-1, forms the horizon. The space above it is south of the horizon; the space below it is north.

The ascendant (**AS**) is intersected by the meridian, the axis that connects the Midheaven (**MC**) and the Nadir or Imum Coeli (**IC**). The space to the left of the meridian is east; the space to the right is west.

These directions are the opposite of what they usually are because we live in the northern hemisphere, "on top" of the planet. This means the sun is due south when it reaches the peak of its daily arc at noon.

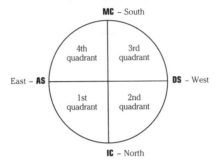

Figure 1-1

The birth chart in Figure 1-2 shows an ascendant in Pisces, a Sun in Virgo, and a Moon in Virgo. The numbers inside each of the pie shapes represent the houses. In the lower left-hand corner is a graph that depicts the various aspects of the chart.

This is a child's chart (1989 birth year). It's quite straightforward, and shows clearly defined areas of the *soul's intent*. We'll be referring back to it in later chapters as you begin to put together everything you've learned.

Past Life Astrology

Even if you don't believe you've lived before, your astrologer probably believes it and can pinpoint elements in your chart that seem to confirm it.

Jeanne Avery, writing in *Astrology and Your Past Lives*, emphasizes the sign, house placement, and aspects to the planet Saturn as hints about lives you might have lived. Mary Devlin, author of *Astrology & Past Lives*, contends that "the incarnating entity chooses the time most astrologically advantageous for its mission on Earth."

Edgar Cayce, the famed sleeping prophet of Virginia Beach, gave many readings that included astrological information on past lives. These readings were studied by the Association of Research and Enlightenment, the organization that Cayce's sons and grandsons perpetuated, and the ARE now offers past life astrology charts based on Cayce's reading.

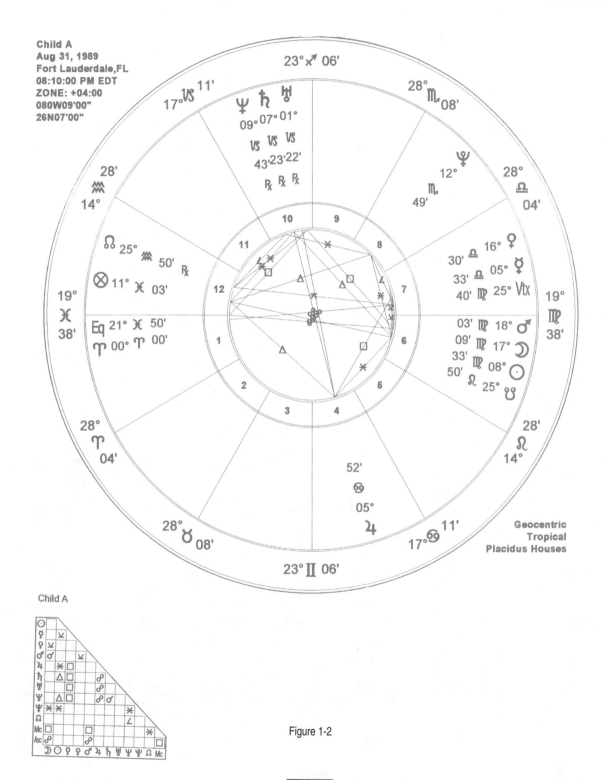

Child A
Aug 31, 1989
Fort Lauderdale,FL
08:10:00 PM EDT
ZONE: +04:00
080W09'00"
26N07'00"

Geocentric
Tropical
Placidus Houses

Child A

Figure 1-2

Other astrologers look to the Moon's nodes for evidence of past lives. Astrologer Martin Schulman, writing in *Karmic Astrology*, says: "To a qualified expert a knowledge of the Sun, Moon, and Nodal positions can reveal the entire life of the individual. It is through the Nodes that Western astrology is now able to make its first inroads into related this divine science to the Hindu concept of reincarnation."

Most astrologers eventually arrive at some aspect or configuration that tells them about the past lives of the people whose charts they erect. It may well be Saturn or the Moon's nodes; but it may be something else. The practice of astrology, particularly in relation to past lives, is a highly individual pursuit.

Avery backs up her research with Saturn through hypnotic regression. Astrologer Mary Devlin accumulated four hundred horoscopes that included reincarnational histories derived through hypnotic regression as the basis for her book, *Astrology & Past Lives*.

She notes that past life birth charts are obtained through two methods, which are sometimes combined. In the first method, research has located the recorded birth date for a past personality. In the second method, an individual, while under regression, is asked to tune in psychically to his or her birth date in a particular past life.

"The birth data is then run through a computer. The resulting natal-chart features are analyzed carefully to make sure they fit the life and personality (as revealed through regression) of the prior incarnation. About one half of our cases involve subjects with one past-life birth chart; the rest have at least two." By studying the patterns in the birth charts, Devlin was able to formulate the theories in her book.

Under Devlin's system, there are five areas of vital importance:

1. **The Sun**, Ascendant and dominant planets in a chart suggest the primary purpose for incarnation.
2. **The twelfth house** may symbolize the incarnation immediately preceding the present life. In chart interpretation generally, any planets found in this house represent unfinished business.
3. **Uranus, Neptune, and Pluto** symbolize different facets of the "karma" an individual brings with him into his present life.
4. **Saturn** symbolizes characteristics which the soul brings with him into the present life.
5. **The Moon** and its phases and Nodes suggest the path the soul should take in "filling out the outlines of Saturn's destiny formula."

Astrological Patterns

CHAPTER 2

The Broad Strokes

During the Sixties, when astrology enjoyed a boom unlike anything it had known since the late 1800s, it seemed that everyone knew everyone else's sun sign, even if no one was clear what exactly it meant.

A Gemini, for instance, was pegged as bright and fun, flighty and flirtatious, but basically two-faced and superficial. Scorpios were viewed with some trepidation because they were known to get even with people who crossed them. But they allegedly made great lovers. Virgos were known as fussy about details, Capricorns were rigid, Taureans were so stubborn you could never win an argument with them.

These generalities weren't wrong, but they were hardly the full story. It was the equivalent of saying that all pit bulls are terrible, vicious dogs and that all Jack Russell terriers are fabulous with kids. It didn't take into account the vast diversity inherent in every human being. But yes, it was a convenient way to immediately get a handle on someone you'd just met.

Your sun sign is the *pattern* of your overall personality and represents your ego. If you're a Scorpio, you may be an intensely sexual individual who is intuitive and possibly quite psychic. I know that I if I cross you, chances are quite good that you won't forget it. But if I'm loyal to you, I'll have a friend for life. Part of who you are involves the imposition of your will on other people. You have charisma and it's apparent in your personal countenance or in some extraordinary talent you possess.

One Scorpio man I knew, for instance, had taught himself the piano. Give him a keyboard and he could play anything that he'd heard at least once, but he couldn't read a note of music. A Scorpio friend of mine, a woman, has the sort of presence that turns heads when she enters a room. Some people consider her beautiful; others think she's attractive but not gorgeous. No one disputes the fact that she commands attention.

Jones's Patterns

But there is much more to these generalities. Another part of the astrological pattern that appears in a natal chart is formed by the distribution of the planets in the twelve houses of the horoscope. The astrologer Marc Edmond Jones identified seven such patterns or shapes and all horoscopes fall into one of them. Even if your chart isn't an exact fit, one will fit more closely than the others.

The Splash

In this particular shape, the planets are dispersed somewhat evenly around the horoscope with no more than two planets occupying a single house. These people are usually adaptable and have many varied interests. They may scatter ideas around through their communication skills, travels, or talents. They may reach restlessly into unfamiliar areas and transform them. They have a universal approach to life and can be capable of great achievements. Immanuel Kant and Emanuel Swedenborg are examples of the splash type.

The downside for these people is that their thinking may be so scattered that they lack focus and concentration and don't achieve much of anything.

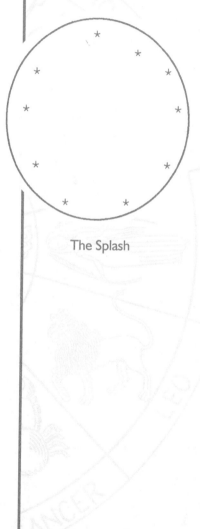

The Splash

The Bucket

This shape has nine planets occupying half of the chart and one planet, often referred to as a "singleton," that occupies the other half. It indicates that most of the individual's activities in life are centered in the occupied portion of the chart. However, the single planet, which forms the bucket's handle, is the focus of the action and often indicates a particular talent or gift.

Sometimes the handle may consist of a pair of planets in conjunction within one degree of each other. The position of the handle is significant. When the handle is upright, energy is intensified. Napoleon is a prime example of this type.

The Bucket

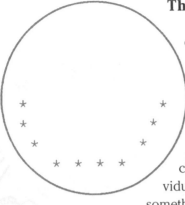

The Bowl

The Bowl

The typical bowl shape has a concentration of planets in half of the chart, with the other half completely devoid of planets. These people tend to be self-contained. They generally aren't the types who look to others for approval or confirmation.

The occupied hemisphere of the chart identifies the areas in which these people make their contributions; the unoccupied half represents the challenge. The planet leading away from the unoccupied part of the chart (the first planet moving clockwise that leads the planets) tells you how the bowl individual can overcome the challenge. These people generally have something to offer others.

The most important element to remember about the bowl is the tilt of the chart. In the child's chart in Figure 1-2, the concentration of the planets lie in the western hemisphere—houses 4–10. The leading planet is Jupiter—♃. Abraham Lincoln and Helen Keller are examples of the bowl type.

The Bundle

In the bundle, the ten planets fit into a space of about 120 degrees, into four, possibly five houses. This shape isn't common and usually indicates some sort of unique quality or trait in the individual. There is a certain narrowness of vision with this shape, which may be enhanced or mitigated by other elements in the chart. Since the planets are concentrated in only a third of the chart, experience tends to be limited to the occupied houses. But the activity in those house is often very powerful. Mussolini and William James are examples of bundle types.

The Bundle

The Seesaw

In this shape, two distinct groups of planets fall opposite each other in the chart. The groups don't have to have an equal number of planets, but all ten planets should be within the two groups. People

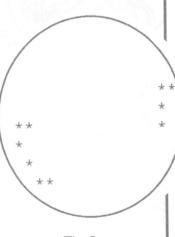

The Seesaw

with this shape to their charts generally seek balance. They weigh all sides of an issue before making a decision. At times, this shape may lead to indecisiveness. But in a strong chart, there's excellent perspective and harmony that can lead to unique achievement. The poet Percy Bysshe Shelley and Rudyard Kipling had seesaw charts.

The Locomotive

The ten planets in this shape fall within nine of the twelve houses. With this configuration, look for self-motivated, charismatic individuals with seemingly endless reservoirs of energy. These people are goal-oriented, action-driven achievers. Isaac Newton and George Washington are examples of the locomotive type.

The Locomotive

The Splay

At first glance, this shape could be what fits when nothing else does. But it actually possesses a particular pattern: two or more planets are bunched together at various points in the chart. These people are often loners who buck the system. They're individualists with their own unique agendas and interests. Henry VIII and the composer Richard Wagner are examples of the splay type.

When interpreting these patterns in charts, it's important to look at the aspects—conjunctions, oppositions, sextiles, squares, trines, and any special aspects like grand trines. Aspects are covered in depth in Part Three of this book.

When you're interpreting a chart, these patterns usually will be the first thing you notice, simply because they're so obvious.

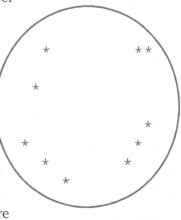

The Splay

Jones's Patterns

Marc Edmund Jones wrote the seminal book on Jones's Patterns in *The Guide to Horoscope Interpretation*. He not only explains the patterns in depth, but offers valuable information in the art of horoscope interpretation.

Sun Signs: An Overview

The Sun symbolizes the ego and how it expresses itself. The sign in which your sun falls influences the goals you choose and how you accomplish those goals.

I have included general comments on health issues that might concern each sun sign and a physical description. An individual's physical appearance, however, is usually influenced more strongly by the ascendant or rising sign, which rules the first house of self.

The twelve sun signs are divided roughly by months, but because those divisions don't follow the months exactly, you may have been born on the cusp between two signs. If you were, then read the interpretations for both signs. If, for instance, you were born on April 19, the cutoff date for Aries, also read the interpretation for Taurus, because some of those attributes probably apply to you.

The signs are grouped according to triplicities (the elements) and quadruplicities (types of activity and adaptability to circumstances). The elements are earth, air, fire, and water; the quadruplicities are cardinal, fixed, and mutable. Planets are also grouped according to gender. Table 2-1 shows these groups for easy reference.

The descriptions of sun signs are broken down into several categories: overview of the sign, women, men, kids, compatibility, romance, work, finances, physical, and spirituality. Under compatibility, a safe rule of thumb is that a given sun sign usually gets along with signs that are sextile—sixty degrees away or one sign removed on either side. An Aries, for instance, gets along with Aquarius and with Gemini. Remember, however, that you can't gauge compatibility with any depth without comparing the natal charts of the people involved.

Table 2-1: Triplicities and Quadruplicities

Triplicities

Air Signs (masculine): Gemini, Libra, Aquarius

Air signs deal with mental abilities and intellectual attributes. Geminis generally have an ease for acquiring, using, and communicating information. Libras weigh, balance, and compare information. Aquarians apply what they know to universal principles.

Fire Signs (masculine): Aries, Leo, Sagittarius

The fire triplicity is characterized by aggression and some kind of leadership. Aries people are good at launching new projects and ideas. Leos excel as managers, CEOs, and the central figure around whom other people gather. Sagittarians are often spiritual and philosophical leaders.

Earth Signs (feminine): Taurus, Virgo, Capricorn

Practicality is the hallmark of earth signs. The pragmatism manifests in the houses where earth planets are found. In Taurus, the practicality may show up as an ability to accumulate and manage material resources. In Virgo, this talent is evident in intellectual matters, in a practical application and use of material resources. Capricorns are terrific organizers and managers of financial and material resources.

Water Signs (feminine): Cancer, Scorpio, Pisces

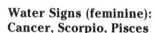

The focus of the water triplicity is on emotion and feeling, intuition, and deeper psychic levels of life. In Cancers, this quality usually manifests around home and family. In Scorpio, it centers around issues that involve death, joint resources, sexuality, and metaphysics. In Pisces people, this quality is most evident in a deep connection to the unconscious. The water signs are also "fruitful," because they are related to fertility.

Quadruplicities

The qualities below apply only in a general sense and should be considered in light of the rest of the chart.

Cardinal Signs: Aries, Cancer, Libra, Capricorn
These people tend to be outgoing and social and initiate new ideas and projects. Their challenge is that they often lack endurance to see new projects to the end.

Mutable Signs: Gemini, Virgo, Sagittarius, Pisces
The hallmark here is adaptability. Mutable signs react to new situations by adapting to them. Their challenge is that they can be too changeable or malleable.

Fixed Signs: Taurus, Leo, Scorpio, Aquarius
These people resist change and continue to act and react according to fixed patterns. They have persistence, but their challenge is inflexibility and stubbornness.

Aries ♈

THE RAM (MARCH 21–APRIL 19)

Element: Fire	**Quality:** Cardinal
Keyword: Leadership, the pioneer spirit	**Planetary Ruler:** Mars
Rules: Head and face; natural ruler of first house	

The pioneering spirit of the typical Aries is the same spirit that settled the United States. These are the people who set out in wagon trains across a vast wilderness more than two centuries ago because they wanted to know what was there. These are the type of people who conceived the NASA space program, who will eventually colonize other planets.

They are bold, courageous, resourceful. They always seem to know what they believe, what they want from life, and where they're going. Aries people are dynamic and aggressive in pursuing their goals, whatever they might be. They're survivors.

The challenge with this sign is persistence. Aries people sometimes lose interest if they don't see rapid results. But this tendency is compensated for by their ambition and drive to succeed. They can be argumentative, lack tact, and have bad tempers. On the other hand, their anger rarely lasts long.

Aries Woman

The bottom line with an Aries woman is don't offend or anger her. If you do, she'll never forget it and you won't see much of her after that. She'll turn her energy to someone or something else. If you're involved with an Aries woman, the relationship had better be one of equality or she won't stick around. This isn't a woman who tolerates chauvinism.

Professionally, she's driven. She sets goals and pursues them with all the relentless energy she possesses. She's great at initiating projects, at launching ideas, and putting things into action. But she isn't particularly good at seeing a project or idea through to its completion, unless she passionately believes in it. She's the type who, way back when, got the wagons rolling westward, went along for part of the journey, and jumped ship long before the wagon train reached California.

She can hold her own in most situations and certainly can compete with any man on the professional front. She exudes an aura of success and dresses to enhance that aura. In romance, her passions are fervent and sometimes all consuming.

Aries Man

He's as bold and brash as his female counterpart and just as impatient and driven. Thanks to his innate courage, he may take up daredevil sports, but with a certain recklessness. He wants to prove himself and takes unnecessary chances and risks.

He's an excellent executive, the kind of man who relies on his own judgment and intuition to make decisions. Like the female Aries, he projects a successful image even if he has failed at endeavors in the past. Some women may find the Aries man too audacious for her tastes, but life with him is never boring. This is the guy who, on a whim, flies to the Caribbean for a long weekend simply to see what's there.

Once an Aries man is smitten, watch out. He brings his considerable energy and drive to the relationship and pursues the woman in a whirlwind of romance. But if the emotion isn't reciprocated quickly, he'll be gone in a flash.

Aries Kids

On a playground filled with children, an Aries child is easy to pick out. He's organizing the others and directing the action. Or he and several of his cronies are out exploring, turning over rocks in a search of interesting bugs.

An Aries child, just like the adult Aries, fears nothing, which is sure to send an over-protective parent into occasional fits. When he doesn't get his own way, watch out for an explosion of temper. But when he's feeling good, he's fun, loving, and tender.

Compatibility

Aries, because it's a fire sign, is often attracted to other fire signs—Sagittarius or Leo. But generally, unless aspects in the chart indicate otherwise, romance with another fire sign can be explosive. Aries gets along well with air signs—Gemini, Libra, Aquarius—or a sign that's sextile (60 degrees) or trine (120 degrees) from Aries. Sometimes, an earth sign helps ground all that Aries energy. In chart comparisons, a Venus or moon in Aries in the other person's chart would indicate compatibility.

Romance

Watch out! Romance with an Aries is an experience you don't quickly forget. Man or woman, these people are all passion and fire. They often form impulsive, rash attachments, but they don't hold back

Notable Aries People

Marlon Brando
Richard Chamberlain
Howard Cosell
Betty Ford
Aretha Franklin
Erica Jong
Henry Mancini
Steve McQueen
Eddie Murphy
Leonard Nimoy
Lawrence Olivier
Debbie Reynolds
Diana Ross
Rod Steiger
Gloria Steinem
Spencer Tracy
Vincent Van Gogh

emotionally. They need to know, however, that they're appreciated and loved in return.

Romance with an Aries means movement, activity, and being on the go to museums, movies, midnight walks by the ocean, good food in good restaurants, and more exotic things like hang gliding, parachuting, or rock climbing. Remember that these people are fearless and they bring that courage to their relationships.

Work

An Aries excels at anything in which leadership ability is paramount. They like giving orders and they're terrific at delegating responsibilities. They have numerous ideas and want to put them all into effect yesterday. As a fire sign, they pour energy into whatever they do. They aren't particularly interested in having power over others. They simply want the power to do what they want without restriction.

Finances

No two ways about it: Aries people spend money as fast as it comes in. An Aries knows something should be tucked away, but retirement seems such a long ways off and besides, money always comes in when needed! The challenge for an Aries is to develop the habit of saving.

Physical Aries

These people often have ruddy complexions, arched brows, narrow chins, and in men, profuse body hair. An Aries requires adequate rest and good nutrition to replenish all the energy he burns. They shouldn't eat much red meat and will benefit from herbs that belong to this particular sign: mustard, eye-bright, and bay.

Since Aries rules the head and face, these areas are considered to be the weakest parts of the body. Common ailments are tension headaches, dizziness, and skin eruptions.

Spirituality

Aries is likely to sample a little of everything before deciding on which spiritual belief fits best. He might live in an ashram, delve into paganism, or even try out a more conventional religion. While involved with a particular spiritual path, he will be passionate about it. But unless his passion is sustained, an Aries will eventually get bored and move on to something new.

Taurus ♉

THE BULL (APRIL 20–MAY 20)

Element: Earth | **Quality:** Fixed

Keywords: Endurance, perseverance, stubbornness | **Planetary Ruler:** Venus

Rules: Neck, throat, cervical vertebrae; natural ruler of second house

While Aries is out pioneering and discovering new lands, Taurus is settling it, cultivating the land, and using his resources for practical purposes. His stubbornness and determination keep him around for the long haul on any project or endeavor.

These individuals are the most stubborn in the zodiac. They are also incredibly patient, singular in their pursuit of goals, and determined to attain what they want. Although they lack versatility because of the fixed nature of the sign, they compensate for it by enduring whatever they have to in order to get what they want. Long after other contestants have fallen out of the race Taurus individuals are still in the running. As a result, they often win when others fail.

Most Taureans enjoy being surrounded by nice things. They like good art, good music, and many have considerable musical ability. They also have a talent for working with their hands—gardening, woodworking, and sculpting.

It takes a lot to anger a Taurus person, but once you do, clear out. The "bull's rush" can be fierce. But thanks to Venus ruling this sign, Taurus people are usually sensual and romantic. They are also physically-oriented individuals who take pride in their bodies.

Taurus Woman

She's loyal and dedicated to whatever she loves most. The place around which her life is centered reflects her particular tastes in art, color, and decor. She enjoys beauty, whatever its guise. If she's into clothing, then she dresses well and tastefully. If sports and physical activity are her passion, she pursues them diligently and with tremendous patience.

Since the Taurus woman is Venus-ruled, she's a romantic. Court her with flowers, moonlit walks on a beach, poetry. She's a generous, ardent lover who probably has a love of music. She may even play an instrument or sing. If you want to change her opinion on something, go about it in a gentle way. Don't ever back her into a corner. She'll dig in her heels and refuse to budge.

As an earth sign, she likes to putter in the garden and perhaps grows and cultivates herbs. She benefits from any time spent outdoors doing something she finds pleasurable. Animals are important to her and if she has pets, they reflect her own tastes in beauty.

Taurus Man

Like his female counterpart, he works hard and patiently at what he loves. His patience and perseverance make him good at finishing what other people have started. This guy isn't impetuous. Considerable thought goes into most things that he does. It's not that he's cautious; he's merely purposeful. If he doesn't understand the reason for doing something, he won't do it and nothing you can say will change his mind.

Both men and women in this sign can be jealous and possessive. But this tendency is mitigated considerably if the Taurus man knows you're as sincere as he is. He may have a deep connection with nature and the natural world that manifests in camping and solo sports. If he works out in a gym, he probably does it alone without a trainer. He may be into yoga, alternative medicine, and health foods.

His romantic nature may not always show up in flowers and gifts, but he does others things that tell you he cares. In return, he enjoys a good massage, likes having his neck rubbed, and melts in front of a fireplace.

Taurus Kids

This kid may be a loner or prefers one or two friends to a group of buddies. When she plays, she has fixed ideas about how the play should proceed. She has her own script and won't be persuaded to change it unless she understands the reason why and agrees it's the best way to play the game. When she gets tense, it shows up in the neck area. She benefits from massage and physical exercise.

Encourage Taurus kids to explore their own creativity, whether it's art, music, drama, or simply an appreciation of these things. They benefit from the rhythms of nature, from being outside and engaged in physical activity.

Forget time out for a Taurus child; he or she will simply outwait you. Better to explain what you object to and why, then ask for a promise not to repeat the act again.

Compatibility

Conventional wisdom says that we're better off with people who share the same element we do or with people who feed our element (earth with water, for instance). This makes Taurus compatible with other earth signs (Virgo and Capricorn) and with the water signs.

Quite often, Taureans are fatally attracted to Scorpios, their polar opposites. Although their elements, earth and water, should make them compatible, it tends to be superficial. Beneath the surface, they are probably at war with each other.

Romance

In romance with a Taurus, a lot goes on under the surface, out of sight. They're subtle and quiet about what they feel. Once they fall, they fall hard and their fixed natures simply won't allow them to give up. As a Venus-ruled sign, Taureans are true sensualists and romantic lovers. Their romantic attachments ground and stabilize them.

Work

They excel at work that requires persistence, stability, and relentless drive. They're able to take abstract ideas and make them concrete and practical. This means they're good at behind-the-scenes work, especially if the work is artistically creative—writing, costume design, gourmet cooking, musical composition, or anything to do with nature. You won't find a more tireless worker in the zodiac.

Finances

Despite the Taurean need for material security, they enjoy spending money. But the spending is rarely frivolous because Taurean tastes are quite specific and usually refined. Books, art, travel, and shamanic workshops may offer security for the Taurus.

Physical Taurus

They are recognizable by their necks, which are often thick and sturdy. They tend to be attractive people with broad foreheads and many retain their youthful appearances long after the rest of us begin to show our age. They benefit from a daily regimen of physical exercise and should be moderate in their consumption of fattening foods. This, of course, is undoubtedly true for all signs, but particularly true for the slower metabolism of the bull.

Spirituality

Taurus, due to the fixed, earth temperament of the sign, often seeks spiritual answers in nature. While camping, hiking, or engaged in some sort of physical activity outside, he or she connects with the deeper levels of self. Music and the arts can have the same effect on a Taurus.

Notable Taurus People

Candice Bergen
Frank Capra
Cher
Joan Collins
Ulyssess S. Grant
Joseph Heller
Audrey Hepburn
Dennis Hopper
Reggie Jackson
Soren Kierkegaard
Shirley MacLaine
Ann Margaret
Rod McKuen
Maureen O'Sullivan
Michelle Pfeiffer
Katherine Porter
Barbara Streisand

Gemini ♊

THE TWINS (MAY 21–JUNE 21)

Element: Air	**Quality:** Mutable
Keyword: Versatility	**Planetary Ruler:** Mercury
Rules: Hands, arms, lungs, nervous system; natural ruler of the third house	

After Aries and Taurus have discovered and cultivated the new land, Gemini ventures out to see what else is there and seizes upon new ideas that will help their communities expand. The innate curiosity of this sign keeps these people on the move.

Geminis, because they're ruled by Mercury, tend to use the rational, intellectual mind to explore and understand their personal worlds. They need to answer the single burning question in their minds: Why? This applies to most facets of their lives, from the personal to the impersonal. This need to know may send them off to foreign countries, particularly if the sun is in the ninth house, where they can explore other cultures and traditions.

These individuals are fascinated by relationships and the connections among people, places, and objects. Their rational analysis of everything, from ideas to relationships, drives them as nuts as it drives everyone else around them. When this quality leads them into an exploration of psychic and spiritual realms, it grounds them.

Geminis are changeable and often moody. Their symbol, the twins, means they are often at odds with themselves, the mind demanding one thing, the heart demanding the opposite. To someone else, this internal conflict often manifests as two very different people; as a significant other, you may reach a point where you wonder which twin you're living with.

In romance, the heart of a Gemini is won by a seduction of the mind.

Gemini Woman

At first glance, she seems to be all over the place. She can talk on any number of topics and sounds like she knows what she's talking about, until you discover that her knowledge on most things is superficial. But if you hit one of her passions, her knowledge is

deep and thorough. She excels at communication; the form this talent takes depends on other aspects in her chart.

In her twenties, she tends to be flirtatious and flighty, unable or unwilling to commit to a relationship. On the one hand, this girl loves her freedom; on the other, relationships are important to her. If she marries young, she may marry at least twice. In her thirties and forties, she begins to settle in. By this time she has made a kind of peace with herself. She has a better understanding of her moods, needs, and emotions. By fifty, the Gemini woman knows who she is; now she must begin living that truth.

If you want to change this woman's attitude or opinion, you have to prove that your attitude or opinion is more logical. Remember that her concept of logic may differ from yours.

Gemini Man

He's quick, witty, enigmatic. Just when you think you've got him figured out, he says or does something that blows your concept of who he is. Don't expect a courtship from this guy; he doesn't possess the sensual appreciation of beauty that a Taurus man has. But if you appeal to his intellect, if you court him mentally, he might dedicate his next book to you.

Like his female counterpart, the Gemini man often seems to be two people inhabiting one body. One twin is attentive to your every need and whim; he's solicitous. But the other twin could care less. You won't change this particular quality, you simply have to learn to live with it.

The Gemini man makes a good editor, writer, or orator. He may hold down two jobs and is certainly capable of working on more than one project at a time. Once he commits to something, whether it's a profession or a relationship, he needs to know that he is appreciated.

Gemini Kids

As toddlers, their personalities are marked by impatience. They don't bother learning to crawl; they're trying to walk as soon as their legs are strong enough to support them. Once they learn to communicate, watch out. They challenge you at every step with questions. Why this, why that, why why why.

Notable Gemini People

Joan Collins
Jacques Cousteau
Clint Eastwood
Sigmund Freud
Dashiell Hammett
Susan Hayward
Lillian Hellman
Bob Hope
Hubert Humphrey
John F. Kennedy
Stan Laurel
Paul McCartney
Marilyn Monroe
Joe Namath
Whitley Streiber
Orson Welles

These kids are as precocious as Aries children, but inconsistent in the way they express it. Some days a Gemini leads the neighborhood kids into anarchy; the next day he or she might keep company with a book, a microscope, or a pet. They like the furry warmth and security of a pet and enjoy observing how animals live on a daily basis.

As a parent, you can forget trying to pigeon hole your Gemini child. It just isn't going to happen. So accept the fact, provide a learning environment in which your Gemini can explore who and what he or she is, and be prepared for a wild ride.

Compatibility

Geminis are social enough to get along with just about anyone on a superficial basis. They feel most at home with other air signs, particularly Aquarians, whose minds are as quick. They also get along with Sagittarius, their polar opposites in the zodiac, who share some of the same attributes. Again, though, these are broad generalizations. For compatibility purposes, compare the individual charts.

Romance

IGeminis love first with their minds. Even a relationship that begins primarily because of a sexual attraction won't last if there's no mental camaraderie. Quite often, Geminis seek friendship first with the opposite sex and once a mental rapport is established, the friendship deepens to love. They can be quite fickle in their affections, sometimes carrying on simultaneous relationships. But once their hearts are won, they love deeply.

Work

Geminis excel in any line of work that provides diversity. It doesn't matter if it's with the public or behind the scenes, as long as it isn't routine. They make good counselors because one of the twins is always willing to listen. Their love of language gives them a talent for the written word. Acting, politics, libraries, research: all of these fields fit Gemini. The bottom line is simple: Boredom to a Gemini is like death.

Finances

How a Gemini handles money depends on which twin holds the purse strings—the spendthrift or the tightwad. Either way, Geminis enjoy spending money on the things they love, such as books, movies, theater, and travel. As the old Grace Slick song goes, "these things feed their heads."

Physical Gemini

They generally are slender and wiry people, filled with nervous energy. All this energy can be difficult to rein in sometimes, particularly on nights when they work late and their heads race with ideas. Geminis benefit from breaks in their established routines and need physical exercise to ground their thoughts. They are prone to respiratory and nervous ailments.

Spirituality

Geminis are so restless mentally that they generally don't do well within organized religions, unless they've chosen that path for themselves. They sample spiritual belief systems the way other people sample new foods. Once they find a spiritual path that makes sense to them, they generally stick with it.

Cancer ♋

THE CRAB (JUNE 22–JULY 22)

Element: Water	**Quality:** Cardinal
Keyword: Nurturing, emotional drive	**Planetary Ruler:** Moon
Rules: Breasts, stomach, digestive system; natural ruler of the fourth house	

Now that the first three signs have discovered, settled, and expanded their new land, the Cancer comes along and tames it. Civilizes it. These people need roots, a place or even a state of mind, that they can call their own. They need a safe harbor, a refuge, to retreat for solitude.

Imagination, sensitivity, and the nurturing instinct characterize this sign. Cancerians are generally gentle and kind people, unless they're hurt. Then they become vindictive and sharp-spoken. They forgive easily, but rarely forget.

Cancerians tend to be affectionate, passionate, and even possessive at times. As parents, they might be over-protective. As spouses or significant others, they may smother their mates with love and good intentions.

Emotionally, Cancers act and react in the same way the crab moves—sideways. They avoid confrontations and usually aren't comfortable in discussing what they feel. They're reluctant to reveal who they are and sometimes hide behind their protective urges, preferring to tend to the needs of others rather than to their own needs. They're intuitive and sometimes quite psychic. Experience flows through them emotionally.

Cancers are often moody and always changeable; their interests and social circles shift constantly. Once a Cancer trusts you, however, he lets you in on his most private world.

Cancer Woman

At first she seems enigmatic, elusive. She's so changeable in her moods that you never know where you stand with her. Beneath her gentle and sympathetic nature, beneath her bravado, she's scared of being pinned down and insecure about who she is.

She needs roots—her own home, preferably near water—but she can establish a base of operation anywhere. She nurtures everything—

animals, her own children, waifs and orphans of all shapes, sizes, and species. This woman is emotion distilled into its purest form. She feels first, then thinks. Sometimes she's a psychic sponge who absorbs every emotion around her.

If she doesn't have children of her own, she probably has some sort of connection with children. Or her animals or people in need are her children. Somehow, her nurturing instinct finds expression.

Cancer Man

Like the female Cancer, the male has liquid eyes that communicate a kind of forlorn nostalgia for what has passed. He's kind, affectionate, and nurturing, but only to a point. When he feels his personal space has been infringed upon, he retreats just like the crab—rapidly to the side. Then he buries himself in sand by retreating to his special place—his own home, his RV, his tent, whatever his refuge is. Like the female Cancer, he is often nurturing and gets along well with kids.

This guy is hard to figure. Sometimes he courts you with flowers and candlelight; other times he's sacked out on the couch lost in his own gloom. Your best course of action is to let him be. Don't prod him when he's in this kind of mood. You won't get anywhere even if you do.

If he's interested in spiritual issues, chances are he's in deep. In this sign, you're likely to find psychic healers and clairvoyants, people who use their intuition in highly developed and sophisticated ways.

Cancer Kids

The Cancerian youngster definitely listens to a different drummer. Don't expect loquacious explanations about what your Cancerian is feeling. If she's in the mood she might tell you how so and so hurt her feelings today at school. But if she's not in the mood, nothing you can say will prod her to explain.

This kid is often dreamy. She would rather watch TV or read a book than run around outside, unless the activity or sport happens to interest her. In a group, she's likely to take the easy way out and go along with the crowd. Or remain completely passive about the situation, hiding inside of "I don't know" or, worse, "I don't care."

The Cancerian child needs to feel that he or she is an integral part of the family unit and is appreciated. As a parent, your best

Notable Cancer People

Dan Aykroyd
James Brolin
Mel Brooks
Tom Cruise
Olivia De Haviland
Harrison Ford
Merv Griffin
Franz Kafka
Helen Keller
George Orwell
Jason Robards
Linda Ronstadt
Ringo Starr
Meryl Streep
Donald Sutherland
Henry David Thoreau

route to communication with a Cancer child is acceptance and gentle prodding.

Compatibility

On the surface, Scorpio and Pisces, as the other water signs, would seem to be the most compatible with a Cancer. But Scorpio's intensity might swallow up Cancer's innate gentleness, and the duality of Pisces probably would drive a Cancer person crazy. Earth signs—Taurus, Virgo, Capricorn—are particularly good for Cancers with Taurus and Virgo as the preferred because they are both sextile to Cancer.

Romance

Cancers can be evasive when it comes to romance. They flirt, they're coy, and all the while they're feeling their way through the maze of their own emotions. They enjoy entertaining at home because it's where they feel most comfortable, surrounded by all that's familiar to them. Some Cancers dislike the courtship of romance altogether and prefer to get right down to the important questions: Are we compatible? Do we love each other?

To live with and love a Cancer, you have to accept the intensity of their emotions and their imaginations.

Work

Cancers may be happiest when they work out of their own homes. Due to the intensity of their feelings, they do well in medicine working directly with patients. For the same reason they also make good psychic healers, counselors, and psychologists. Teaching kids, running a daycare center, or even taking care of other people's homes are also good for the Cancerian personality.

Finances

Cancers aren't lavish spenders except when it comes to their homes and families. Then, nothing is too expensive. Otherwise, they tend to be big savers. As kids, they stash their allowance in cookie jars; as adults, they stick their money in long-term CDs.

Physical Cancer

This sign is more recognizable than some of the others because of the roundness of the face. The entire body, in fact, may be rounded, though not necessarily overweight. Cancerians benefit from water sports, a day at the beach, or anything having to do with water. If they have hangups about their earlier lives, particularly child-hood, hypnosis might be a good way to dislodge and work through the past. It's important that a Cancer doesn't cling to past hurts and injuries, as these emotions eventually lodge in the body and create health problems.

Spirituality

Introspection is key with Cancers and it doesn't matter if it's pro-vided in the guise of organized religion or some New Age belief system. When they feel the rightness of a particular set of beliefs, they stick with it, explore it, and draw on their innate intuition to understand it.

Leo ♌

THE LION (JULY 23–AUGUST 22)

Element: Fire	**Quality:** Fixed
Keyword: Action, power	**Planetary Ruler:** Sun
Rules: Heart, back, and spinal cord; natural ruler of the fifth house	

Yes, Leos roar. They love being the center of attention and often surround themselves with admirers. To remain in the proud kingdom of a Leo, their admirers have to think like he thinks, believe what he believes, and hate and love who he hates and loves. To a Leo, this is loyalty. In return, Leo the king offers generosity, warmth, and compassion.

Leos have an innate dramatic sense and life is definitely their stage. Their flamboyance and personal magnetism extend to every facet of their lives. They seek to succeed and make an impact in every situation. It is no surprise that the theater and allied arts fall under the rulership of Leo.

Don't ever argue to change the opinions and beliefs of a Leo. As a fixed sign, they stand firm in their belief systems. They have found what works for them and don't understand why their beliefs may not work for someone else.

In general, they are optimistic, honorable, loyal, and ambitious.

Leo Woman

She's up front about what she feels and invariably is disappointed when she finds that other people may not be as forthright. You'll never have to guess where you stand with a Leo woman, unless there's something in the aspects of her chart that say otherwise. She loves flattery, romantic courtships, and is an ardent lover.

The Leo woman exudes confidence and because of it, other people place their trust in her. She needs to be at the helm in her workplace—a manager will do but a CEO would be better. She dislikes playing second fiddle on any level.

In a marriage, don't expect her to be content with staying home, unless she's running her business from there. If she's a mother, she's not just a mother. She has a career, hobbies, and passions. She may be involved somehow with children even if she doesn't have her own, because Leo rules children.

She likes nice clothes and probably dresses with flair and style in bright, bold colors. Remember, she's an actress and adept at creating

certain impressions and moods through the way she looks and acts. She likes order in her world, but it has to be her order.

Leo Man

Give him center stage and he's at his best; tell him what to do and he's at his worst. Once you accept that about the Leo man, he's easy to get along with because you really want to like this guy. He's warm, outgoing, and fun. Kids love him because in many ways he's like they are, full of magic.

People are attracted to him because they sense his leadership abilities. They like his frankness, abundant energy, and ambition. If you're a Leo's significant other, get used to sharing him with his "court," whoever they might be. But rest assured that if your Leo commits to you, he means it.

Neither the male nor the female Leo do well in subservient jobs. But give them distinction and the power to command and they do it exceptionally well.

Leo Kids

As toddlers, they keep you running. Their abundant energy fuels them from sunrise to midnight, and by the time you fall into bed, you're ragged. As they mature, Leo kids are surrounded by other kids, so your house is likely to be the gathering place for your Leo's youthful tribe.

The innate generosity of this sign manifests itself early. Leo kids feel compassion toward people less fortunate than they are. They're likely to bring home strays of all shapes and sizes. They also tend to be fearless, accept every dare, and take risks that turn you gray before your time. Life with a Leo kid is never boring!

Compatibility

Another fire sign is good for a Leo simply because their energy levels are similar. Any sign that is sextile (Gemini, for instance) or trine (Aries) would be fine, too. The polarity between Leo and Aquarius, its polar opposite sign, might elevate a Leo's consciousness to where it succeeds best: to the wider world beyond himself, the family of man.

Romance

Leos are passionate. They can also be impulsive, particularly when their egos are stroked. For the most part, Leos need to feel needed and need to know they are loved before they commit entirely. Once they're

Notable Leo People

James Baldwin
Lucille Ball
Peter Bogdanovich
Rosalynn Carter
Geraldine Chaplin
Robert DeNiro
John Derek
Michael Douglas
Samuel Goldwyn
Dag Hammarskjold
Mata Hari
Dustin Hoffman
Mick Jagger
T.E. Lawrence
Jacqueline Kennedy
　Onassis
Ogden Nash
Roman Polanski
Arnold Schwarzenegger

committed, everything is bigger than life and brighter than the sun. Courtship is often a series of dramatic gestures: five dozen roses that arrive at your office, an erotic call at three a.m., or a chopper ride over Manhattan.

Work

A Leo excels at work in front of the public. Actor, orator, Speaker of the House, CEO: forget the menial job for a Leo. Leos are good at teaching because the classroom becomes their stage and their students become their audience. They also tend to be good with animals and enjoy training, caring for, and loving them.

Finances

If Leo wants it, Leo buys it. If he can't afford it, he charges it. If his charge cards are maxed out, then he hocks his Rolex or his collection of baseball cards to buy it. Saving for a rainy day just isn't in the picture because for a Leo there aren't any rainy days! There are, of course, exceptions to all these generalities. A Moon in an Earth sign, combined with a Leo sun, would mitigate the flamboyance, particularly if the Moon were in Capricorn.

Physical Leo

Jacqueline Kennedy Onassis was the physical epitome of a Leo female with her compelling eyes, thick hair, and regal bearing. Leos generally benefit from low-fat diets because one of the weakest parts of their bodies is the heart. Exercise, even if on the light side, is needed to channel some of that abundant energy.

Spirituality

The Leos I've known were probably sun-worshipping pagans in past lives and now they're sampling everything else along the spectrum. Unless aspects in the chart indicate otherwise, a Leo isn't likely to stay within the confines of organized religion unless it suits him. If he does it out of obligation, then in his mind he's doing it for his kids. A Leo's greatest spiritual contributions come when he expands beyond the parameters of the self and reaches for the universal.

Virgo ♍

THE VIRGIN (AUGUST 23–SEPTEMBER 22)

Element: Earth	**Quality:** Mutable
Keyword: Order, detailed, dedication	**Planetary Ruler:** Mercury
Rules: Intestines, abdomen, female reproductive system; natural ruler of the sixth house	

The popular image of Virgos as people who are picky, critical, and compulsively tidy, is misleading. If one or all of these traits manifest obviously, the natal chart reveals other aspects that enhance this characteristic.

Virgos equal Geminis in mental quickness and agility. Due to their attention to detail, they tend to delve more deeply into subjects they study. Even though they are career-oriented people, they seem to be more interested in doing their jobs efficiently and well. They're happiest when engaged in something that benefits society at large. In other words, duty is important to Virgos.

They tend to be attracted to people who are intellectually stimulating or eccentric in some way. Their standards are high when it comes to romantic relationships and unless the mental connection exists, the relationship won't last long.

Since Virgos, like Geminis, are Mercury-ruled, they need outlets for all that nervous energy. Writing, pets, reading, and education all serve this purpose.

Virgo Woman

Physically, she's distinctive in some way—intriguing eyes, exquisite bone structure in her face, or meticulous grooming. She possesses a certain vibrancy and energy that other people sense even when she's not trying to project an image. In romance, she is attracted first when a mental spark exists. As the mental camaraderie deepens, so do her emotions.

The Virgo woman, like her male counterpart, is often insecure and tends to fret over everything. This trait usually evens out as the Virgo woman matures. It can be irritating to a significant other, particularly when her fretting turns to a constant critique of everything other people say and do.

She usually is aware of health and hygiene issues, especially when it concerns cutting-edge research. She may not always apply what she knows to her own life, but she has the knowledge.

She enjoys spending money on items like books and pieces of art that strike her fancy. She's sensitive to her surroundings, so her home is comfortable. If she's a mother, she's conscientious, tactful, and loving. She usually has a real soft spot for animals.

Virgo Man

He looks good and possesses an indisputable presence. He's mentally quick, intellectually curious, and is an excellent worker. His humor is often biting but rarely malicious.

He can be quite fussy about his personal environment. This is the kind of man who insists on having his own bathroom or, at the very least, his own side of the bathroom counter. If he cooks, then he probably is quite good at it and possessive about the kitchen while he's creating. Like the female of the sign, the Virgo man enjoys pleasant surroundings and usually owns several special items that he keeps for the sake of nostalgia.

He's prone to taking himself too seriously and benefits from any activity that forces him to lighten up. He's always hardest on himself, overly critical of what he does or doesn't do and can be quite critical of others as well. He rarely seeks praise for his efforts and in the less evolved Virgo man, won't give praise even when it's deserved.

Virgo Kids

You'd better know how to think quickly when you're around a Virgo child. They're impatient, want everything yesterday, and possess boundless energy. They love to learn and their curiosity prompts them to poke around in everything. When they feel passionate about something, they bring the full power of their being to that particular endeavor.

This child is inclined to fluctuating moods in the same way that Cancer kids are. But for a Virgo, the cause of the fluctuation originates first in the mind, rather than in the emotions. If they can't

understand something, their frustration mounts until they either explode or understand the problem. Their attention span improves with age and maturity. The compassion that marks them at a young age usually deepens with time. They love animals.

As the parent of a Virgo child, provide him or her with books, learning tools, and plenty of positive feedback and praise.

Compatibility

Virgos are attracted mentally to Geminis, but sometimes find the twins a bit hard to take for the long run. The grounding present in other earth signs may seem appealing on the surface, but leave it to a Virgo to find fault with his fellow earth signs. Scorpios and Cancers may be the best bets, with the mystical Pisces a close second.

Romance

Virgos are often inscrutable in the affairs of the heart. They seem remote and quiet, then open and talkative. One moment they're glad to see you, then the next they act like they could care less. This is only the Virgo need to perfect what is. Virgos generally don't entertain romantic illusions; they see what's there in finely carved detail, like an X-ray, and then they try to improve on it. Don't take it personally. A Virgo is never harder on the people she loves than she is on herself.

Work

Virgos bring sincere striving for perfection to their work and careers. They do best when working for others—social work, in hospitals, clinics, hospice programs, with their children. The challenge in every area of a Virgo's life is to serve without self-sacrifice. Their striving for perfection compels them to evolve and change.

Finances

When Virgos are big spenders, they usually pull back at some point and question what they buy and why. What need does it fill? If they are tight with money, then something happens that impels them to loosen their hold, to spend money for enjoyment. Virgos follow an arc of evolvement toward perfection in everything they do. They

Notable Virgo People

Elizabeth Ashley
Anne Bancroft
William Golding
Buddy Hackett
Michael Jackson
Elia Kazan
Ken Kesey
Jean Claude Killy
B.B. King
Stephen King
Roddy McDowall
Bill Murray
Maxwell Perkins
William Saroyan
Peter Sellers
Leo Tolstoy
Lily Tomlin

analyze the patterns in their lives and seek to change those that don't work.

Physical Virgo

They usually have slender builds and are physically attractive. There may be a sharpness about their features. Since Virgos fret and worry so much, their physical ailments usually manifest first in their stomachs. Colic in infancy, stomach upsets as a youngster, ulcers as an adult. But because Virgos are generally fussy about their diet and health, they grow into their innate wisdom about their own bodies.

Spirituality

The evolved Virgo is capable of great vision and an intuition that often borders on prescience. They are likely to sample different spiritual beliefs until they find one that appeals to their eminently practical side.

Libra ♎

THE SCALES (SEPTEMBER 23–OCTOBER 22)	
Element: Air	**Quality:** Cardinal
Keyword: Balance	**Planetary Ruler:** Venus
Rules: Lower back and the diaphragm; natural ruler of the seventh house	

Librans seem to come in three distinct types: those who are decisive, those who aren't, and those who seek harmony for its own sake. The typical Libra seeks to mediate and balance, to act democratically and fairly.

They love beauty in all of its guises—art, literature, classical music, opera, mathematics, and the human body. They usually are team players who enjoy debate but not argument. They're excellent strategists and masters at the power of suggestion.

Even though Librans are courteous, amiable people, never presume they're pushovers. They use diplomacy and intelligence to get what they want. They're natural romantics and flourish in enduring partnerships. They are fair-minded people, but avoid anything that is grim, crude, vulgar, and garish. Adversely afflicted, they have trouble making decisions and may lose themselves in sensual pleasures. In highly evolved Librans, the human mind is perfect in its balance and discretion.

Libra Woman

Watch out. She's a flirt who is seductive and romantic, and she bowls you over with the small luxuries she brings you. If she cooks, she probably does it well, using herbs and seasonings. She sets the mood, too, with candlelight, fresh flowers, and soft music. She's a romantic, tender lover, enjoys companionship, and flourishes in partnerships.

Her home reflects her refined tastes in art, books, and good music. She may not be extravagant and probably doesn't squander the money she has. But she derives enormous pleasure from whatever she buys. If she likes opera or the ballet, she attends regularly; these extravagances feed her soul. She may play a musical instrument and have a fondness for chess.

Libra Man

He needs companionship, just like his female counterpart, and generally works better as part of a team. But he also needs to retain his individuality in any partnership, which may be quirky at times. Once you've won his heart, he's loyal and considerate and seeks to perfect the union until it fits his idealized vision of what is possible.

He enjoys pleasant, harmonious surroundings in his work and personal environment. He often finds himself in the role of peacemaker simply because he seeks balance in all things. He shares many of the same artistic interests as his female counterpart.

A Libra man rarely expresses anger; he would rather work around whatever problems crop up. But if he lets loose, he doesn't leave anything unsaid. Every transgression and insincerity is spelled out. Although his anger passes quickly, such outbursts leave him shaken and sometimes ill because he has such an intense dislike for anything unpleasant.

Libra Kids

Chances are good that you won't find a Libra child rolling around in a sandbox or looking for bugs. Their sensibilities usually are too refined for that. The typical Libra child is more likely to be reading a book or listening to the music in the cool comfort of his or her own room.

Libra kids enjoy group activities and get along well with others kids in a group. They usually have one special friend in whom they confide. Don't be alarmed if your Libra toddler has an imaginary friend that she talks about and plays with. Many creative people had imaginary friends as youngsters. It's part of what makes their personalities different. You're better off never shouting at a Libra child. Just tell him or her what behavior you object to and extract a promise that the problem won't be repeated.

Compatibility

Librans are so sociable they can get along with just about anyone. They are most compatible with other air signs, Leo, and Sagittarius. They gravitate toward people who reflect their refined tastes and aesthetic leanings. Sometimes, an earth sign may provide a certain grounding that a Libran needs. Or a water sign, like Cancer, may offer a fluidity of emotion that a Libran may lack.

Romance

Libras are drawn to beauty, whatever its form. The only thing they enjoy as much as beauty is harmony. Even when a relationship has gone sour, a Libra hesitates to be the one who ends it. They can't stand hurting anyone's feelings; emotional rawness is one of those ugly realities that they don't like to see. As a result, they may remain in a relationship longer than they should just because disharmony is so distasteful. Libras seek harmony because in their heart they know that enlightenment lies at the calm dead center of the storm.

Work

The Libra's obvious choice for a profession is an attorney or judge because of Libra's finely tuned sense of fair play. But Librans excel in any profession that calls for an acutely balanced mind and sensitivities. They make good editors, musicians, accountants, artists, and parents. The work itself is less important in the long run than what it teaches Libra about making decisions, in spite of their ability to see all sides of an issue.

Finances

A sense of balance allows Libras to strike the right note between spender and miser. Libras tend to save, but enjoy spending when they can afford it. Most Libras know their limit.

Physical Libra

As a Venus-ruled sign, these people are usually physically distinctive in some way—compassionate eyes or well-formed bodies. They tend to be slender, very attractive, and seem to know instinctively how to bring out the best in their companions. Since Libra rules the lower back and diaphragm, unvented emotions manifest first in those areas of the body. Libras benefit from physical exercise, particularly anything that strengthens the back and maintains general flexibility.

Spirituality

Evolved Libras understand instinctively that they must unite human duality with divine unity. They seek idealized balance, the perfect equilibrium. For some, this is accomplished within the parameters of organized religion. For others, spirituality is sought through community efforts or in their immediate family.

Notable Libra People

Lenny Bruce
Michael Douglas
Dwight Eisenhower
Graham Greene
Richard Harris
Helen Hayes
Rita Hayworth
Jim Henson
Charles A. Jayne
Buster Keaton
Ralph Lauren
Groucho Marx
Roger Moore
Mickey Rooney
Eleanor Roosevelt
Susan Sarandon
Wallace Stevens
Ben Vereen

Scorpio ♏

THE SCORPION (OCTOBER 23–NOVEMBER 21)

Element: Water	**Quality:** Fixed
Keyword: Regeneration, transformation	**Planetary Ruler:** Mars and Pluto
Rules: Sexual organs, rectum, and reproductive system; natural ruler of the eighth house	

Note the sharp point at the tip of the glyph that represents this sign. Symbolically, it's the scorpion's stinger, which characterizes the biting sarcasm often associated with Scorpios. These people are intense, passionate, and strong-willed. They often impose their will on others. In less aware people, this can manifest as cruelty, sadism, and enmity; in the more evolved Scorpio, this characteristic transforms lives for the better.

Like Aries, they aren't afraid of anything. But they have an endurance that Aries lacks and it enables them to plow ahead and overcome whatever opposition they encounter.

Scorpios don't know the meaning of indifference. They tend to live in black and white worlds, dealing with either/or issues. They either approve or don't approve, agree or disagree. You're either a friend or an enemy; there are no shades of gray. Once you've gained their trust, you've won their loyalty forever, unless you hurt them or someone they love. Then they can become vindictive and may attempt to get even.

Scorpios possess an innate curiosity and suspicion of easy answers that compels them to probe deeply into whatever interests them. They dig out concealed facts and seek the meaning behind facades. Most Scorpios are exceptionally intuitive, even if they don't consciously acknowledge it. The more highly evolved people in this sign are often very psychic, with rich inner lives and passionate involvement in metaphysics.

Scorpios are excellent workers, industrious and relentless. They excel at anything associated with the eighth house—trusts and inheritances, mortuaries, psychological counselors, the occult.

Scorpio Woman

She smolders with sexuality. This is a woman who turns heads on the street, who walks into a room filled with strangers and instantly grabs attention through nothing more than the power of her presence. If you seek to win a Scorpio woman's heart, you'd better be up front and honest right from the beginning. If she ever catches you in a lie or if you hurt her, she'll cut you off cold.

She's a passionate lover and can be jealous and possessive. You won't ever figure out what she's thinking or feeling just by the expression on her face, unless she's angry and then watch out. Her rage takes many forms—an explosion, sarcasm that bites to the bone, or a piercing look that makes you shrivel inside.

If her intuition is developed, it borders on clairvoyance. This inner sense often shines forth in a Scorpio woman's striking eyes.

As a mother, the Scorpio woman is devoted, loving, and fiercely protective. She strives to create a comfortable and loving home for her kids that is also a refuge from the outside world.

Scorpio Man

Like the female of the sign, he's intense, passionate, and very private. There is always something compelling about a Scorpio man—his eyes, the way he dresses, or the enigma of his presence. He isn't just a flirt. He often comes on like a locomotive with sexual energy radiating so powerfully that he's difficult to ignore even if you aren't attracted to him.

The Scorpio man often has a marvelous talent of some kind that he pursues passionately, but which may not figure into his income. In others words, this talent is his avocation—music, art, writing, acting, astrology, tarot cards. Or, he may pour his considerable talent into nurturing his own children.

Many Scorpio men (and women) enjoy sports. They have a distinct preference for more violent sports like football and hunting. His choice of sports is sometimes a reflection of his personal struggle with emotional extremes.

Scorpio Kids

From infancy, these children are usually distinctive in some way. They form their opinions early, based on what they experience and

Notable Scorpio People

Howard Baker
Fanny Brice
Prince Charles
Michael Crichton
Richard Dreyfuss
Linda Evans
Sally Field
Goldie Hawn
Katherine Hepburn
Billie Jean King
Timothy Leary
Pablo Picasso
George Patton
Carl Sagan
Jonas Salk
Martin Scorcese
Jaclyn Smith
Marlo Thomas

observe. The intensity and depth of their emotions may result in outbursts of temper when they don't get their way or terrible bouts of crying when their feelings are hurt.

As the parent of a Scorpio child, there are times when you're completely puzzled about your child's behavior. Instead of trying to guess what's wrong, just be forthright and ask. Your child's response may astonish you. Scorpio children flourish in an environment that is rich with variety, but they definitely need their own space and sanctuary.

Compatibility

Scorpio is usually compatible with Taurus, because the signs are polar opposites and balance each other. The water of Scorpio and the earth of Taurus mix well. However, both signs are fixed, which means in a disagreement neither will give in to the other. Scorpios can be compatible with other Scorpios as long as each person understands the other's intensity and passions. Pisces and Cancer, the other two water signs, may be too weak for Scorpio's intensity, unless a comparison of natal charts indicates otherwise.

Romance

You don't know the meaning of the word intensity unless you've been involved with a Scorpio. No other sign brings such raw power to romance. The rawness probably isn't something you understand or even like very much, but there's no question that it's intricately woven through the fabric of your relationship.

The odd part is that you're never quite sure how the intensity is going to manifest: jealousy, fury, endless questions, or unbridled passion. Sometimes, the intensity doesn't have anything to do with the relationship, but with the personal dramas in the Scorpio's life. So don't try to figure it out. If you're in for the long haul, then accept your Scorpio the way he or she is. If you're not in for the long haul, then hit the road.

Work

They make excellent actors, detectives, spies, even teachers. There's just no telling where all that rawness of perception can take a Scorpio.

Finances

Scorpios are masters at using other people's money to build their own fortunes. This is as true of a Mafia don as it is of a Wall Street entrepreneur. Scorpio attaches no moral judgment to it; this is simply how things are. In return, Scorpios can be extravagantly generous in charity work or anonymous donations to worthy causes. Your Scorpio may even rewrite the last act of your rejected screenplay and get it to sell big time.

Physical Scorpio

All Scorpios seem to share the same compelling, intense eyes. Regardless of body height or size, they generate a powerful sense of presence and usually have low, husky voices. Due to the unusual will power inherent in the sign, Scorpios often work to the point of exhaustion. Any illness usually has a strong emotional component.

Spirituality

Some Scorpios take to organized religion like a duck to water. They like the ritual and the sense of belonging. Others, however, delve into unorthodox belief systems seeking spiritual answers. Whatever form spirituality takes for a Scorpio, he or she brings passion and sincerity to the search.

Sagittarius ♐

THE ARCHER (NOVEMBER 22–DECEMBER 21)

Element: Fire	**Quality:** Mutable
Keyword: Idealism, freedom	**Planetary Ruler:** Jupiter
Rules: Hips, thighs, liver, and hepatic system; natural ruler of the ninth house	

These people seek the truth, express it as they see it, and don't care if no one else agrees with them. They see the large picture of any issue and can't be bothered with the mundane details. They are always outspoken and can't understand why other people aren't as candid. After all, what's there to hide?

This is a mentally oriented sign where logic reigns supreme. But the mentality differs from Gemini, the polar opposite of Sagittarius, in several important ways. A Gemini is concerned with the here and now; he needs to know how and why things and relationships work in his life. A Sagittarian, however, focuses on the future and on the larger family of humanity. Quite often, this larger family includes animals—large, small, wild, or domestic—and the belief that all deserve the right to live free.

Despite the Sagittarian's propensity for logic, they are often quite prescient, with an uncanny ability to glimpse the future. Even when they have this ability, however, they often think they need an external tool to trigger it such as tarot cards, an astrology chart, or runes.

They love their freedom and chafe at any restrictions. Their versatility and natural optimism win them many friends, but only a few ever really know the heart of the Sagittarian.

Sagittarius Woman

She's hard to figure at first. You see her in a crowd and notice that she commands attention. She's humorous, vivacious, outspoken. One to one, she's flirtatious. But the moment you mention having dinner or catching a movie, she's gone. It's not that she's coy; it's simply that you're just a face in the crowd.

If you catch her attention, however, it's because you talk well and quickly about something that interests her. Animal rights, for instance, or paradigm shifts in worldwide belief systems. The lady thinks big and if you want to win her heart, you'd better think just as big.

Sagittarian women excel in jobs and careers that don't confine them. If they have children, they allow their offspring such great latitude that to other people it may appear that they're indifferent. This is hardly the case. A Sagittarian mother is loving and devoted, but believes that her children should find their own way. She offers broad guidelines and her own wisdom but doesn't force her opinions.

Sagittarius Man

He's a charmer, flirtatious and witty, the kind of man everyone loves to have at a party. He's also candid and opinionated, with firm ideas on how things work and should be done. His frustration is that what often seems so obvious to him seems oblique to other people. He fails to understand that not everyone sees the world as he does.

His vision is broad and often grandiose. He does everything in a big way and is rarely satisfied with what he achieves. On his way to attaining a particular goal, he gets carried away with the momentum he has built up and ends up taking on more than he can handle.

He enjoys traveling, particularly foreign travel, and is too restless for a sedentary lifestyle. During his free time, this man is out horseback riding, practicing archery, or maybe whitewater rafting. He's always moving and aiming toward the future.

The less evolved men of this sign sometimes lose sight of the difference between need and greed. They want everything and they want it immediately. This is as true in business as it is in romance. Sagittarian men often have more than one relationship going on at a time, which suits their need for freedom. For this reason, Sagittarius is also known as the bachelor sign.

Sagittarius Kids

From the time they are old enough to have friends, your phone will never stop ringing. Sagittarius kids possess an optimism and vivaciousness that makes other kids feel good about themselves. A Sagittarius kid is always the center of attention. Their candor may be welcome with friends but not with adults in their life. A Sagittarius child may refuse to surrender his or her opinion to anyone.

As a parent of a Sagittarian child, your best approach is to establish the parameters of authority early. Always allow her the freedom to say what she thinks and believes, even if you don't agree. The Sagittarian child needs to know she won't be reprimanded for standing up for what she believes.

Notable Sagittarius People

Woody Allen
Jeff Bridges
Dale Carnegie
Emily Dickinson
Walt Disney
Jane Fonda
Betty Grable
Jimi Hendrix
Chet Huntley
Don Johnson
Caroline Kennedy
Brenda Lee
Mary Martin
Margaret Mead
Agnes Moorehead
Nostradamus
Frank Sinatra
Dionne Warwick

Compatibility

Other fire and air signs are compatible with Sagittarius. The Sagittarius-Gemini polarity confers a natural affinity between the two signs.

Romance

Remember the movie *Two for the Road* with Audrey Hepburn and Albert Finney? The romance between Hepburn and Finney definitely fell under a Sagittarian influence. The exotic place, their individual searches for truth, and the truths they ultimately found in each other are Sagittarian themes. No matter who a Sagittarian loves or marries, a part of him or her is always slightly separate and singular, aware of the larger picture.

Work

Constraint isn't in the Sagittarian vocabulary. Or if it is, the word and the reality influence other people's lives, not the Sagittarian's. They work best in jobs and fields where they have complete freedom to call the shots: an owner of an airline, CEO, small business owner, entrepreneur, actor, writer, or traveling salesman. The point isn't the work so much as the freedom of the work. That is always the bottom line with Sagittarius.

Finances

A Sagittarius has plenty of options about where to spend his or her money—travel, education, workshops, seminars, animals, or books—and that's often the problem. How can they narrow their choices? What should they buy first? More than likely they will toss all their choices into the air and seize the one that hits ground first.

Physical Sagittarius

Many people born under this sign are tall and wide through the shoulders. They may have a tendency to gain weight because they indulge their appetites. Jupiter, the planet of expansion, rules this sign and often expands the physical body as well. The face tends to be oval and elongated.

Spirituality

As the natural ruler of the ninth house, which governs philosophy, religion, and higher education, Sagittarians generally sample a vast array of spiritual beliefs. Once they find a belief system that suits them, they generally stick with it. In this way they are much like their polar opposites, Gemini. The difference, though, is that Sagittarius delves very deeply.

Capricorn ♑

THE GOAT (DECEMBER 22–JANUARY 19)

Element: Earth	**Quality:** Cardinal
Keyword: Materialism, self-discipline	**Planetary Ruler:** Saturn
Rules: Knees, skin, and bones; natural ruler of the tenth house	

Capricorns are serious-minded people who often seem aloof and tightly in control of their emotions and their personal domain. Even as youngsters, there's a mature air about them, as if they were born with a profound core that few outsiders ever see.

This sign's nickname, the goat, represents Capricorn's slow, steady rise through the world. They're easily impressed by outward signs of success, but are interested less in money than in the power that money represents. Like Scorpio, they feel the need to rule whatever kingdom they occupy whether it's their home, work place, or business. Like Scorpios, they prize power and mastery over others, but they tend to be more subtle about it.

Capricorns are true workers—industrious, efficient, and disciplined. They deplore inertia in other people. Their innate common sense gives them the ability to plan ahead and to work out practical ways of approaching goals. More often than not, they succeed at whatever they set out to do.

In a crowd, Capricorns aren't particularly easy to spot. They aren't physically distinctive the way Scorpios are, and they aren't the life of the party like Sagittarians. But they possess a quiet dignity that's unmistakable.

Capricorns are natural worriers. Even when they've done their homework and taken all precautions they can possibly take, they fret that they've forgotten something. They benefit from the cultivation of "perfect faith" that whatever they do will work out fine.

Capricorn Woman

At first glance, she appears to be tough as nails, a determined, serious woman who seems to know where she has been, where she is, and where she's going. But when you get to know her, you discover she's not tough at all; she's merely guarded and reserved. Don't expect her to welcome you into her life with open arms. You have to prove yourself first.

This woman has certain parameters and boundaries that she simply won't cross. She isn't the type to throw herself recklessly into a casual affair. Once you've proven you're worth her while, she opens up emotionally and her depth may astonish you. She plays for keeps in love.

As a mother, she's devoted and often runs her home with the efficiency of a business. Due to the Saturn influence on this sign, the Capricorn woman can sometimes be too rigid with her spouse and children. She expects a lot and, supported by other aspects in her chart, may enforce her will to the point of dominance. She has a soft spot for animals, which often bring out the best in her simply because she opens to them emotionally.

Capricorn Man

He's well prepared for any journey he undertakes and it doesn't matter whether the journey is physical, emotional, or spiritual. He doesn't like surprises. He shies away from getting involved in people's lives and this detachment him allows him to focus on his goals. As a boss, he can be dictatorial, ordering people around with absolute impunity. As an employee, you won't find a harder worker.

He enjoys the company of vivacious women, perhaps because they make him feel lighter and less driven. Once he's committed, he tends to be monogamous. Life seems to improve for him as he ages, perhaps because he has learned that discipline is not nearly as important as compassion.

Capricorn Kids

Capricorn children can converse as easily with other kids as they can with adults. They are at ease with adults and, in some respects, actually consider them equals. This doesn't mean that they never act like kids. When they loosen up, they can be wild and unpredictable, but probably never reckless.

Like their adult counterparts, Capricorn children attack whatever they do with efficiency and patience. They often exhibit deep

compassion for people less fortunate. As the parent of a Capricorn child, teach him or her to lighten up!

As a parent, he is similar to the Capricorn mother's emphasis on rules, and parameters.

Compatibility

Virgos may be too mental and picky and Taureans too fixed, but because they have the earth element in common, they get along with Capricorns. Of the water signs, the intensity of Scorpios may be overwhelming and the ambivalence of Pisces may drive them nuts. Capricorns get along well with Cancers because both are cardinal signs.

Romance

At times, Capricorns need a partner who is serious, while other times they need the comic, the lighthearted innocent who makes them laugh. Which mate they end up with depends on where they are in life. That may be true for all of us to one extent or another, but it's especially true for the Capricorn.

Ultimately, the Capricorn's path is always serious business. No matter how hard you make them laugh, their path always leads back to the same riddle. Regardless of how hard they work, how far they climb, or how emotionally or physically rich they become, it's never enough. It only leads back to the solitude of self.

Work

Capricorns excel in any profession that is structured, such as engineering, medicine, editing, politics, ceramics, building, architecture, and leatherwork. Their strong desire to succeed is colored by traditional values and a conservative approach. In some Capricorns, these traits make them exceptionally good workers who progress slowly and successfully toward their goals. With other Capricorns, the tradition and conservatism hold them back.

Finances

Thriftiness is the hallmark for Capricorn finances. They build their finances the same way they build their careers, one penny at a time. They do seek status and the acquisition of material goods that reflect what they seek, so they go through periods where they overspend.

Notable Capricorn People

Humphrey Bogart
David Bowie
E. L. Doctorow
Faye Dunaway
Jose Ferrar
Cary Grant
J. Edgar Hoover
William James
James Earl Jones
Diane Keaton
Martin Luther King, Jr.
Mary Tyler Moore
Sir Isaac Newton
Dolly Parton
Edgar Allan Poe
Elvis Presley
J.D. Salinger
Albert Schweitzer
Josef Stalin

Physical Capricorn

They aren't the body-builder types. But because they are earth signs, they generally appreciate the benefits of exercise and have something physical that they do regularly. Their knees tend to trouble them. Because the sign is sometimes repressed emotionally, Capricorns benefit by venting what they feel, which in turn improves their physical bodies.

Spirituality

Capricorns flourish within structured and firmly established parameters. Ritual speaks to them and inspires them. They bring the same serious efficiency to their involvement with spiritual beliefs as they do to other areas of their lives. In less evolved types, the expression of spiritual beliefs can manifest as dogma. In the highly evolved Capricorn, the soul clearly understands its purpose in this life.

Aquarius ♒♒

WATER BEARER (JANUARY 20–FEBRUARY 18)	
Element: Air	**Quality:** Fixed
Planetary Ruler: Uranus	**Keyword:** Altruism, individuality, freedom
Rules: Ankles, shins, and circulatory system; natural ruler of the eleventh house	

Aquarians are original thinkers, often eccentric, who prize individuality and freedom above all else. The tribal mentality goes against their grain. They chafe at the restrictions placed upon them by society and seek to follow their own paths.

Aquarius is the sign of true genius because these people generally have the ability to think in unique ways. Once they make up their minds about something, nothing can convince them to change what they believe. This stubbornness is a double-edged sword; it can sustain them or destroy them. When the stubbornness manifests in small rebellions against the strictures of society, energy is wasted that could be put to better use.

Even though compassion is a hallmark of this sun sign, Aquarians usually don't become emotionally involved with the causes they promote. Their compassion, while genuine, rises from the intellect rather than the heart. The Uranian influence confers a fascination with a broad spectrum of intellectual interests.

Aquarius Woman

Even when you know her well, she's hard to figure because she's so often a bundle of paradoxes. She's patient but impatient; a nonconformist who conforms when it suits her; rebellious but peace-loving; stubborn and yet compliant when she wants to be.

She likes unusual people and has a variety of friends, both male and female. Economic status doesn't impress her, so her friends tend to come from a broad spectrum of backgrounds. Like the people she associates with, the Aquarian woman has many interests. She may dabble in tarot or astrology, have a passion for invention or writing, or may be a budding filmmaker. Whatever her profession, it allows her latitude to do things her way.

In romance, the only given with this woman is that she's attracted to someone who is unusual or eccentric in some way. Even if the significant other appears to be conventional, he isn't. As a mother, she allows her children the freedom to make their own decisions, revels in their accomplishments, and never lets them down.

Aquarius Man

He's often as inscrutable as his female counterpart and for the same reasons. He wants companionship, but not at the expense of his individuality. Even when he marries, he retains his independence to often irritating extremes. He might, for instance, fly off to some exotic place, leaving his wife or significant other to tend to his affairs at home.

The Aquarian man is fascinated by unusual people and places. Even though his attention is focused on the future, he may be interested in the mysteries of ancient cultures—how the pyramids were built, the true nature of Stonehenge, or the disappearance of the Anasazis. His travel to foreign cultures is often connected to these interests.

Aquarian men and women are both natural revolutionaries. If the restrictions placed on them are too confining, they rebel in a major way. But both need a place to which they can return, a sanctuary where they can refresh themselves. When the Aquarian man returns from his exotic journeys, he's eager to indulge himself in his family. As a parent, he may seem remote at times and perhaps somewhat undemonstrative, but his love for his offspring runs deep.

Aquarius Kids

They don't recognize barriers of any kind among people, so their friends span the gamut of the social and economic spectrum. They tend to be extroverts, but can also be content in solitary pursuits, their little minds busy with the stuff of the universe. They can be as stubborn as a Taurus, particularly when it comes to defending something they believe in.

Even though these kids get along well with their peers, they aren't followers. They aren't afraid to disagree with the consensus opinion. Within a family structure, they need to know they have the freedom to speak their own minds and that their opinions are heard. They may chafe at rules that are too rigid and strict.

Compatibility

Due to the lack of prejudice in this sign, Aquarians usually get along with just about everyone. They're particularly attracted to people with

whom they share an intellectual camaraderie. A sign that's sextile or trine to Aquarius is usually very compatible as is Aquarius's polar opposite, Leo.

Romance

Aquarians need the same space and freedom in a relationship that they crave in every other area of their lives. Even when they commit, the need doesn't evaporate. They must follow the dictates of their individuality above all else. This stubbornness can work against them if they aren't careful. Aquarians usually are attracted to people who are unusual or eccentric in some way. Their most intimate relationships are marked by uniqueness.

Work

They work best in avant garde fields: film, the arts, cutting-edge research in electronics, computers, or psychology. Many have raw psychic talent that can be developed into clairvoyance, remote viewing, and precognition, and most are very intuitive. The main element they seek in their work is freedom.

Finances

Aquarians are generous with their families and loved ones and that compassion extends to the larger scope of humanity as well. They stash money away, but the accumulation of wealth isn't the point; their freedom is.

Physical Aquarius

The typical Aquarian is usually tall and slender with a complexion that is lighter than his or her ethnic group. With Uranus ruling the sign, Aquarians have a sensitive nervous system and can be easily excitable. They should guard against exhausting their energy reserves; their minds are incessantly busy.

Spirituality

The revolutionary nature of the sign definitely extends to spiritual issues. Even if an Aquarian is born into a family that follows the dictates of an organized religion, he or she probably won't stick to it. Aquarians insist on finding their own path and seek a broader spiritual spectrum that honors "the family of man."

Notable Aquarius People

Alan Alda
Tom Brokaw
Natalie Cole
James Cromwell
Christian Dior
Farrah Fawcett
Zsa Zsa Gabor
Gene Hackman
Charles Lindberg
James Michener
Graham Nash
Paul Newman
Burt Reynolds
Tom Selleck
Emmanuel Swedenborg
John Travolta

Princess Diana and Astrology

Within hours of Princess Di's death in Paris on August 31, 1997, the astrology boards on the web literally hummed. Her birth chart and transits to her chart went up like billboards along the information highway. Every astrologer had an opinion about the celestial movements that had caused the accident.

Some astrologers focused on aspects that clearly indicated that alcohol or drug abuse had been involved. Other astrologers pinpointed aspects that spoke tomes about her relationship with the royal family. Some speculated that a conspiracy might be behind it because of her relationship with Dodi al Fayed.

In *The Mountain Astrologer*, an eminent magazine in the astrology field, one astrologer wrote: "At her death, transiting Neptune exactly conjoined her Saturn, while Uranus conjoined Jupiter, the ruler of her chart. Neptune dissolved the structure and Uranus, as shocking as it was, set her free."

To an astrologer, this language is eloquent; it precisely describes celestial movements that affected physical life. But what, exactly, do the words mean?

In yet another article about Diana's death, an astrologer notes that Diana's natal Venus was conjunct Caput Algol, the fixed star at 25 degrees Taurus. This star is known as "the evil one" and is associated with violent death. In Diana's chart, it is placed in her fifth house of children. At the very least, this would suggest her children might be taken from her through divorce. But, as Dawne Kovan wrote, "The tragic reality is that it is she who has been taken from them."

Kovan goes on to explore the prominent role that eclipses played in Diana's life. Her marriage to Prince Charles occurred within two days of a solar eclipse; Prince William was born during an eclipse; Diana's separation from the prince was announced on a lunar eclipse; and she died less than twenty-four hours before a solar eclipse on September 1, 1997.

All of this is as fascinating as Diana's life. But the bottom line is that death in a chart is fairly easy to spot after the fact and nearly impossible to predict before the fact. Astrologer Grant Lewi allegedly predicted his own death, but we don't know whether that was astrology speaking or the voice of his own intuition.

What might Princess Diana's astrologer have said to her? At best, she might have warned the princess that certain patterns would be taking shape that might endanger her. She might have warned the princess to be careful on the highway, to stay clear of any driver who had been drinking. She might have advised her to stay put between certain dates. But for the most part, these kinds of warnings are common sense. It's doubtful that Diana's astrologer told her she might die around the time of the solar eclipse on September 1, 1997. Doubtful because most contemporary astrologers realize that an individual's free will governs the blueprint of the birth chart.

Pisces ♓

THE FISH (FEBRUARY 19–MARCH 20)

Element: Water	**Quality:** Mutable
Keyword: Compassion, mysticism	**Planetary Ruler:** Neptune
Rules: The feet and is associated with the lymphatic system; natural ruler of the twelfth house	

Pisces need to explore their world through their emotions. They feel things so deeply that quite often they become a kind of psychic sponge, absorbing the emotions of people around them. Because of this, they should choose their friends and associates carefully.

People born under this sign usually have wonderful imaginations and great creative resources. They gravitate toward the arts in general and to theater and film in particular. In the business world, they tend to make powerful administrators and managers because they are so attuned to the thoughts of the people around them.

Pisces people need time alone so that they can detach from the emotions of people around them and center themselves. Without periodic solitude, it becomes increasingly difficult for them to sort out what they feel from what other people feel. They are very impressionable. They also tend to be moody because they feel the very height of joy and the utter depths of despair.

Love and romance are essential for most Piscean individuals. It fulfills them emotionally and they generally flourish within stable relationships.

Pisces, represented by the fish swimming in opposite directions, can be ambivalent and indecisive simply because they're so impressionable. In highly evolved types, mystical tendencies are well developed and the individuals possess deeply spiritual connections.

Pisces Woman

She's mysterious, with an air of complexity about her, as if she knows more than she's telling. Her eyes are large, gentle, and almost liquid with compassion. The lady is all feeling and possesses a quiet strength that hints at inner depths.

Don't ever be dogmatic with her. She refuses to be limited or restricted by anyone or anything that might inhibit her freedom of expression. This is reflected in her job, her home, and her relationship with her family and friends. This tendency may sometimes work against her, but she doesn't care. It's against her nature to be otherwise.

Even though she needs companionship, she also craves her solitude. It's as essential to her well-being as harmony is to a Libra. When she doesn't have her time alone, she may be prone to alcohol or drug abuse. Properly channeled, her energy can produce astonishing works in art, literature, and music. In this instance, she becomes a mystical channel for the higher mind.

As a mother, her psychic connection to her children allows her to understand what they're feeling even when they don't understand it themselves.

Pisces Man

His quiet strength and self-containment fascinate women. He's a good listener, the kind of man who gives you his full attention when you're talking. He's also a fine friend to people he trusts, always there when his friend are in need. But, like his female counterpart, he's a sucker for a sob story; he can't stand seeing tragedies or heartbreaks in others.

In affairs of the heart, the Pisces man is a true romantic, even if he doesn't want to admit it to himself. He likes candlelight dinners and intimate conversation. It may take him a while to fall head over heels in love, but once he does, his emotions run deep and eternal.

The Pisces man may gravitate toward the arts or, because the sign rules the twelfth house, may work behind the scene in some capacity. Whatever his path, he needs to learn to balance the demands of his inner life with his responsibilities in the external world.

Pisces Kids

In a crowd, the easiest way to pick out a Pisces child is by the liquid eyes. Their gaze seems wise, ancient, as if they have seen worlds the rest of us haven't even imagined. Pisces kids tend to have vivid dreams and many of them manifest an early interest in

psychic phenomena. If the mystical tendencies are nurtured and encouraged, a Pisces child can grow into a true medium, clairvoyant, or healer.

These kids feel everything with such intensity that a cross look is probably all a parent needs to keep them in line. If you raise your voice to a Pisces child, it's the equivalent of a physical assault. Their feelings are easily hurt.

Compatibility

Other water signs seem the obvious choice here.
But Scorpio might overpower Pisces and Cancer might be too clinging. The signs sextile to Pisces are Capricorn and Taurus. While Capricorn might be too limited and grounded for the Piscean imagination, Taurus probably fits right in. Gemini, because it's a mutable sign like Pisces, can also be compatible.

Romance

Through the heart, sensitive Pisces experiences his subjective reality as real, solid, perhaps even more tangible than the external world. For some Pisces, romance can be the point of transcendence, the source where he penetrates to the larger mysteries that have concerned him most of his life. To be romantically involved with a Pisces is to be introduced to many levels of consciousness and awareness. If you're not up to it, then get out now because your Pisces isn't going to change.

Work

Pisces do well in anything that is behind the scenes. Due to their dreamy imaginations and mystical leanings, they excel in the arts, literature, and drama, or as monks, mystics, even inventors. Piscean Edgar Cayce, the "sleeping prophet," is probably the best example of what a Pisces is capable of doing in metaphysics. Piscean Albert Einstein is one of the best examples of Pisces as scientific genius.

Finances

Pisces is usually less concerned about money and material goods than he is about enjoying what he does to make a living. Can

Notable Pisces People

Michael Caine
Frederic Chopin
Albert Einstein
Mikhail Gorbachev
Peter Graves
Jean Harlowe
George Harrison
Rex Harrison
Ron Howard
Andrew Jackson
Jerry Lewis
Liza Minnelli
B.F. Skinner
Elizabeth Taylor

he transcend himself through his work? Does his tremendous compassion find expression through his work? If not, then he will undoubtedly change his work again and again, until he finds the job or profession that suits him.

Physical Pisces

There are two types of Pisces individuals—the whale and the dolphin. The first tends to be physically large—in height and in weight. The second tends to be smaller, more graceful. The whale often looks awkward when he walks, as if his feet are too small for the rest of him. His dolphin counterpart is, in contrast, like a dancer, at home in his body. The extraordinary eyes that are typical of the Pisces individual are exemplified in the violet eyes of Elizabeth Taylor.

Since Pisces rules the feet, most individuals with a Pisces Sun, Moon, or Ascendant benefit from foot massage and foot reflexology.

Spirituality

Not all Pisces people are psychic, of course, or mystically inclined. Not all of them want to become monks or nuns, either. But most Pisces people are born with a deep intuitive sense, even if it's latent. And this sense is what connects them to a higher power. It may manifest within the parameters of organized religion—or it may veer into something less structured. Whatever form it takes, the intuitive side of Pisces seeks expression.

The Planets

CHAPTER
3

Astrology and Intuition

When I was eight or nine, one of my uncles took me, my sister, and several cousins on an adventure I've never forgotten. It took place in his back yard in Oklahoma, on a clear summer night, when each of us got a turn to peer through the magical lens of his new telescope.

That night, I saw the rings of Saturn, the red dust of Mars, the stark landscape of the moon. And suddenly, the stories about the Greek and Roman gods that my mother read to me leaped to life. The outer evidence fused with an inner certainty, intellect joined intuition, pieces slammed together. In a moment of utter clarity, I understood why Mars was the god of war, why Mercury was the messenger, why Neptune ruled the seas and everything beneath them. I intuitively sensed connections.

And intuition is what brings any natal chart interpretation into clarity. It links the pieces into a coherent whole, a living story. Without it, you're just reading symbols. You're a traveler in a foreign country equipped with only a phrase book; you can get by, but not much else.

Planets are the expression of energy. They are classified as benefic or malefic, good or bad. These terms are misleading since planetary energy isn't positive or energy; our use of the energy determines whether it's positive or negative. Traditionally, Jupiter is the great benefic, the planet that blesses. Venus comes in a close second. The Sun, Moon, and Mercury line up after that. Saturn is the great malefic, the big bad guy of the group whose lessons tend to be harsh. He's followed by Mars, Uranus, Neptune, and Pluto.

Inner and Outer Planets

Planets orbit the sun at different speeds. The closer a planet is to the sun, the faster it travels through its orbit. The Moon, for instance, travels through the zodiac in about twenty-eight days and spends two to three days in each sign. Mercury orbits the Sun in eighty-eight days. Pluto, which lies the farthest from the sun, completes its orbit in 248 years. The faster moving planets—Moon, Mercury, Venus, Mars—are known as inner planets. Jupiter, Uranus, Neptune, and Pluto are known as outer planets.

The inner planets are considered to be personal because they relate to the development of our individual egos, our conscious selves. The outer planets relate to the outer world. Since the outer planets move so much more slowly through the zodiac, their pattern of influence is often felt by an entire generation of people.

The luminaries—Sun and Moon—also have transpersonal qualities. The Sun represents not only our ego, but fundamental cosmic energy. The Moon, which concerns our most intimate emotions and urges, links us to what astrologer Robert Hand calls, "One's Ultimate Source."

Planetary Motion

Planetary motion is either direct (D), retrograde (R), or stationary (S). In reality, all planetary motion is direct but relative motion isn't.

The Sun and the Moon can never turn retrograde, but all of the other planets do. A retrograde planet is one that appears to move backward in the zodiac, but this backward motion is actually an optical illusion. Imagine being in a train as another train speeds past you. You feel as if you're moving backward, when in actuality you're only moving more slowly than the other train. Retrograde motion doesn't change the fundamental essence of a planet; it merely means that the expression of its energy is altered somewhat.

Earth

During a Mercury retrograde, for instance, communications tend to get fouled up and travel plans are disrupted. During a Jupiter retrograde, the beneficial aspects of the planet are turned down somewhat. Some astrologers contend that if there are three or more retrograde planets in a chart, certain past life patterns may prevail in the present life. But even if it is true, our point of power lies in the present, in this life, this moment.

During a retrograde, the nature of that planet is forced inward, where it creates tension and stress. The outlet for this tension is usually worked out in relationships with others.

Planets in direct motion have more influence than retrograde planets. Stationary planets, those that are about to turn direct or retrograde, have greater influence in a chart than either retrograde or direct moving planets. This is due to the concentrated energy of the planet.

Strengths and Weaknesses of the Planets

The strength or weakness of a planet depends on its sign, placement in the houses, aspects, and motion. A planet that occupies a sign it rules is *dignified*—Mercury in Gemini, for instance, or Venus in Libra.

When a planet is *exalted*, its drive and essential qualities are expressed more harmoniously. An example would be the Sun in Aries or the Moon in Taurus. Exalted planets are assigned specific degrees and are said to function smoothly within those degrees. These specifics are summarized in Table 3-1.

A planet is in the sign of *detriment* when it occupies the sign opposite that of its dignity. An example is Mercury in Sagittarius; Mercury is in detriment here because it rules Gemini and Sagittarius is Gemini's polar opposite. In a detriment, the energy of the planet is considered to be at a disadvantage.

When a planet lies in the sign opposite that of its exaltation, it's said to be *in fall*. A Moon in Scorpio is in fall because the Moon is exalted in Taurus. Its energy is watered down.

Mutual reception occurs when two planets are placed in each other's sign of dignity. The Sun and the Moon, for instance, are in mutual reception if the Sun is in Cancer or Taurus and the Moon in Leo or Aries. This happens because the Sun rules Leo and is exalted in Aries, and the Moon rules Cancer and is exalted in Taurus.

When a planet is placed in its natural house of the horoscope (Mercury in the third house, for instance), it's *accidentally dignified* and strengthened.

One of the most important planets in a chart is the one that rules the ascendant or rising. This planet is usually, but not always, considered the ruler of the chart. A Libra rising, for example, means that Venus is the chart ruler because Venus rules Libra.

The Nodes of the Moon

The lunar nodes are the degrees where the plane of the Moon's orbit intersects or crosses the ecliptic (Earth's orbit around the sun). The nodes are important in the interpretation of a chart, but astrologers differ about what they mean.

Astrologer Robert Hand believes that nodes "relate to connections with other people; that is, they are an axis of relationship. In this context, the North Node has a joining quality, while the South has a separating quality."

In Hindu astrology, both nodes are considered to be malefic. In Western astrology, the North Node, called the Dragon's Head, is considered an easier aspect, the equivalent of Jupiter, and the South Node or Dragon's Tail is considered the equivalent of Saturn.

Another theory ties the nodes in with reincarnation. In this theory, the South Node represents our karma, deeply embedded patterns of behavior and thought we acquired in previous lives. We need to overcome these patterns through the North Node, which represents the area of our most profound growth in this life.

In *The Inner Sky*, astrologer Steven Forrest writes: ". . . the South Node of the Moon symbolizes our karma . . . it shows a kind of behavior that is instinctive and automatic . . . it speaks of mindset and a pattern of motivations that arise spontaneously . . ." The North Node, according to Forrest, ". . . represents the point that puts the most unrelenting tension on the past. As we allow ourselves to experience it, we open up to an utterly alien and exotic reality. We are stretched to the breaking point . . ."

I dislike the word karma because it implies a negation of free will. I prefer to think of the South Node as an unconscious bias—either from previous incarnations or that builds up during our lives. It's what we need to release in order to grow. The North Node sign and house placement indicate the area of our lives we need to expand so we can evolve toward our fulfillment as spiritual beings in this life.

Sometimes, the nodes seems to work in a symbiotic relationship with Saturn. As we encounter restrictions in the area where Saturn sits in our chart, we are seemingly forced to rid ourselves of South Node prejudices by working through our North Node energies.

The North Node also represents the types of people we gravitate toward and the South Node represents the types of people we avoid.

Critical Degrees

Certain planets are strengthened in a horoscope when they fall within a certain range of degrees. A planet that is dignified by house or sign or one which is well-aspected is infused with more power when it falls in one of these degrees.

Critical Degrees

SIGN	DEGREES
Aries ♈	0–26°
Cancer ♋	
Libra ♎	
Capricorn ♑	

SIGN	DEGREES
Taurus ♉	9–21°
Leo ♌	
Scorpio ♏	
Aquarius ♒	

SIGN	DEGREES
Gemini ♊	4–17°
Virgo ♍	
Sagittarius ♐	
Pisces ♓	

Part of Fortune

There are at least thirty-seven Arabian parts that are vestiges of Medieval times when Arabian astrology found its way into Western astrology through the influence of Moslem thought. These parts are imaginary spots in a chart that are computed from the addition and subtraction of three or more points. The most commonly used Arabian part in Western astrology is the Part of Fortune.

The Part of Fortune is considered a fortunate point in the horoscope, a point of harmony, success, and ease. In *Joy and the Part of Fortune*, astrologer Martin Schulman notes, "The Part of Fortune represents that place in the horoscope where, within himself, the individual knows he must not compromise his ideals."

The house indicates the area in which we find fortune and success and the sign shows how the energy of the part can best manifest in our lives. To calculate the Part of Fortune, the Moon's position is added to the position of the Ascendant, and the position of the Sun is subtracted from this sum. The formula is: AS + Moon - Sun.

Table 3–1: Exaltations and Critical Degrees

This list includes the exact degree of dignity for the exaltations. Detriments are the same degree in the opposite sign.

Planet		Exaltation		In Fall	
☉	Sun	19° ♈	Aries	19° ♎	Libra
☽	Moon	3° ♉	Taurus	3° ♏	Scorpio
☿	Mercury	15° ♍	Virgo	15° ♓	Pisces
♀	Venus	27° ♓	Pisces	27° ♍	Virgo
♂	Mars	28° ♑	Capricorn	28° ♋	Cancer
♃	Jupiter	15° ♋	Cancer	15° ♑	Capricorn
♄	Saturn	21° ♎	Libra	21° ♈	Aries
♅	Uranus	7° ♏	Scorpio	7° ♉	Taurus
♆	Neptune	18° ♋	Cancer	18° ♑	Capricorn
♇	Pluto	17° ♌	Leo	17° ♒	Aquarius

Calculating the Part of Fortune

In calculating the Part of Fortune, the signs are converted to the number of their natural position in the zodiac: Aries = 1, Taurus = 2, and so on. Sixty minutes equals one degree.

Let's say that that we're working with the following: rising at 00°50' Scorpio; Moon at 29°54' Capricorn; and a Sun at 16°12' Gemini. Scorpio is the eighth sign, so the converted rising is: 8 00°50'; Capricorn is the tenth sign, so the Moon's conversion is: 10 29°54'. Gemini is the third sign, so the Sun's conversion is 3 16°12'. Now let's put it together.

Rising:	8	00°	50'
Moon:	10	29°	54'
	18	29°	104'

	18	29°	104'
minus the Sun	- 3	16°	12'
	15	13°	92'

This figure must now be reduced to its lowest units. There are 12 signs, so that figure must be subtracted from 15 for a total of 3. Since there are 30 degrees in each sign, we need to reduce the 92' to its lowest unit: 92'–90', for a total of two. Three minutes are then added to the 13':

	15	13°	92'	
- 12				
	3	13°	92'	
-			90'	(90' = 3°)
	3	13°	02'	
+		3°		
	3	16°	02'	

This means that the Part of Fortune is in the third sign of Gemini at 16°02'. This figure is then entered into the appropriate house.

Key Words for the Planets

Sun: Vitality, ego, self-image.

Moon: Emotions, intuition, the yin.

Mercury: Culling and communication of information, mental quickness.

Venus: Love, romance, aesthetics, serenity.

Mars: Aggression, individuation, will.

Jupiter: Expansion, luck, higher mind.

Saturn: Discipline, limitations, building a solid foundation.

Uranus: Sudden and unexpected, disruption, genius, innovative.

Neptune: Illusion, inspiration, creative genius.

Pluto: Transformation, regeneration, the occult.

North Node: The point through which we break free of unconscious or past-life bias and evolve fully as spiritual beings.

South Node: The release of old, deeply embedded patterns we need to break.

Part of Fortune: A point of luck, success.

The Planets

The Sun: Your Ego ☉

Think beach, blue skies, sunlight spilling across the white sand. The Sun is the very essence and energy of life, the manifestation of will, power, and desire. It represents the ego, individuality, the yang principle and is the thrust that allows us to meet challenges and expand our lives. The Sun represents a person's creative abilities and the general state of his or her physical health.

The Sun embraces the fatherhood principle and in a chart, symbolizes a person's natural father and a woman's husband. As natural ruler of the fifth house, it rules children in general and the firstborn in particular. Since the Sun also symbolizes authority and power, a strongly placed Sun confers leadership ability. A Sun that is badly aspected or which is weakly placed lessens the natural vitality and may make it difficult for the person to express basic drives and desires.

The Sun spends about a month in each sign, with a mean daily motion of 59'8". It rules occupations of power and authority—royalty and religious and spiritual rulers. Its natural house is the fifth and it governs the sign of Leo. It rules the heart, back, spine, and spinal cord.

The Moon: Your Emotions ☾

The inner you. Intuition. The feminine. The mother. The yin principle. Coupled with the Sun and the Ascendant, the Moon is one of the vital parts of a chart. It describes our emotional reactions to situations, how emotions flow through us, motivating and compelling us—or limiting us and holding us back.

The Moon symbolizes a person's mother and the relationship between mother and child. In a man's chart, the Moon represents his wife; in a woman's chart, it describes pregnancies, childbirth, and intuition. Symbolically, the Moon represents our capacity to become part of the whole rather than attempting to master the parts. It asks that we become whatever it is that we seek.

As Earth's satellite, the Moon moves more swiftly than any of the planets, completing a circuit of the zodiac in less than twenty-eight days. It rules activities and professions dealing with children and those that concern the sea. Its natural house is the fourth and it governs the sign of Cancer. The stomach, breasts, mammary glands, womb, conception, and the body fluids in general are ruled by the Moon.

Mercury: Your Intellect ☿

Mental quickness. Verbal acuity. Communication. Our mental picture of the world. Mercury is the messenger; it speaks in terms of logic and reasoning. The left brain is its vehicle. Mercury represents how we think and how we communicate those thoughts. Mercury also is concerned with travel of the routine variety—work commutes, trips across town, weekend excursions, or a visit with siblings and neighbors—rather than long distance travel.

Restlessness is inherent to Mercury because it craves movement, newness, and the bright hope of undiscovered terrains. Mercury often tackles something new before the old has been assimilated. On a higher level, Mercury seeks to understand the deeper connections between the physical universe and the divine.

Mercury orbits the Sun in about eighty-eight days. It goes retrograde every few months and during that time communications and travel plans go haywire. Your computer may go down, lightning may blow out your electricity, or you may spend hours in an airport waiting for a flight that is ultimately canceled. It's best not to sign contracts when Mercury is retrograde.

Mercury rules any profession dealing with writing, teaching, speaking, books, and publications. Mercury is the natural ruler of the third and sixth houses and governs Gemini and Virgo. It rules arms, hands, shoulders, lungs, the solar plexus, abdomen, intestines, the thymus gland, and the nervous and respiratory systems.

Mercury

Venus: Your Love Life ♀

Romance. Beauty. Artistic instinct. Sociability. Venus governs our ability to attract compatible people, to create close personal relationships and to form business partnerships. It expresses how we relate to other people one-on-one and how we express ourselves in marriage and in romantic relationships.

Since Venus determines our spontaneous attractions to other people, it's one of the areas to look at when doing chart comparisons for compatibility. When Venus falls in another person's Sun sign, it enhances the initial attraction and bodes well for overall compatibility. This planet, along with the Moon, is associated with maternal love in that it gives what it has freely and without strings attached.

Venus is associated with the arts and the aesthetic sense, and it has enormous influence on our tastes in art, music, and literature.

Venus

The sign and placement of Venus, as well as its aspects, determine our refinement—or lack of it. This planet also has some bearing on material resources, earning capacity, and spending habits. A strong Venus enhances these things; a poorly placed or badly aspected Venus generates laziness, self-indulgence, extravagance, and discord in partnerships.

Venus orbits the Sun in 255 days. It spends about four weeks in a sign when moving direct and is retrograde for about six weeks. It rules all professions having to do with the arts and music. Its natural houses are the second and the seventh, and it governs Taurus and Libra. It rules the neck, throat, thyroid gland, kidneys, ovaries, veins, and circulation of the venous blood. It shares rulership with the Moon over the female sex organs.

Mars: Your Energy ♂

Dynamic expression. Aggression. Individualism. Sexual drive. Action. Mars dictates our survival energy and the shape that energy assumes as we define ourselves in terms of the larger world. It represents the individualization process, particularly in a romantic relationship. A weak Mars placement in a woman's chart may make her too passive and submissive in a love relationship, especially if her significant other has a strongly placed Mars.

Mars rules athletes and competitions. The true Mars individual seeks to take himself to the limit—and then surpass that limit. He refuses to compromise his integrity by following another's agenda. He doesn't compare himself to other people and doesn't want to dominate or be dominated. He simply wants to be free to follow his own path, whatever it is.

Mars' energy can be either constructive or destructive; it depends on how it's channeled. Rage, violence, and brutality can manifest if the energy is poorly channeled. When properly channeled, Mars' energy manifests as stamina and achievement.

Mars orbits the sun in 687 days. It spends six to eight weeks in a sign. When retrograde, it sits in a sign for two and half months.

As the god of war, Mars governs the military, rules Aries, and is co-ruler of Scorpio. Its natural houses are the first and the eighth. It rules the head, general musculature of the body, the sex organs in general—the male sex organs in particular—the anus, red corpuscles, and hemoglobin.

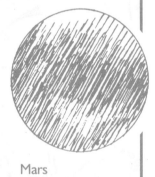

Mars

Jupiter: Your Luck, Your Higher Mind ♃

Philosophy. Religion. Higher education. Expansion and integration. Growth. Tradition views Jupiter as the great benefic planet, associated with luck, success, achievement, and prosperity. But it can also indicate excess, laziness, and other less desirable traits. The bottom line, though, is that Jupiter's energies are usually constructive.

This planet's energy is what allows us to reach out beyond ourselves and expand our consciousness. It confers a love of travel and a need to explore religious and philosophical ideas. Jupiter also allows us to integrate ourselves into the larger social order—church or religion, community, and corporation.

Since Jupiter rules the abstract mind, it describes our intellectual and spiritual interests in the most profound sense. In terms of the body, Jupiter can often lead to a physical expansion as well: weight gain.

Jupiter takes about twelve years to traverse the zodiac and averages a year in every sign. It governs publishing, the travel profession, universities and other institutions of higher learning, and traditional organized religions. Its natural houses are the ninth and the twelfth. It rules Sagittarius. Jupiter oversees the blood in general, arteries, hips, thighs, and feet (with Neptune).

Saturn: Your Responsibilities, Karma ♄

Discipline. Responsibility. Limitations and restrictions. Obedience. Building of foundations. No free rides. Saturn has long been known as the great malefic. While it's true that its lessons are sometimes harsh, it also provides structure and foundation, and teaches us through experience what we need in order to grow. It shows us the limitations we have and teaches us the rules of the game in this physical reality.

Astrologer Jean Avery, writing in *Astrology and Your Past Lives*, says: "The description of Saturn's placement, aspects, and rulerships in the horoscope is most important in the process of uncovering past life experiences." Even if you don't believe in reincarnation, there's ample evidence that Saturn holds a key to what the soul intends to accomplish in this life.

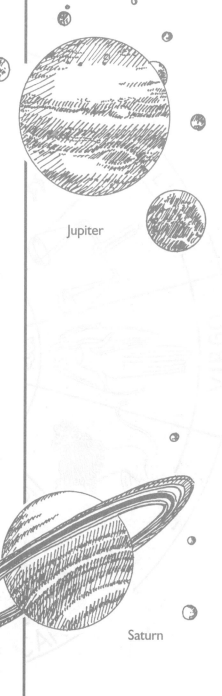

Jupiter

Saturn

People with a well placed or well aspected Saturn tend to have a practical, prudent outlook. When poorly aspected, Saturn creates rigid belief systems, restricts growth, and closes us off to other possibilities. A delicate balance must be grasped about Saturn influences. Even though it pushes us to understand and work with limitations, it can also cause us to settle for too little, to deny our creative expression because we don't want to see what is really possible.

As one of the outer, slowly moving planets, Saturn takes twenty-nine and a half years to cross the zodiac. Its natural houses are the tenth and the eleventh. It rules Capricorn. This planet governs the bones and joints, skin, and teeth.

Uranus: Your Individuality ♅

Sudden, unexpected disruptions. Breaks with tradition and old patterns to make room for the new. Genius. Eccentricity. Astrologer Steven Forrest considers Uranus the ruler of astrology; Robert Hand calls Uranus, Neptune, and Pluto "transcendental planets" that can be dealt with constructively only with an expanded consciousness. Unless we nurture a larger perspective, Uranian disruptions appear to bring unpleasant and unexpected surprises. In reality, these disruptions liberate us, revolutionize the way we do things, and blow out the old so that the new can flow in.

Uranus, like the other outer planets, remains in a sign for so long that its effect is felt on the masses. Today, nearing the twenty-first century, this planet's influence is visible in the breakdown of old paradigms of belief within most of the large structures we have taken for granted: health care, medicine, science, religion, lifestyle, education, social programs. We stand at the brink of a new century with old structures crumbling around us. But in the shadows, the new paradigms are forming, bubbling with vitality, gathering momentum. This is all part of the Uranian influence.

Uranus

In a horoscope, Uranus dictates the areas of our life in which these disruptions occur and how we utilize this energy. Do we feel it? Think about it? Seize it? Pull it deep within us so that it becomes rooted in who we are? Are we so afraid of it that we deny it? Uranus also indicates the areas in which we are most inventive, creative, and original.

This planet takes eighty-four years to go through the zodiac. Its natural house is the eleventh and it rules Aquarius. Traditionally, before the discovery of Uranus in 1781, Saturn ruled this sign. But Saturn's rigidity just doesn't fit Aquarius. It governs electricity, inventions, the avant garde, everything that is unpredictable or sudden.

Neptune: Your Visionary Self, Your Illusions Ψ

Hidden. Psychic. Spiritual insights. Illusions. The unconscious. This planet stimulates the imagination, dreams, psychic experiences, artistic inspiration, flashes of insight, mystical tendencies. On the down side, it deals with all forms of escapism—drug and alcohol addiction, as well as delusion.

Neptune

Neptune, like Uranus, overpowers Saturn's rigidity. Where Uranus disrupts the rigidity, Neptune simply negates it. This planet is considered the higher octave of Venus, and when it operates in the chart of an evolved soul, its music is extraordinary. Edgar Cayce, known as the "sleeping prophet," was such an individual. While asleep, he was able to diagnose physical ailments for people he'd never met, using nothing more than their names.

Most of us experience Neptune through synchronous events and flashes of insight that seem to come out of nowhere. Or we lose ourselves in the illusions we've created. The best way to appreciate Neptune's energy is from a standpoint of quiet contemplation—meditation, yoga, listening to music, writing imaginative fiction, or through some activity that involves water.

As Steven Forrest writes in *The Inner Sky,* "Neptune asks us to go beyond the universe of ego, hunger, and aggression without sacrificing our ability to function as a personality."

Neptune takes 165 years to cross the zodiac and spends about fourteen years in each sign. The twelfth house is its natural domain and it rules Pisces. It governs shipping, dance, film, and the arts in general, and is associated with mediums, clairvoyants, psychic healers, and both white and black magic.

Pluto: How You Transform and Regenerate Your Life ♀

Destiny. Transcendence. Redemption. Purge. Power. Afterlife. Good and evil. Pluto's influence is never ambivalent or passive. Although it sometimes works in subtle ways, its repercussion in our lives is far-reaching and transformational. Its two extremes are best symbolized by Hitler and Gandhi, each man possessed of a vision that he manifested in physical reality. Both had a mission, a sense of destiny, but one caused massive destruction and the other elevated mass consciousness.

In our personal lives, Pluto's influence is no different. Pluto tears down our habits and belief systems, the very structures that Saturn has helped us build, thus forcing us to transcend the ruin—or to smother in the debris.

Pluto

A Pluto placement in Sagittarius, in the ninth house of philosophy and spiritual beliefs, would mean you evolve through expansion of your beliefs in these areas. But before you do, Pluto will destroy your old beliefs, collapsing them like a house of cards.

Pluto, discovered in 1930, is the most distant planet from the Sun. It exists at the very edge of our solar system, its light so dim it seems almost etheric. It takes 248 years to complete a circuit of the zodiac. Popular astrological theory says that Pluto, like Uranus and Neptune, wasn't discovered until humanity had evolved to the point to be able to understand its energy.

"Through it," writes Steven Forrest, "we embody the visions and terrors of humanity. We represent them. We serve as a living symbol of some communal need or fear." Through Pluto, we tap into that which is larger than our individual selves. We tap into the collective mind in all its hypnotizing horror and magnificent beauty.

Since Pluto's discovery, its influence has been observed in only Cancer, Leo, Virgo, Libra, and Scorpio. In the late fall of 1995, Pluto slipped into Sagittarius. The transformation under this influence is apt to be enormous and far-reaching, completing the collapse of old paradigms and belief systems.

Pluto, the higher octave of Mars, governs various types of occult practices: black magic, levitation, witchcraft, and reincarnation. On a personal level in a horoscope, Pluto's influence is most powerful when it occupies a prominent place or rules the chart.

EXERCISE

Practice Exercise 1: Planets and Their Symbols

Just for fun, match the symbols with the planet. See answers that follow.

♃ ☉ ♂ ♀︎⃝ ♀ **AS** **PF/⊕** ☾ ♄ ☊ ♆ ☋ ☿ ♅

Sun _____

Moon _____

Mercury _____

Venus _____

Mars _____

Jupiter _____

Saturn _____

Uranus _____

Neptune _____

Pluto _____

North Node _____

South Node _____

Part of Fortune _____

Ascendant _____

EXERCISE

Answers to Practice Exercise 1: Planets and Their Symbols

Sun	☉
Moon	☽
Mercury	☿
Venus	♀
Mars	♂
Jupiter	♃
Saturn	♄
Uranus	♅
Neptune	♆
Pluto	♇
North Node	☊
South Node	☋
Part of Fortune	PF/⊕
Ascendant	AS

EXERCISE

Practice Exercise 2: Sun Signs and Their Symbols

Now, just for review, do the same thing with the sun signs and their symbols. See answers that follow.

♏ ♉ ♓ ♌ ♐ ♈ ♋ ♍ ♊ ♒ ♎ ♑

Aries _____

Taurus _____

Gemini _____

Cancer _____

Leo _____

Virgo _____

Libra _____

Scorpio _____

Sagittarius _____

Capricorn _____

Aquarius _____

Pisces _____

Answers to Practice Exercise 2: Sun Signs and Their Symbols

Aries	♈
Taurus	♉
Gemini	♊
Cancer	♋
Leo	♌
Virgo	♍
Libra	♎
Scorpio	♏
Sagittarius	♐
Capricorn	♑
Aquarius	♒
Pisces	♓

Planets and Nodes in the Signs

CHAPTER 4

The sign a planet or a node occupies describes how that particularly energy permeates your personality and influences your life. If you have eight out of ten planets in fire signs, then you probably have abundant energy and a fierce temper and tend to initiate action and experience. If you have mostly air planets, your approach to life is primarily mental.

This section is arranged with the faster-moving planets first. For a more concise understanding of the energies involved, planets in their signs should be read in conjunction with planets in their houses.

The Moon in the Signs

The Moon expresses your emotions, the inner you, that which makes you feel secure.

Aries Moon

Your emotions are all fire. You're passionate, impulsive, headstrong. Your relationships, especially when you're younger, can be impulsive. Your own actions ground you. You take pride in your ability to make decisions and to get things moving.

Taurus Moon (exalted)

You don't like to argue. You need time alone and thrive in your private spaces, whatever they might be. You enjoy your creature comforts and being surrounded by belongings that hold personal meaning. Your emotional well-being depends on the harmony of your emotional attachments.

Gemini Moon

You thrive on change and variety. Your emotions fluctuate and sometimes you think too much, analyzing what you feel and why. Your capacity for adaptability, however, sees you through the many changes you experience.

Cancer Moon (dignified)

You have strong family ties and feel a need to nurture or nourish others. At times, you're very psychic; other times you're merely moody. When you're hurt, you tend to withdraw and brood. You don't like emotional confrontations and seek to sidestep them.

Leo Moon

Your emotions are often dramatic. You feel cheerful and optimistic about life in general. You enjoy the limelight and being recognized for what you do and what you are. You take deep pride in your children and family.

Virgo Moon

You tend to be somewhat reticent about what you feel. You're interested in health and hygiene and how these issues relate to you and the people you care for. You feel happy when you're of service to others and take pride in your meticulous attention to details. You can be overly critical of your personal relationships and of yourself.

Libra Moon

Discord makes you feel anxious. You thrive on harmony in your personal environment and need compatible relationships for your emotional well-being. You go out of your way to avoid confrontations. Music, art, ballet, and literature lift your spirits.

Scorpio Moon (in fall)

Your emotions and passions run deep. You feel a profound loyalty to your family and the people you love. You possess great strength and are able to draw on it during times of crisis. Your dreams, premonitions, and many of your experiences border on the mystical. You rarely forget it when someone has slighted you.

Sagittarius Moon

You need emotional freedom and independence. You need your own space so you can explore everything that fascinates you—foreign cultures, inner worlds, or the distant future. None of this means that you love your significant other any less; you simply need your freedom. You enjoy animals.

Capricorn Moon (detriment)

You need structure of some sort to feel emotionally secure. This need can show up in any area of your life; it depends on what issues are important to you at a given time. You aren't as emotionally aloof as some people think; you just don't wear your heart on your sleeve.

Aquarius Moon

Your compassion extends to humanity—the beggar on Seventh Avenue, the children dying in Africa, or the AIDS patients whose families have turned against them. You bleed for them. Your home life is important to you, but it's definitely not traditional. You don't recognize boundaries or limitations of any sort.

Pisces Moon

When your emotions flow through you with the ease of water, you feel and sense what is invisible to others. Sometimes, you're a psychic sponge; you soak up emotions from others and may even manifest those emotions. Your compassion sometimes makes you gullible and impractical. Your artistic sensibilities are strong.

The Nodes of the Moon in the Signs

The Moon's nodes are always in opposite signs, thus directly opposed to each other in a chart. The North Node symbolizes the future we move toward, the route to our greatest spiritual fulfillment. The South Node represents the prejudices we need to overcome, the areas in our lives that hold what we need to release, so that we can grow.

North Node in Aries, South Node in Libra

With assertiveness and initiative, you overcome indecisiveness and reliance on others.

North Node in Taurus, South Node in Scorpio

A relentless practicality and drive allow you to release deeply embedded prejudices concerning power and sexuality.

North Node in Gemini, South Node in Sagittarius

By learning to appreciate other people's viewpoints and communicating what you've learned, you realize that truth begins within. This realization allows you to finally commit to people and issues in an intimate, personal sense.

North Node in Cancer, South Node in Capricorn

You grow spiritually through an emotional sensitivity to others, thus conquering a tendency to react with emotional coolness and selfishness.

North Node in Leo, South Node in Aquarius

By developing the strength of your will and emotional warmth toward others, you overcome eccentric and impersonal attitudes that hold you back.

North Node in Virgo, South Node in Pisces

You need to build inner confidence and to crystallize your goals so that you overcome a tendency for escapism through your compassion for others.

North Node in Libra, South Node in Aries

By learning to cooperate with others and to balance all issues, you overcome the selfishness tendencies of your "me first" attitude. You learn you aren't always right.

North Node in Scorpio, South Node in Taurus

Through the regenerative powers of Scorpio, you learn to release your need for security.

North Node in Sagittarius, South Node in Gemini

Through integrity and ethical actions, you overcome a tendency for deceit and cunning. You learn to remain undivided in your search for the truth.

North Node in Capricorn, South Node in Cancer

Through discipline and hard work, by creating a structure for what you do, you release your dependency on your family. You learn to rely on yourself first.

North Node in Aquarius, South Node in Leo

Through humanitarian ideals and pursuits and a spiritual understanding for the suffering of others, you master your egotism.

North Node in Pisces, South Node in Virgo

Through compassion for others and delving into your own mystical nature, you conquer your criticisms of others.

Mercury in the Signs

The sign Mercury occupies describes how you express your mental habits, how you gather information, how you study, and how you communicate your ideas.

Mercury in Aries

Quick, decisive mind that makes snap judgments. Often argumentative. Intuitive about the dynamics of relationships.

Mercury in Taurus

Practical, determined mind with strong likes and dislikes. Intuitive about the practical aspects of relationships. Love of beautiful, flowing language. Can be quite stubborn.

Mercury in Gemini (dignified)

Quick, inventive mind. Up to date on current events. Shrewd powers of observation. Adaptable, versatile intellect. Ease with language. Intuitive about the structure of relationships. Enjoys travel.

Mercury in Cancer

Sensitive, imaginative mind with excellent powers of retention. Changes opinions quickly. Interest in psychic matters, often has psychic abilities as well. Intuitive about the inner connections in relationships.

Mercury in Leo (in fall)

Great willpower and lofty ideals. Intellect can be self-centered, but intuitive. Mental aspirations may revolve around children, pets, drama, and sports. Intellectual efforts often carry your personal and unique style.

Mercury in Virgo

Facility with language and as a linguist. Mentally, you display a great attention to detail, which can collapse into criticism and nit-picky tendencies. Deep interest in mystery, the occult, magic. Excellent intellect overall.

Mercury in Libra

A refined intellect, capable of broad scope. Excellent at balancing issues, intuitive about the innate balance in relationships. Good placement for any artistic pursuit, particularly music.

Mercury in Scorpio

Suspicious, but deeply intuitive intellect capable of probing beneath the obvious. Mental need to perceive the hidden order of things, to pierce that order and pull out the truth. Can be sarcastic and wry in communication.

Mercury in Sagittarius (detriment)

Idealistic and intellectually versatile. Mental and intellectual development comes through philosophy, religion, law, publishing, and travel. Personal opinions sometimes are inflated and become principals rather than just personal opinions.

Mercury in Capricorn

Mental discipline and organizational ability. The intellect is sometimes structured in a way that inhibits imagination. Much serious and thoughtful contemplation.

Mercury in Aquarius (exalted)

Intellect is detached from emotion and endlessly inventive. Mental interests tend to be progressive, unusual, and often eccentric. Interest in the occult and science.

Mercury in Pisces (detriment)

Psychic impressions are often so pronounced that reasoning ability is clouded. Great imagination and creativity are indicated and much information is culled through intuitive means.

Venus in the Signs

The sign in which Venus falls describes your artistic nature and what you are like as a romantic partner, spouse, or friend. Venus's sign also indicates financial and spending habits.

Venus in Aries (detriment)

Aggressive social interaction. Passion in romantic relationships. You form impetuous, impulsive ties and are self-centered in love. Good initiative in making money, but it usually goes out as fast as it comes in. Marriage may happen early or in haste.

Venus in Taurus (dignified)

Heightened artistic expression. You attract money and material resources easily. Deeply emotional love attachments. Strong financial drive. Marriage is sometimes delayed.

Venus in Gemini

Great charm and wit. Flirtatious. Good conversationalist. You're popular, enjoy reading and travel. Tendency for short-lived relationships which can occur simultaneously. You're a spendthrift who earns money from a variety of sources. You will have several occupations and, possibly, several marriages as well.

Venus in Cancer

Home and marriage are important and offer you a sense of security. Family ties are strong. You spend money on home and family, but also squirrel it away in savings. There can be a tendency for secret love affairs and a deep interest in the occult. You benefit through houses and land.

Venus in Leo

Ardent in relationships, gregarious nature. You may have a pronounced talent in one of the arts. You like to entertain and gamble and have a strong attraction to the opposite sex. You gain through investments and speculation.

Venus in Virgo (in fall)

Secret romances, disappointment through love, possibly more than one marriage. You're too analytical and criticize romantic relationships and emotions. You're a perfectionist about artistic self-expression.

Venus in Libra (dignified)

Kind, sympathetic nature. Love of the arts, music, drama. Happy marriage, with talented children. You earn money through areas that Venus rules and seek harmony in all your relationships.

Venus in Scorpio (detriment)

Passionate nature, dominant sex drive. Marriage can be delayed, relationships are often stormy. Your friends may have mystical and occult talents. You gain financially through inheritances, taxes, insurance, and the occult.

Venus in Sagittarius

Generous nature and ardent emotions in love. If your relationships threaten your personal freedom, however, your emotions cool rapidly. Love of arts, travel, and animals, with a particular fondness for horses. There can be more than one marriage.

Venus in Capricorn

Restraint in emotions. Some disappointment in love and romance. Marriage is usually for practical reasons and may be to someone older and more established financially. The partner may be cold and indifferent. Your emphasis is on acquiring financial and material assets.

Venus in Aquarius

Friends from all walks of life. Strange, unexpected experiences in romance and friendships. Need for intellectual stimulation in romantic partnerships. Erratic financial habits. Gain through friends, partnerships, speculations.

Venus in Pisces (exalted)

Charitable, compassionate nature. More than one marriage is likely. Romantic love and emotional attachments are necessary to your well-being. Great sensitivity to others. Psychic abilities are likely.

Mars in the Signs

The planets Mars describes how you use energy, your physical stamina, the expression of your desire for personal achievement, and the nature of your sexual drive.

Mars in Aries (dignified)

You go after what you want. Your strong sex drive sometimes manifests selfishly, with little regard for the partner. Initiative and drive are highly developed, but due to haste and impulsiveness, there can be a tendency not to finish what you've started.

Mars in Taurus (detriment)

You're not easily thwarted or discouraged by obstacles. Your sheer determination and strength of will are well-developed, but may not be used to the fullest. You prefer purposeful, practical action to achieve what you want. Your sexual nature is sensual, but can be somewhat passive. You find pleasure through your profession.

Mars in Gemini

Energy is expressed mentally, through a keen intellect and versatile mind. You tend to take on too many projects that scatter your energy. Your mental restlessness needs a creative outlet or otherwise you become argumentative. You enjoy travel, science, and law. Good placement for writing.

Mars in Cancer (in fall)

You take everything personally and find it difficult to be objective about issues that are important to you. Your sex drive is overshadowed with deep emotional needs.

Mars in Leo

Passion rules the expression of your energy. You possess good leadership ability, a fearless nature, and a determined will. You need to be appreciated for who you are and as a lover. Mechanical or musical skill may be indicated.

Mars in Virgo

You express your energy through efficient, practical pursuits. You're an excellent worker, particularly if the work involves attention to detail. You apply your will quietly, with subtlety. Your sexual drive may be somewhat repressed, with the energy channeled into work. Good placement for work in medicine, healing, writing.

Mars in Libra (detriment)

You benefit through partnerships and express your energy best with and through other people. This placement of Mars is good for a lawyer or surgeon. Marriage may happen later in life. Your children may be gifted. You're a romantic when it comes to sex.

Mars in Scorpio (dignified)

Your drive and ambition are legendary. It's difficult and sometimes downright impossible for you to compromise. Secrecy surrounds your personal projects. You make a formidable enemy and ally. Your sex drive is powerful.

Mars in Sagittarius

You have the courage to act on your convictions. Good placement for orators, crusaders, evangelists, New Age leaders. You have a passionate sex drive but are often impulsive and noncommittal in your relationships. Good sign for competitive sports, travel, and adventure.

Mars in Capricorn (exalted)

Your worldly ambitions may take you into public life. You're able to plan well and to work practically to realize your ambitions and goals. You tend to keep a tight rein on your sex drive and may get involved with people who are older than you are.

Mars in Aquarius

Your unique approach may brand you an eccentric. You act independently to achieve your goals, which are often directed toward humanity in general. Your approach to sex is apt to be rather unemotional.

Mars in Pisces

This placement can go one of two ways. You're either inconsistent in what you seek to achieve or you're able to pull together various facets of a project and make them work. Sex drive is intimately linked with emotions. Excellent placement for a detective, occult investigator. You try to avoid conflict and confrontations.

Jupiter in the Signs

The sign in which Jupiter falls describes how you seek to expand your understanding of life, the benefits you receive, and how you express your intellectual, moral, religious, or spiritual beliefs. Jupiter is the first of the outer planets, which relate to the larger social world.

Jupiter in Aries

You're zealous in your beliefs and are convinced you're right, whether you are or not. Everything for you is personal and immediate. You expand your life through personal initiative, seizing opportunities when you see them or creating your own opportunities. You gain through travel, children, law, and friends.

Jupiter in Taurus

Your approach is practical. You seek to apply spiritual and philosophical principles to daily life. You gain through children and marriage and greatly love your home. Fixed in your religious or spiritual views, your generosity to others is a result of their need rather than your sympathy.

Jupiter in Gemini (detriment)

The hunger for knowledge and the acquisition of information and facts expand your world. You need to communicate what you learn through writing, speaking, or maybe even film. Your travels are usually connected to your quest for understanding larger philosophical or spiritual issues. Benefits come through publishing, education, and psychic investigations.

Jupiter in Cancer (exalted)

You hold onto the spiritual and moral ideals of your parents and pass these teachings down to your own children. Your spiritual beliefs are expanded through your compassion for others. Benefits come through your parents, family, and home-related matters.

Jupiter in Leo

Your beliefs are dramatized; you act on them, promote them, live them. In doing so, you attract others who help expand your world. Your exuberance, however, may be interpreted by some as outright pride. You gain through overseas trips that are connected with education, sports, or diplomatic issues.

Jupiter in Virgo (detriment)

Through your work ethic and service to others, you expand your philosophical and spiritual horizons. However, your work must be purposeful. You bring a critical and analytical mind to your profession. Travel is primarily related to business. You gain through employees, business and professional pursuits.

Jupiter in Libra

You expand your life through your associations with other people and through marriage and partnerships in general. You benefit from the opposite sex. Your sense of fair play and justice are well developed. The risk with this placement is that you may sacrifice your own interests to maintain harmony.

Jupiter in Scorpio

It's as if you were born with your spiritual beliefs already intact. You expand through your relentless search to understand these beliefs and how they relate to the nature of reality. Your willpower and determination are your greatest assets in overcoming any obstacles in your search. You gain through inheritances, psychic investigation, and any areas that Scorpio governs.

Jupiter in Sagittarius (dignified)

Your deep need to understand spiritual and philosophical issues broadens your life. Travel, foreign travel in particular, and education benefit your search. This is a lucky placement for Jupiter and usually denotes success in the area described by the house in which it falls. You benefit through all things associated with Sagittarius.

Jupiter in Capricorn (in fall)

Your philosophical and spiritual expansion happens mostly through your own efforts. You seek to accumulate wealth, have a great appreciation for money, and tend to be guarded in your financial generosity. You gain through your father, employers, and commercial affairs.

Jupiter in Aquarius

Your progressive views and willingness to explore all kinds of spiritual beliefs expand who and what you are. Your tolerance for other people's beliefs deepens your understanding of beliefs that differ from yours. Benefits come to you through your profession and through group associations.

Jupiter in Pisces (dignified)

Your compassion, emotional sensitivity, and imagination expand your philosophical and spiritual foundations. Benefits come through psychic and occult investigations and anything to do with behind-the-scenes activities. Look toward the sign and house placement of the Part of Fortune and aspects to Pisces to find out what pushes your buttons.

Saturn in the Signs

The restrictions and structure inherent to Saturn are expressed through the sign it occupies. The sign shows how you handle obstacles in your life, deal with authority, and how you cope with serious issues. It's also thought to be the "karmic" planet of the zodiac. The house placement is more personally significant because it shows what area of your life is affected.

Saturn in Aries (in fall)

Circumstances force you to develop patience and initiative. Your impulsiveness needs to be mitigated, otherwise setbacks occur. With this position, there's a capacity for great resourcefulness which, constructively channeled, can lead to innovative creations. On the negative side, you can be self-centered and defensive.

Saturn in Taurus

You feel a deep need for financial and material security. But material comfort is earned only through hard work, discipline, and perseverance. As a result, you need to cultivate reliability and persistence in your chosen profession. The downside to this placement is that there can be a tendency for stubbornness and excessive preoccupation with material affairs.

Saturn in Gemini

Discipline and structure are expressed mentally through your systematic and logical mind. Problems must be thought through carefully and worked out in detail, otherwise difficulties multiply. You seek practical solutions.

Saturn in Cancer (detriment)

Your crablike tenacity sees you through most obstacles and difficulties. You choose a course, which may not always be the best, that doesn't threaten your emotional and financial security. There's a certain emotional restraint with this placement because so much is internalized. Psychic and intuitive resources are sometimes stifled.

Saturn in Leo (detriment)

Your ego and need for recognition can be your worst enemies. If you try to solve your difficulties in a self-centered way, you only compound the problem. Cooperative ventures and consideration of mutual needs work wonders for this placement.

Saturn in Virgo

You're such a perfectionist you tend to get bogged down in details. You need to separate the essential from the inconsequential. An intuitive approach to obstacles and challenges is an enormous help with this placement.

Saturn in Libra (exalted)

You overcome obstacles and difficulties by cooperation and a willingness to work with others. The best way to achieve your goals is in partnership with others. You have the opportunity to develop an acute sense of balance and timing with this placement.

Saturn in Scorpio

You handle your difficulties in an intense, secretive manner, which increases the suspicion of those around you. By being more open and up front about what you're doing, you're able to overcome obstacles. Work to discipline your intuition; it can be an infallible guide.

Saturn in Sagittarius

You need to loosen up. Any kind of rigid approach only increases your problems and difficulties. Your best bet is to structure your life by incorporating your ideals into practical, daily life. Your intense intellectual pride makes you vulnerable to criticism by peers.

Saturn in Capricorn (dignified)

No matter what challenges you face, your ambition conquers them. You know that everything has a price and strive to make your contributions to the larger world. You respect the power structures that you see. For you, life itself is serious business. Don't get locked into rigid belief systems; remain flexible.

Saturn in Aquarius (dignified)

Your emotional detachment and objectivity allow you to meet challenges head on. Your innovative and unique approach to problems is best funneled through a quiet, practical application to daily life. Your peers help you to learn discipline.

Saturn in Pisces

Astrologers don't look kindly on this placement. But much of what might manifest negatively can be mitigated by practical use of the innate psychic ability of Pisces. Instead of letting yourself become trapped in memories of the past, use past triumphs as a springboard to the future. Your psychic ability is a doorway to higher spiritual truths but must be grounded in some way, perhaps through meditation or yoga.

Uranus in the Signs

Uranus remains in the same sign for about seven years, so its influence in the signs has only a general application. The sign indicates the ways in which your urge for freedom and individuality are manifested. The house placement is more significant on a personal level because it shows what area of your life is impacted.

Uranus in Aries

Your spirit of adventure is quite pronounced and prompts you to seek freedom at almost any price. In its most extreme form, this need for freedom can cause estrangement and a complete severance of ties with your past. You're blunt, outspoken, and can have a fiery temper. You need to develop more consideration for others.

Uranus in Taurus (in fall)

You're looking for new, practical ideas concerning the use of money and financial resources, so that the old way of doing things can be reformed. You have tremendous determination and purpose. Carried to extremes, your stubbornness can impede your progress. Your materialistic attachments may limit your freedom of expression and stifle spiritual impulses.

Uranus in Gemini

Your ingenuity and intuitive brilliance impel you to pioneer new concepts in the areas where you're passionate. But your deep restlessness can make it difficult for you to follow an idea through to completion. Self-discipline will help you

to bring your ideas to fruition. You travel frequently, seeking exposure to new ideas and people. You have the ability to break out of habitual living patterns and need to draw on that talent to succeed in whatever you're trying to do.

Uranus in Cancer

You pursue freedom through emotional expression and seek independence from parental authority that restricts you in some way. Your own home is unusual, either in decor or in the way you run your domestic life. There can be great psychic sensitivity with this placement, which may manifest as occult or spiritual activities in the home. This placement also carries a certain amount of emotional instability.

Uranus in Leo (detriment)

Your route to freedom and independence can touch several different areas: love and romance, leadership, and the arts. Sometimes it can encompass all three. Regardless of how it manifests, you chafe at existing standards, so you create your own. The risk of egotism in this placement indicates that your best channel for expression lies in issues that affect universal rather personal concerns.

Uranus in Virgo

You have original and unique ideas regarding health, science, and technology. You seek your independence through meticulous intellectual research in whatever you undertake. There can be erratic health problems with this placement, which may spur you to look into alternative medicine and treatments.

Uranus in Libra

You seek independence through marriage and partnerships. As a result, there may be a tendency for disharmony in your personal relationships. Your unconventional ideas about law and the legal system may prompt you toward reform in that area. This placement can also produce gifted musicians.

Uranus in Scorpio (exalted)

Your independence comes through drastic and profound change in whatever house Uranus in Scorpio occupies. This is an intensely emotional placement, with an innate psychic insight that allows you to perceive the nature of all that is hidden. Your temper can be quite fierce

and you may feel compelled to bring about change regardless of the consequences.

Uranus in Sagittarius

Your individuality is expressed through unique concepts in religions, philosophy, education, or spirituality. You seek out the unusual or the eccentric in foreign cultures in an attempt to incorporate other spiritual beliefs into your own. You have a deep interest in reincarnation, astrology, and other facets of the occult.

Uranus in Capricorn

This generation of people (born 1989–1994) will bring about vital changes in government and business power structures. They won't dispense with the past traditions entirely, but will restructure old ideas in new ways. Their ambitions are as strong as their desire to succeed. Look to the house placement to find out which area of life is affected.

Uranus in Aquarius (dignified)

You don't hesitate to toss out old ideas and ways of doing things if they no longer work for you. You insist on making your own decisions and value judgments about everything you experience. Your independence is expressed through your impartial intellect and an intuitive sense of how to make connections between seemingly disparate issues. Future trends are born in this placement.

Uranus in Pisces

You bring about change and seek independence through heightened intuition. You have the capacity to delve deeply into the unconscious and receive inspirations through your dreams that you can use in your daily life. Be cautious, however, that your idealism isn't impractical; face and deal with unpleasant situations as they arise.

Neptune in the Signs

Neptune spends about twice as long in each sign as Uranus—fourteen years. This makes the sign placement far less important than the house placement, unless Neptune figures prominently in the chart. The sign attests to the capacity of your imagination and your

How do you see yourself?

spiritual and intuitive talents. It also addresses the area of your life where you cling to illusions: your blindspots.

Neptune in Aries

This placement fires the imagination on many levels and allows you to act on psychic impulses. Your point of illusion may be your own ego.

Neptune in Taurus

Imagination and spiritual energies are channeled into concrete expression. Your point of illusion can be your own materialism.

Neptune in Gemini

Heightened intuition bridges the left and right brains. Imagination and spiritual issues are channeled through logic and reasoning. Your blindspot may be that you believe you can take on anything. It's a sure route to burnout.

Neptune in Cancer (exalted)

The enhanced psychic ability with this placement makes you impressionable. You need to be acutely aware of the fine line between illusion and reality.

Neptune in Leo

Bold creative and artistic concepts characterize this placement. Imagination finds expression in artistic performance. Your ego may hold you hostage.

Neptune in Virgo (detriment)

Imagination and spiritual issues are carefully analyzed and fit into a broader, concrete whole for practical use. Strive not to over analyze.

Neptune in Libra

Imagination and spiritual concepts find expression through beauty and harmony. Misplaced idealism can accompany this placement.

Neptune in Scorpio

Great imagination allows you to pierce the depth of esoteric subjects. You may be blind, however, to your own consuming interest in psychic matters. This placement can also induce drug and alcohol abuse and a sexual identity crisis.

Neptune in Sagittarius

Your intuition allows you to understand broad spiritual issues and to fit them into your personal search for truth. Your blindspot may be your need for creative freedom. In a broad, generational sense, this placement can give rise to religious cults.

Neptune in Capricorn (in fall)

Spiritual ideals and concepts are given a practical structure in which to emerge. The risk lies in being so practical that the voice of the imagination is stifled.

Neptune in Aquarius

In a societal sense, heightened intuition and spiritual enlightenment bring about vast and innovative changes and discoveries under this influence. The blindspot personally is learning to apply this energy to your own life.

Neptune in Pisces (dignified)

A vivid imagination allows you to connect to deeper spiritual truths. The risk with this placement is becoming separated from reality and losing yourself in a world of illusion.

Pluto in the Signs

First, Pluto sweeps in and collapses the old. Then it rebuilds, transforms, and regenerates. The sign it's in describes how your personal transformations are likely to happen; the house placement explains which area of your life is affected.

About the time that Pluto entered Sagittarius, in late 1995, many people experienced difficulties in whatever houses Pluto occupied in their birth charts.

Due to the length of time it spends in a sign, its personal significance lies primarily in the house it occupies. The definitions that follow apply in broad terms to the larger world.

Pluto in Aries

It begins the reform, but doesn't have the staying power to finish what it starts. This transit will begin in 2082 and end in 2101. Perhaps the Aries pioneers will be heading out into the solar system to explore new frontiers on other planets.

Pluto in Taurus (detriment)

Resists the initial change, yet slides in for the long haul once the process has started. Pluto goes into Taurus in 2101 and stays there for thirty-one years; the Taurean energy will help settle the new frontiers.

Pluto in Gemini

Regeneration manifests through the dissemination of ideas and through communication. In 2132, Pluto will go into Gemini for thirty years. New forms of communication and new ways to disseminate information will be found under this influence.

Pluto in Cancer

Regeneration comes through deep emotional involvement with the home and all that involves the home and homeland. Pluto in this sign will domesticate new worlds.

Pluto in Leo (exalted)

Regeneration manifests dramatically through power struggles on an international level. The last time Pluto was in Leo, a power struggle led to World War II. Hopefully, when this transit comes around again, war will be obsolete and Leo's power struggles will have to take place on other levels.

Pluto in Virgo

Purging occurs through a careful analysis of what is and isn't essential. Under the last transit in Virgo, great advances were made in medicine and technology. Given the rapid change in both fields, there's no telling where the next transit through Virgo may lead!

Pluto in Libra

Regeneration comes through a revamping of views towards relationships, marriages, and partnerships. By the time this transit comes around again, marriage and family may bear no resemblance at all to what they are now.

Pluto in Scorpio (dignified)

This is the eleventh hour placement of Pluto, which prevailed from 1983 to 1995. We suddenly realized that global warming wasn't just a buzz word; it's a fact. AIDS became a terrible reality. Alternative medicine became the most popular kid on the block. Gender, racial, sexual, and legal issues—everything pertinent to our survival as a society and a species—was on the evening news.

Pluto in Sagittarius

In this sign, the transformation will either succeed or fail. If it succeeds, then it's quite possible that we'll be bound as nations through our spiritual beliefs rather than our profit and loss statements. If it fails, chaos ensues.

Pluto in Capricorn

This rolls around in 2017. With typical Capricorn practicality and discipline, the pieces that Sagittarius spat out will be sculpted and molded into something useful. This will be the reconstruction period of the Aquarian Age. Kinks will be worked out, rules established. During Pluto's last appearance in Capricorn, the United States was founded and the Declaration of Independence was signed.

Pluto in Aquarius (in fall)

In 2041, the new order will be ready for Aquarius's humanitarian reforms.

Pluto in Pisces

This begins in 2061, nearly sixty-five years in the future. Who besides Nostradamus would presume to predict what might be happening? One thing is sure, though. With Pluto in Pisces, we'll at least have a deeper understanding of who and what we are and what makes it all tick.

Part of Fortune in the Signs

The significance of this Arabian point is more pronounced according to the house it occupies and the aspects that are made to it. In the signs, it describes your best approach to creating the Part of Fortune in your life.

Part of Fortune in Aries

Your drive and energy allow you to create your pot of gold. But you have to know what you want, set clear goals to attain it, and then see it through to the end. The more open and receptive you are to the forces and synchronicities in your life, the easier the process will be.

Part of Fortune in Taurus

Your greatest joy lies in what is stable and enduring. You attain it through your considerable patience and perseverance. Don't get hung up in the destructive forces of your polar opposite (Scorpio); this will only deter you from your path. Rather than resisting change, surrender to it.

Part of Fortune in Gemini

Your greatest joy manifests in learning and communicating what you learn. Guard against becoming judgmental. As long as you follow your impulses and listen to your inner prompting, your intellectual passions will lead you to your pot of gold.

Part of Fortune in Cancer

Your profound emotions seek to nurture and nourish ideas and people from birth to maturation. You find your greatest joy through family and the home, in your role as a nurturer, and in activities that revolve around these things.

Part of Fortune in Leo

You achieve your pot of gold through following your own code of excellence and integrity. You should remain generous to others, but realize they must follow their own paths. Once you incorporate this tenet into your approach, whatever you achieve also benefits the wider social order.

Part of Fortune in Virgo

By avoiding the polarity tug of Pisces to live in the past, you are more firmly rooted in the here and now. You should strive to create an organized and efficient framework in which to live in the present. By tempering your logic with Pisces' compassion, your pot of gold lies at your fingertips.

Part of Fortune in Libra

Through unselfish cooperation and partnership with others, you attain your greatest joy. This doesn't mean, however, that you should allow your own desires to be subsumed. By seeking the ideal balance between self and others, your pot of gold flows into your life.

Part of Fortune in Scorpio

Your best vehicle to manifesting your Part of Fortune is through your intense desire to pierce the meaning of hidden, mystical truths. Once you realize that you can't control other people's beliefs and actions, that you can only enlighten them about what you've discovered, your pot of gold flows into your life with utter ease.

Part of Fortune in Sagittarius

Your best approach to manifesting the Part of Fortune is to be who you are. Let your sense of adventure and your natural curiosity about universal truths lead you to your greatest fulfillment. Understand that you can't transfer your happiness to someone else.

Part of Fortune in Capricorn

To manifest your greatest joy, you need only do what you already do best: erect structure in your life, have clearly defined goals, and an underlying plan. Once you've charted your course, stick to it until you achieve what you set out to do. Your pot of gold is literally what you win through your own determined efforts.

Part of Fortune in Aquarius

Your universal awareness allows you to live with one foot in the future. This isn't how other people conduct their lives, but so what? Once you accept the fact that you're different, your path unfolds. It leads you to a pot of gold that benefits not only you, but everyone around you.

Part of Fortune in Pisces

To fully realize this placement of the Part of Fortune, you must cultivate the inner attunement necessary to hear the powerful voice of your intuition. Your fertile imagination and deep compassion then take you where you need to go. With this placement, the pot of gold is the rainbow itself.

Practice Exercise 1: The Sun Signs

Next to each Sun sign, jot a short description without using the book or the key word chart. For practice, add the glyph for each sign.

Scorpio: _____

Aries: _____

Taurus: _____

Virgo: _____

Sagittarius: _____

Capricorn: _____

Pisces: _____

Libra: _____

Gemini: _____

Leo: _____

Cancer: _____

Aquarius: _____

EXERCISE

Practice Exercise 2: The Planets, Nodes, and Part of Fortune

Jot the name of a planet, node, or the Part of Fortune next to the appropriate key phrases. The answers follow.

1. Aggressiveness, individuation _____

2. Restrictions, limitations _____

3. Expansion, luck _____

4. Mental quickness _____

5. Love, romance _____

6. The purifier, transformation, regeneration _____

7. Emotions, the feminine, home, the mother _____

8. Luck and success _____

9. Ego, vitality _____

10. Sudden, unexpected, genius _____

11. What we must release _____

12. Illusion, psychic abilities _____

13. What we can evolve toward _____

EXERCISE

Answers to Practice Exercise 2:
The Planets, Nodes, and Part of Fortune

1. Mars

2. Saturn

3. Jupiter

4. Mercury

5. Venus

6. Pluto

7. Moon

8. Part of Fortune

9. Sun

10. Uranus

11. South Node

12. Neptune

13. North Node

THE
HOUSES

PART
2

On the world island we are
all castaways,
so that what is seen by one
may often be dark or obscure
to another.

—LOREN EISELEY
The Immense Journey

Reading a Birth Chart

CHAPTER
5

The Four Angles

A birth chart is a map, a symbolic representation of how the heavens looked at the moment you were born. It's also a blueprint of certain personality characteristics.

In the chart in Figure 5-1, notice that the horoscope circle is divided into twelve equal parts, numbered counterclockwise. These are the houses that represent certain types of activities and areas of life. The lines that divide the houses are called cusps. The horizontal line that cuts through the middle of the chart is called the ascendant (**AS**) or rising sign.

The ascendant is one of the most important features of a natal chart. It's determined by your birth time. The ascendant determines which planets govern the twelve houses and rules the first house of Self. It's the first of the four angles in a chart that you look at in any interpretation.

In the chart in Figure 5-1, the ascendant is 19♓38 or 19 degrees and 38 minutes in Pisces. It means that Pisces governs the first house. Directly opposite the first house cusp is another set of numbers and another glyph: 19♍38. This is 19 degrees and 38 minutes in Virgo, which rules the cusp of the seventh house or the descendant. The cusp of the seventh is the second angle you consider in any interpretation. The line that connects the two is called the ascendant-descendant axis and symbolizes the horizon.

At the top of the chart in Figure 5-1 you'll find another set of numbers: 23♐06. This is 23 degrees and 6 minutes in Sagittarius, which rules the cusp of the tenth house or the Midheaven, abbreviated as **MC**. Directly opposite this, at the bottom of the chart, you'll find the fourth house cusp or **IC** at 23♊06. The **MC** and **IC**—the cusps of the tenth and fourth house—are the third and fourth angles to consider.

At the moment you're born, certain planets are rising above the horizon and certain planets are sinking beneath it. Some planets are stationary or stalled, others are moving direct, and still others are moving retrograde. You may have a cluster of them in one sign or the planets may be scattered throughout the zodiac. The sign and degree of each planet determines which house it occupies. Your starting point in the placement of those planets is the ascendant.

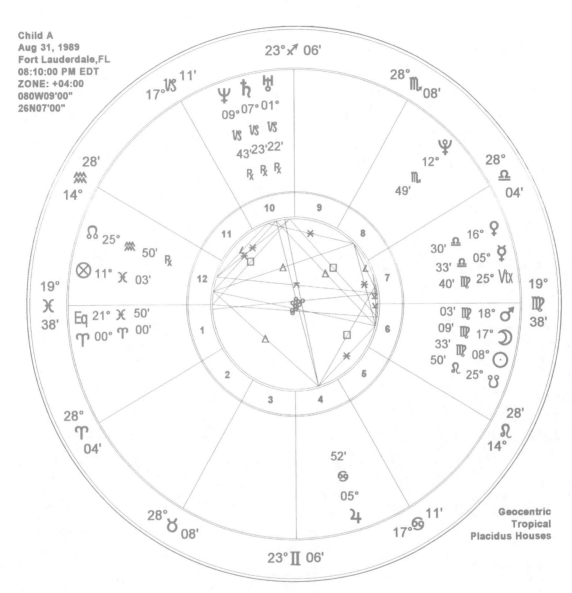

Child A
Aug 31, 1989
Fort Lauderdale,FL
08:10:00 PM EDT
ZONE: +04:00
080W09'00"
26N07'00"

Geocentric
Tropical
Placidus Houses

Child A

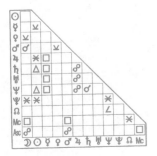

Figure 5-1

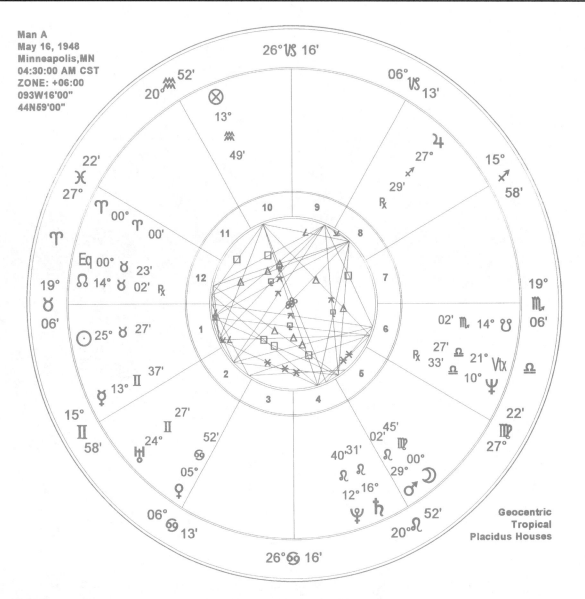

Man A
May 16, 1948
Minneapolis, MN
04:30:00 AM CST
ZONE: +06:00
093W16'00"
44N59'00"

26° ♑ 16'

06° ♑ 13'

20° ♒ 52'

⊗ 13° ♒ 49'

22' ♓ 27°

06° ♐ 29' ♃ 27' Rx

15° ♐ 58'

♈ 00° ♈ 00'

19° ♉ 06'

Eq 00° ♉ 23'
☊ 14° ♉ 02' Rx

☉ 25° ♉ 27'

10 9

11   8

12   7

1   6

2   5

3 4

19° ♏ 06'

02' ♏ 14° ☋

27' ♎ 21' Vtx
Rx 33' ♎ 10' ♆

22' ♍ 27°

☿ 13° ♊ 37'

15° ♊ 58'

♅ 24° ♊ 27'

52' ♋ 05'

♀

06° ♋ 13'

02' 45' ♍
40' 31' ♌ 00° ♌
♌ ♌ 29' ☽
12° 16° ♂
♆ ♄

20° ♌ 52'

Geocentric
Tropical
Placidus Houses

26° ♋ 16'

Man A

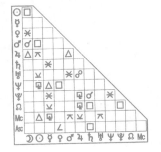

Figure 5-2

The Ascendant and Hemisphere Emphasis

When evaluating a birth chart, notice how planets fall in relation to the horizon or ascendant. A balanced chart has an equal number of planets above and below the horizon.

In Figure 5-1, six of the ten planets are placed above the horizon. Of the four that lie under the horizon, Mars ($\male$) and the Moon ($\leftmoon$) are only one and two degrees away from the horizon (the descendant). This is close enough so that their energy is felt in the seventh house as well as the sixth.

With a predominance of planets above the horizon, most experiences for this person are expressed openly. Not much is hidden. This hemisphere is concerned with conscious thought. As astrologer Steven Forrest notes, "A visible event marks every important developmental milestone on her path. The event may be a move to another city. A marriage. A journey to the East . . . . For such a person there is a perceptible life ritual signaling every major evolutionary step."

The birth chart in Figure 5-2 is almost the complete opposite of the one in Figure 5-1. In Figure 5-2, all the planets except one are under the horizon. A person with this type of placement is less obvious in what he does, more circumspect. As Forrest writes in *The Inner Sky,* "Emotion and intuition flavor all his perceptions . . . His life is a search for an inner state."

Some astrologers say that people who have most of the planets above the horizon tend to be more outgoing, affable, and generally sociable than those who don't. In others words, the first is active, the other is intellectually passive. But this isn't necessarily true. The horizon placement of planets has more to do with how you approach and assimilate experience.

The imaginary line that divides a chart vertically is called the **MC-IC** or vertical axis. The space to the left of this axis is called the eastern hemisphere; this is where planets are rising. This includes houses one, two, three, ten, eleven, and twelve. The space to the right of the vertical axis is called the western hemisphere; this is the twilight where planets are setting. It includes houses four, five, six, seven, eight, and nine.

People with the majority of their planets to the left of the axis tend to be self-determined; they act on their choices. Astrologer Robert Hand, however, notes: "The planets in the east should not be ones that, like Saturn, tend to frustrate action or, like Neptune, weaken the basis on which one should act."

When a majority of the planets lie in the western hemisphere, an individual considers his or her choices before acting. Opportunities may be somewhat restricted by the society in which the person lives.

The Midheaven and the IC

The Midheaven or **MC** is the highest point in a chart. In Figure 5-1, this point is 23♐06; in Figure 5-2, this point is 26♑16. The **IC** lies opposite the Midheaven in the same degree.

Even though the Midheaven doesn't provide much information about the personality, it's vital in understanding someone's life because it pertains to social roles, your public life, your relationship with authority, and status. Since it rules the cusp of the tenth house, which is concerned with an individual's professional life and career, the Midheaven also helps define what a person does for a living.

"Perhaps the most important attribute of the Midheaven," writes Robert Hand, "is that it helps to identify what people need to do with their lives in order to grow."

If the **MC** defines the externalization of the self, then the **IC**, as its opposite, represents the internalized self. The **IC** concerns the roots laid down in early childhood, the home, the nurturing parent, and the end of life.

Any planet that is placed closely to the cusps of the first, fourth, seventh, or tenth houses—the four angles—manifests with considerable strength. In the chart in Figure 5-1, such planets would be Mars (♂) at 18♍03 and the Moon (☾) at 17♍09. Both are nearly conjunct the descendant or seventh house cusp. In the tenth house, Uranus (♅) at 1♑22R is within seven degrees of the Midheaven at 23♐06, close enough to be particularly significant.

In the chart in Figure 5-2, the Sun (☉) in the first house exerts a particualry strong influence.

The Houses

The sign in which a planet falls tells us how we express who and what we are; the houses explain the conditions and areas in our lives where that expression occurs. Without them, we only have part of the picture. This is what makes your birth time so important to a natal chart; the time you were born personalizes your horoscope. Otherwise, all you know are the signs of the planets that were rising and setting on your birthdate.

If you don't know your time of birth, your chart can be rectified according to particular events in your life. An example of chart rectification is covered in Chapter 14.

Beginning with the ascendant, each house falls within a particular sign. That sign is governed by a particular planet, which rules that house. The planet that rules a house exerts an archetypal influence over the affairs of that house, which are interpreted as psychological and personality characteristics. In the chart in Figure 5-2, Taurus (♉) lies on the ascendant so it rules the first house of Self. Since Taurus is governed by Venus, that means everything associated with the first house focuses on aesthetics, sociability, relationships, and tastes in art and literature.

In this same chart, the second house of money and material concerns falls in Gemini (♊), ruled by Mercury. Everything which deals with second house affairs will be colored by communication and versatility, the characteristics of Gemini and Mercury.

Houses are classified into three types. *Angular* houses are the first, fourth, seventh, and tenth houses. *Succedent* houses are numbers two, five, eight, and eleven. The *cadent* houses are three, six, nine, and twelve.

In traditional astrology, angular houses indicate action, and planets placed in these houses motivate you to action. Succedent houses tend to be viewed as resource houses, the things that stabilize our lives. Cadent houses represent diversification. But not all astrologers agree with the traditional views on the types of houses.

Astrologer Robert Hand, for instance, believes these classifications are outmoded. He views them in groups of threes. In his system, houses one, five, and nine are personal houses; houses two, six, and ten are practical; houses three, seven, and eleven are social; houses four, eight, and twelve are unconscious houses.

Planetary Rulers of the Signs

SIGN	RULER
Aries	Mars
Taurus	Venus
Gemini	Mercury
Cancer	Moon
Leo	Sun
Virgo	Mercury
Libra	Venus
Scorpio	Pluto/Mars
Sagittarius	Jupiter
Capricorn	Saturn
Aquarius	Uranus
Pisces	Neptune

As you delve into your own chart and the charts of family and friends, you'll develop your own opinions on what the houses mean and how they should be grouped. But for now, stick to the traditional meanings.

The sidebar on "Keywords for Houses" lists the meanings of the houses. It's intended only as a guideline.

What the Houses Represent

Astrologers generally agree that the houses represent spheres of activity, experience, action, and areas of life impacted by the placement of planets. But they aren't nearly as agreeable when it comes to how the houses are divided.

Astrologer Robert Hand notes: "At least one modern writer has proposed a twenty-four house system. And the Irish sidereal astrologer Cyril Fagan has unearthed ancient references to the *okto-topos,* an eightfold division numbered clockwise from the Ascendant instead of counterclockwise as we are used to." The situation becomes especially muddled when you toss in the ancient Greek traditions and modern Hindu astrology.

The trick is to work with the traditional meanings, then allow your intuition to guide you. You may find, for instance, that you read the mother in the tenth house and the father in the fourth; or that in the horoscope for a man, the mother is in the fourth but for a woman, the father is in the fourth. The point is to develop a system that works for you by studying your own chart first.

If you operate from the premise that the soul chooses all facets of the circumstances into which it is born, then your chart becomes the voice of your soul speaking to you.

First House (Ascendant): Your Mask

Natural sign: Aries
Natural ruler: Mars

All of us are mixtures of intellectual and emotional needs, talents, memories, desires, dreams, fears, and triumphs. These characteristics are streamlined and rolled into our personalities, the face we present to others, our masks. The first house is our social mask.

Keywords for Houses

House 1: *Personality.* The Self, beginnings, physical health, early life, physical appearance

House 2: *Finances.* Personal material resources, assets, expenditures, attitudes toward money

House 3: *Communication.* Intellect and mental attitudes, short journeys, brothers and sisters, neighbors, relatives

House 4: *Home.* Family life, domestic affairs, mother or father, early childhood conditioning, your roots, the end of your life, real estate

House 5: *Children and Creativity.* Pleasurable pursuits, creative outlets, children (the first born in particular), love affairs, sex for pleasure

House 6: *Work and Health.* Working conditions and environment, competence and skill, general health

House 7: *Partnerships and Marriage.* Partnerships in general, marriage, open conflicts, our identification with others

House 8: *Death and Inheritances, the Occult.* Transformation of all kinds, regeneration, sexuality, taxes, death, psychic ability

House 9: *Higher Mind.* Philosophy and religion, law, long journeys, higher education, publishing, foreign travel and interests, ambitions, in-laws and relatives of the marriage partner

House 10: *Career.* Profession, status, mother or father, worldly ambitions, public life, people in power over you, status

House 11: *Friends.* Group associations, hopes and wishes, ambitions and goals, your network of friends

House 12: *Personal Unconscious.* Institutions, confinement, that which we haven't integrated into ourselves, karma

This house, ruled by the ascendant, also governs our physical appearance and the general state of our physical health. The head and face are governed by the first house. When looking for health issues in a chart, always look to the first house, as well as to the sixth and the eighth. In this house, the source of illness can be due to an inability to impact the world in the way or to the degree that we want.

Consider the following descriptions of the ascendant in each of the signs as personality signatures.

Aries: A need to succeed at everything they take on. Impulsiveness. Impatience. Drive. Fiercely independent. Decisive.

Taurus: Determination, patience, practicality, an appreciation of beauty. It takes a lot to anger them, but once they're provoked, get out of their way! People with Taurus rising are often physically attractive, identifiable by short, strong necks.

Gemini: They need versatility and diverse experiences. These people are mentally quick and perceptive. They are often slender, with long arms and fingers, and walk quickly.

Cancer: Their subjective approach to life and a drive to establish some sort of foundation or home base defines who they are. They're intuitive and capable of deep feeling. With Cancer rising, the face is often round. They tend toward stoutness in middle age.

Leo: Think drama, pride, and ambition with this rising sign. They have an excellent ability to organize and direct others, and understand children very well. Physically, these people are handsome and large-boned with hair that is usually thick and beautiful.

Virgo: They possess keen powers of observation and have a fastidious nature. They generally are dedicated to service of others, have a concern for health, and can be very intuitive. Slender bodies and oval faces with a certain softness and charm mark these people.

Libra: They define themselves through social relationships. They seek harmony and fairness in all they undertake and often are so concerned with being fair that they are indecisive. Physically, Libra rising often produces nearly perfectly formed bodies and physical beauty.

Scorpio: With these people, expect intensity, passion, strong sexuality, and a profound perception into the secret nature of life. They are deeply intuitive and possess the ability to drastically alter their personal environment. They tend to have dark hair that is wavy and thick and prominent brows. There's a physical intensity about them as well.

Sagittarius: An adventurous spirit, bluntness in speech, and deep independence: that's it in a nutshell. They have excellent foresight, a respect for all spiritual thought, and a love of animals. Their bodies are usually tall, slender, with a stoop to the shoulders.

Capricorn: They're concerned about status, self-discipline, and ambition. Impulsive activity is generally restrained. They're good at recognizing and defining the overall structure of a problem or challenge. Physically they can be thin and bony, with prominent features.

Aquarius: They are humanitarians, and also possess unusual or eccentric modes of self-expression. People with this rising sign tend to go against the established order and seek their own answers and truths. They have strong, well-formed bodies, with a tendency to plumpness in middle age.

Pisces: Few rising signs possess more emotional sensitivity and profound perception. They are often mystically inclined, impressionable, with multifaceted self-expression. They have exquisitely shaped hands and feet and usually have compelling liquid eyes.

Second House: Your Material Goods

Natural sign: Taurus
Natural ruler: Venus

If the planets and aspects to the ascendant and the first house create issues about self-esteem and self-doubt, the second house can be where we attempt to work them out. This can manifest in any type of behavior that draws attention to our personal material resources: flashy clothes, a flashy car, flashy jewelry, even flashy lovers and spouses. In other words, our self-doubt impels us to prove our own worth through money and possessions.

The second house deals with money and moveable property (not real estate) and our attitudes toward wealth and material possessions. This house also tells us something about our earning capacity, how we meet our financial obligations, and how we save and budget.

Third House: Your Mind

Natural sign: Gemini
Natural ruler: Mercury

A lot of issues are lumped into this house: the intellect, communication, brothers and sisters, short journeys, conscious thinking, neighbors, relatives. But this house actually represents daily activities in our lives, things we do automatically. The mental energy is analytical.

A short journey is a commute to work as opposed to a trip to Europe. Brothers, sisters, neighbors, and relatives refer to our experience of these people, not to the people themselves. It implies an unconscious ease that exists between people who have something in common, whether it's genes or the street they live on.

Fourth House (IC): Your Roots

Natural sign: Cancer
Natural ruler: Moon

This house symbolizes emotional and physical security. For all of us, this begins with our family, homes, parents, and our sense of belonging.

Some discrepancy exists among astrologers as to whether the fourth house represents the mother or the father. I use it to symbolize the primary nurturing parent; the primary provider and authoritarian figure is found in the tenth house. Over the course of a lifetime parents often exchange roles, but generally one will be more nurturing and the other more authoritarian. In later life, this house indicates how we support others.

Quite often, in doing family charts, I find that the Sun sign of a parent or even a grandparent appears on the cusp of the fourth or tenth house. Or the Moon shows up in this house, in the parent's Sun sign. When rectifying a chart, this is one of the things to look for.

My mother's Sun sign (Capricorn) appears on the cusp of my fourth house, with my moon in Capricorn sitting smack on the **IC**. In my daughter's chart, my Sun sign, Gemini, appears on the cusp of her fourth house. Sometimes, you may find that the sun sign of a woman's spouse appears on the **IC**.

In this house we also find issues related to real estate, the collective unconscious, and to the last twenty years or so of a person's life.

Fifth House: Your Pleasures

Natural sign: Leo
Natural ruler: Sun

Pleasure forms the core meaning of the fifth house. But because pleasure is something different to all of us, this can include creativity, children, love affairs, sex, gambling, meditating, running, parties, a nature walk, celebrations, even gazing at a piece of art or reading a book.

The children part of this house also refers to the act of creating them. In this sense, Saturn placed here can indicate a possible stillbirth, abortion, or miscarriage, possibly involving the first born. But it can just as easily indicate a restriction or limitation on the pursuit of pleasure, someone too serious to have fun. The interpretation would depend on whose chart you're reading and the aspects to the house.

I include small animals in this house, even though they are typically covered by the sixth house. But in the world as it is now—rather than five or six hundred years ago—pets and small animals aren't chattel. They bring us pleasure.

Sixth House: Health and Work

Natural sign: Virgo
Natural ruler: Mercury

Centuries ago, one of the definitions of this house concerned servants: handmaidens, stable boys, cooks, and maids—in other words, the chattel. In today's world it refers to the way we extend ourselves for others and the services we perform without any thought of remuneration. It also refers to our general work conditions.

Health issues are also included here. But the illnesses associated with the sixth house are often linked to your work or job. Anything that stifles growth and self-expression—overwork, despising what you do, working just to pay the bills—can lead to illness.

Ultimately, the illness may trigger a transformation in consciousness that forces you to take a vacation, quit your dead-end job, or re-evaluate what you're doing. When that happens, health and hygiene awareness usually increases. In the healing period, it's important to follow your own intuition.

Seventh House (Descendant): Partnerships

Natural sign: Libra
Natural ruler: Venus

This house is about marriage and close partnerships of all kinds. It concerns how you relate to a significant other and how, in doing so, you often deal with an unexpressed aspect of yourself.

When you love someone, you identify with that person. You zip yourself up inside that person's bones, slip into that person's blood, wear that person's shoes. This is the kind of intimate relationships the seventh house addresses. A relationship that implies commitment. A partnership founded on mutual chemistry, on "magic." It can also refer to business partnerships where a commitment is made.

While planets found in this house generally don't describe the significant other, they indicate a great deal about the type of person that would suit you.

Eighth House: Your Instincts

Natural sign: Scorpio
Natural ruler: Pluto and Mars

This house is loaded. It's like an early Woody Allen movie—obsessed with death, sex, and taxes—with the occult tossed in just to muddle the picture. More specifically, it also includes death benefits, insurance, the partner's earning capacity, alimony, joint finances of any kind, and the recycling of goods.

Traditionally, it's known as the house of death. If that strikes you as bleak, then think of the eighth house as one of transformation.

Death is one kind of transformation, sexuality is another, psychic and occult matters are yet another. The house is emotionally loaded because it deals with issues that most of us don't like to dwell on consciously. This emotional impact, however, is why eighth-house events often feel fated or destined. This house relates to the internal energy that seeks outward growth, expansion, and experience.

Ninth House: Higher Mind

Natural sign: Sagittarius
Natural ruler: Jupiter

As the opposite of the third house, the ninth concerns higher ideals, the higher mind, philosophy, religion and spirituality, the law, foreign cultures, and long journeys. Through the ninth house we seek to understand the whole picture and our place in it. We reach out to experience and then try to assimilate the experience into a world view, a belief system. This can be done through reading, education, and travel, all ninth house pursuits. The bottom line is that through this house we break old thought patterns and habits and take chances.

Some astrologers assign higher education to the ninth house, but all educational pursuits fit into this house. The planets found here bear their unique individual stamp on how we experience and assimilate issues associated with this house.

Tenth House (Midheaven): External Achievements

Natural sign: Capricorn
Natural ruler: Saturn

Where the sixth house covers what you do to earn a living, the tenth concerns your career or profession, work that provides a social role in the larger world. It's the work with which we identify ourselves and by which others identify us.

Clerical work, for instance, probably falls into the sixth house unless the individual identifies closely with the job. But if the clerical worker is a nationally known antique car collector who identifies and is identified in that field, then this would fall into the tenth house. This house also represents the authoritarian parent as well as our experience of authority figures.

Astrologer Robert Hand notes that the tenth house often indicates the direction in which a person must evolve toward transcendence. "The tenth can be a calling beyond the mere calling of how we make a living . . . how an individual can grow on the spiritual as well as the mental plane."

Eleventh House: Friends and Ambitions

Natural sign: Aquarius
Natural ruler: Uranus

This house is about manifestation, about the power of manifestation through a group or collective consciousness. It took me a long time to understand that.

In the eleventh house, we don't just get along with certain types of people; there are some people with whom we click immediately. Part of their belief system overlaps and parallels our own. With these people, we have an especially strong affinity and from this affinity rises a certain kind of power: the group or collective mind, the mind that works toward a common end, a shared ideal, and a particular goal.

This house can entail all kinds of networking: group charity work, a theater group, a sewing circle, a writer's group, a group of astrologers or psychics, or bridge players. It also entails computer networking. In each group, the collective mind helps us to stabilize our goals.

Signs and planets in this house offer clues about the types of friends and associations that not only benefit us but whom we might benefit as well. As astrologer Steven Forrest writes: "Establish goals. Find people who support them. Then live in the present moment. That is the secret of successful eleventh house navigation."

Twelfth House: Your Personal Unconscious

Natural sign: Pisces
Natural ruler: Neptune

This house is typically considered to be negative and dark, the psychic garbage pail of the zodiac. In Medieval times it was known as the house of troubles and indicated possibilities of imprisonment, illness, secret enemies, poverty, and dire misfortune. While such possibilities exist with this house, its core meaning is deeper.

Sabian Symbols

In 1925, Marc Edmund Jones worked with a clairvoyant named Elsie Wheeler to list and interpret symbols for each degree of the zodiac. Jones was no stranger to astrology. He had identified certain patterns common to all horoscopes, which he called the Jones's Patterns, and wrote the seminal book on the topic.

In 1953, Jones published *The Sabian Symbols in Astrology*, an expansion of the original list and symbols that he and Wheeler had come up with. The three hundred and sixty symbols, says astrologer Dane Rudhyar, have a complex internal code. In his book *An Astrological Mandala*, in which he expands on the original symbols, he writes: "A set of symbols like the Sabian symbols or the I Ching or the Tarot, confronts us with the challenge of integrating the archetypal and the existential through a symbolic image, scene, or statement in which these two realms are in a state of confluence and interpenetration."

My daughter's sun sign is at eight degrees and thirty-three minutes in Virgo. Since the minutes constitute more than half of a degree, we would look at the Sabian symbol for nine degrees Virgo. It says: "An expressionist painter at work."

Rudhyar's keynote to this symbol reads: "The urge to express one's individualized sense of value regardless of tradition."

My daughter is passionate about art and the keynote description generally fits her overall personality. Since the Sun in astrology is the ego, the symbol for the degree of her Sun characterizes how she perceives herself. Each planet in her chart could be defined according to its Sabian symbol.

To use the symbols as a divination system requires the book itself and an ordinary deck of playing cards. Rudhyar divides the suits into seasons: hearts for the spring; diamonds for summer; spades for autumn; and clubs for the winter. The four kings represent the four cardinal signs of the zodiac: Aries, Cancer, Libra, and Capricorn. The queens represent the fixed signs: Taurus, Leo, Scorpio, and Aquarius. The jacks represent the mutable signs: Gemini, Virgo, Sagittarius, and Pisces.

To find the relevant degree for a question, use the numbered cards of three of the four suits. Hearts, for instance, correspond to the numbers one through ten; diamonds go with the numbers eleven through twenty; and clubs go with the numbers twenty-one through thirty.

I tested this on my husband. I asked him to think of a question and to choose a number between one and three hundred and sixty. He didn't tell me the question. The number he chose was ninety-one. The Sabian symbol for phase ninety-one (which relates to one degree of Cancer) is: "On a ship the sailors lower an old flag and raise a new one." Rudhyar's keynote reads: "A radical of allegiance exteriorized in a symbolical act: a point of no return."

My husband's question was whether a particular publisher would buy a proposal he had submitted. The Sabian symbol seemed to indicate the decision had already been made, he just didn't know about it yet.

The twelfth house represents the personal unconscious, the parts of ourselves that we've disowned, all that is hidden from our conscious perception. Here lie the dregs of early defeats and disillusionments, which ultimately became repressed and weren't integrated into the rest of our personality. Here, too, are aspects of ourselves that for one reason or another we don't want to express openly to others. These hidden parts of ourselves often come out later in life, surfacing as fears, weaknesses, or phobias that work against us.

Sometimes, these repressed aspects find expression in our most intimate relationships. The daughter of an alcoholic parent, for instance, may find herself confronting her childhood experiences in her relationship with an alcoholic spouse.

On a higher level, the twelfth house can embody spiritual, psychic, and mystical experiences that deepen our connection with the divine.

Simple Guidelines for Evaluating the houses in a Chart

When evaluating the houses in a chart, follow these guidelines:

1. Note the ascendant. What element is it in? What does the sign immediately tell you about the individual? Where does the ruling planet fall?

2. Note the cusps of the fourth house (the **IC**); the seventh house (the descendant) and the cusp of the tenth (the Midheaven or **MC**). What do these signs immediately tell you about the person? What do the planets in these houses tell you about the person?

3. What houses do the Sun and the Moon occupy? Are they above or below the horizon? In the western or the eastern hemispheres? In which elements?

4. Note any house where there's a cluster of planets. A house that holds more than one planet indicates activity in that area. It holds a clue as to the soul's purpose in life.

5. Are there are any houses that hold three or more planets within three degrees of each other? This cluster is called a stellium and indicates intensely focused activity in that particular house.

6. Which house holds the Part of Fortune? Where are the Moon's nodes? The placement of these three points provides valuable information about the soul's purpose.

7. Does the chart have a singleton, one planet that stands alone? An example is in the chart in Figure 5-2, with Jupiter sticking up there all alone in the eighth house.

8. What intuitive feelings do you get from the chart?

9. What is the chart's general shape?

A Quick Review

Using the guidelines for evaluating the houses, analyze the birth chart for John Doe, Figure 5-3. Your analysis won't be complete because we haven't covered aspects or the planets in the houses. But you have enough astrological information to provide a general analysis of the man's personality.

John Doe's real name is after this exercise. Don't cheat!

Your Notes on John Doe's Chart

_____

_____

Your Chart

Take a few minutes now to make similar notes on your own chart. Stick to the information we've covered so far; pretend you're interpreting a stranger's chart.

_____

_____

_____

_____

_____

_____

_____

_____

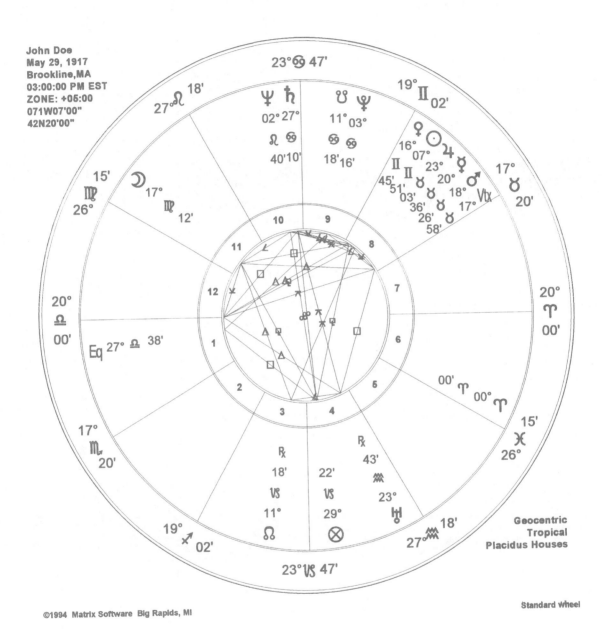

Figure 5-3

_____

_____

_____

_____

_____

_____

_____

_____

_____

_____

_____

_____

_____

Answer: John Doe is John F. Kennedy

Intuition and Interpretation

Astrology is as much an art as it is a science. As with any art, the best impulses and ideas begin somewhere deep inside. They bubble up from the soup of the unconscious, make connections with the right brain, and suddenly leap into your conscious awareness as a flash of intuitive insight. These flashes of insight are invaluable when interpreting an astrology chart.

Several years ago, a friend asked me to interpret his birth chart as well as a progressed chart for the coming year. He recently had been laid off from his job at a computer company, his savings were nearly gone, and his relationship with the woman he'd been seeing for several years wasn't going well. His daughter from a previous marriage was rebelling against everything, and his ex-wife blamed him. To say he was at loose ends hardly covers the flux his life was in at the time.

After I interpreted his birth chart, I glanced at his progressed chart. I figured I would see more of the same problems, because this man is the kind who would rather avoid his problems than confront them. The first thing that struck me was Uranus transiting his fourth house of the home. I blurted that he was going to move suddenly and unexpectedly and that it wasn't just a move across town. I also said it would happen quickly and that he could possibly get married as well.

The man laughed and informed me he couldn't possibly move. He hardly had enough money to buy groceries. As for the marriage part, no way. He'd been married once and look where that had ended up.

Six weeks later, this man was offered a job in Colorado. He sold everything he owned and moved out there. Not long after he arrived, he met a woman, fell in love, and they moved in together. For this man, the commitment to live with her was as good as a marriage.

Uranus transiting your natal fourth house doesn't have to mean a move. It may simply indicate sudden changes in your domestic life, a breaking away from your "roots." But to me, right then, it meant only one thing, a long distance, physical move from one place to another. The repercussions of the man's move, of course, followed the *overall* pattern for Uranus in the fourth house. It transformed his relationship with his family and girlfriend, broke him loose of childhood conditioning, and redefined his concept of security.

So when you have a birth chart in front of you, allow your intuition the freedom to make connections you might not perceive with your conscious mind. Sometimes, those connections are the only ones that matter to the other person. Don't allow the science part of astrology to become dogma. Learn the basics, assimilate them, then get out of the way so your intuition can speak to you.

The practice exercise that follows illustrates how intuition feels as you experience it. The sensation is different for everyone, but it does seem to register somewhere in the body while it's happening. It may be a tightening in your stomach, a sudden pulsing at your temple, or a flash of heat in your hands or fingertips. Once you experience it, you don't forget it.

EXERCISE

Practice Exercise 1: Intuition

This exercise is like a double blind medical experiment in which neither the doctor nor the patient knows whether the patient is receiving a drug or a placebo. It's adapted from Laura Day's excellent book, *Practical Intuition.* You're going to be answering a question that I've asked, which is at the bottom of the next page. Don't peek!

Take a few minutes to get comfortable and make sure that you won't be disturbed for ten or fifteen minutes. Breathe deeply and relax. Now look at the list of words below and write one sentence that uses each word. The sentences can be long or short, simple or complex, silly or logical; it doesn't matter. There aren't any right or wrong answers.

1. Stars _____

   _____

2. My childhood _____

   _____

3. My spouse (or significant other) _____

   _____

4. My career _____

   _____

5. My home _____

   _____

6. My kids _____

   _____

7. My creativity _____

   _____

8. I dream _____

   _____

EXERCISE

9. I hope _____

_____

10. I wish _____

_____

11. My ideal life is _____

_____

Read through your responses as though you've written two or three paragraphs of prose. As you read the question and think about your responses to the list, does your body feel different anywhere? Do you experience a flush of heat or maybe a chill in any part of your body? Do you feel a tightness or an ache in any part of your body?

Jot down any physical or emotional responses you're experiencing. Record anything that zips through your mind—images, thoughts, whatever.

My Responses

_____

_____

_____

_____

_____

_____

_____

_____

The question you answered is: How can astrology improve my life?

Planets in the Houses

CHAPTER
6

The Hologram

A horoscope is like a hologram, a symbolic projection from a level of reality vastly different from our own. It's composed of interconnected parts that we have to understand before we can grasp the meaning of the whole. In our attempt to understand, we interact with the hologram by bringing our own intuitive perceptions to the overall pattern.

Bear this in mind as you read through the descriptions of planets in the houses. To correctly interpret a chart you must consider the other elements we've covered up to this point, as well as the aspects, which will be covered in Part Three. Aspects can dramatically alter the meanings of planets in the houses.

House Cusps

The division between one house and another is called the cusp. The sign on the ascendant sets up the structure of the various house cusps. If, for instance, you have Taurus rising—on the cusp of the first house—then Gemini sits on the cusp of your second house, Cancer on the cusp of the third, and so on around the horoscope circle.

The exception to this structure is an "intercepted sign," which means a sign doesn't appear on the cusp of a house but is completely contained within the house. The chart in Figure 6-1 has such an interception in the sixth house and in the opposite twelfth house as well.

In the first instance, the cusps leap from Virgo on the cusp of the sixth to Scorpio on the cusp of the seventh. Libra has been swallowed. Directly opposite, the cusp of the eleventh house leaps from Taurus on the ascendant to Pisces. Aries has been subsumed.

Some astrologers believe an interception portends trouble for the ruler of the intercepted sign. Others think that the house which holds the interception is more powerful. Actually, it depends on the tenor of the overall chart. Sometimes, with an interception, you're attracted to people born under the subsumed sign. Or you manifest those attributes more strongly than you might otherwise.

In the birth chart in Figure 6-1, ruling planets affected by the interception are Neptune, which rules Pices, and Mars, which rules Aries.

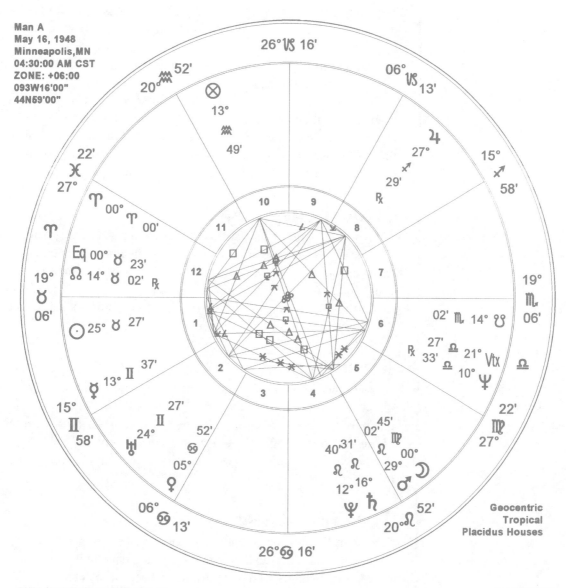

Standard wheel

Figure 6-1

Each house cusp is ruled by the planet that governs the sign on the cusp. In Figure 6-1, Taurus is on the ascendant so Venus rules the first house. Since the Sun is so close to the ascendant in this chart, it could be said to co-rule. Gemini is on the cusp of the second house, so Mercury is the ruler of that house.

However, the natural order of the horoscope begins with Aries, then Taurus, then Gemini, around the zodiac. This means that regardless of what sign is on the cusp, Mars is the natural ruler of the first house because Mars governs Aries. The attributes of the natural rulers must be taken into account when interpreting a chart.

Critical Cusp Degrees

A cusp or a planet is in a critical degree when it's at or greater than 29 degrees. On one level, "critical" simply means a particular tension exists in that part of the chart. On another level, it expresses the soul's intent to get it right this time around.

In the chart in Figure 6-1, there are no cusps in critical degrees. But several are in very late degrees.

Reminders

As you read through these interpretations, remember that a planet is dignified in one of the houses if it's the planet's natural house. If a planet is retrograde or poorly aspected, it can weaken the meanings of the placements. If a planet is stationary, it intensifies the meaning. With a direct planet that is well-aspected, the meanings hold with the descriptions I've given.

The First House

Planets in this house strengthen an individual's personality and personal interests. They also describe physical characteristics, overall health, mannerisms, and attitudes that reflect the nature of the planets' signs. The cusp of the first house (the Ascendant) is a critical point in a chart.

> *Sun.* Self-confidence, initiative, clearly-defined ambitions. You have an optimistic disposition, increased physical vitality, and personal warmth. This position often indicates a leader. With the Sun in this placement, your self-expression is important to you.

Moon. Intuitive, emotional, moody disposition. You're sensitive to your environment, feel social pressure, and usually have a strong need to be appreciated by others. You may go on eating binges when you're stressed out; your weight fluctuates considerably.

If the Moon is in a water sign, intuition may be highly developed and moodiness is more pronounced. In a fixed sign, the nature is more stable. This placement of the Moon is important in a woman's horoscope because the Moon governs monthly periods.

Mercury. Intellectual approach to life. Experiences are filtered through the mind. You're versatile, quick, and enjoy talking about your personal interests and ideas. Your restless nature keeps you on the go. You enjoy literature, books, and the culling of information. You're likely to be found in chat rooms on the Web.

Venus. Charm, friendliness, physical beauty. You may have some unique artistic talent and a deeply sensual nature. There's a certain aesthetic refinement with this placement that manifests as a love of music, literature, poetry, opera, and a fondness for beautiful surroundings. The placement is generally fortunate unless there are bad aspects, then a tendency toward laziness, vanity, and self-indulgence may be apparent.

Mars (accidentally dignified). You're assertive, aggressive, competitive, headstrong, impulsive. You're fearless, imbued with seemingly endless reserves of energy, and have a need to dominate your immediate environment. Your leadership ability is strong, but sometimes you may lack direction. You also may be accident prone.

Jupiter. Vivacious, optimistic, generous. You usually do everything in a big way, particularly if your Jupiter is in Leo. An inclination for travel and adventure are usually apparent with this placement, but the way this is expressed depends on the nature of the sign. A Jupiter in Scorpio, for example, might travel into the hidden nature of reality.

This placement is fortunate and you don't have to work very hard for its benefits. If Jupiter is badly aspected, there can be a tendency for self-indulgence.

Saturn. Serious outlook and disposition. You're dignified and circumspect; you aren't the type to blurt the story of your life on

a first date. You work hard and diligently for what you want. You may have lacked confidence in early childhood, which can delay your success, or some sort of hardship in childhood drives you to rise above it. The second half of life is usually far easier than the early part.

Saturn's lesson here is self-discipline and learning to structure your life so that it's conducive to whatever you strive to accomplish.

Uranus. Individualistic. Originality. Independence. Charismatic. Rebellious. You're totally unpredictable and impossible to categorize. Your life is filled with sudden and drastic changes that work for or against you, depending on aspects to the first house. You despise oppression of any kind and often work out your path in life through dealing with large groups of people.

With this placement, there's probably an interest in the occult, electricity, science, electronic gadgets, and computers. You possess a raw psychic talent.

Neptune. Mysterious, mystical, deeply compassionate, musical ability. Consciously or unconsciously you're psychically attuned to your immediately environment; you're a psychic sponge. You have a Greta Garbo allure and may even possess a Garbo type of beauty. But because Neptune is the planet of illusion, you can be blind to your own faults and shortcomings.

Pluto. Constant regeneration and transformation of the self. This is a powerful position for Pluto. You're very intense, with the capacity to drastically alter your personal environments. General health and recuperative powers are vitalized with this placement.

North Node. By consciously developing natural talents and abilities, you break free of a deep belief that you should place others' needs before your own. This position adds power to your personality and offers the opportunities for honor and recognition.

South Node. Growth comes through learning to balance personal needs against those of spouses, partners, and significant others.

Part of Fortune. Charm, personal magnetism. Through a totally subjective view of yourself, you learn that all power begins inside. You learn to reach for what you want and achieve on your own merits.

The Second House

Planets in the second house trigger activity concerning finances and personal material resources. They also describe the way you handle your financial affairs.

Sun. Good earning capacity, generous with others, tendency to spend extravagantly. You need financial security and enjoy your creature comforts. You gain financially through your father and employers.

Moon. Your finances go through phases, like the moon. Despite the ups and downs, your emotional security is tied to your financial security. Your common sense is well balanced, and you have an intuitive sense about finances in general. You spend freely on your home and family. You benefit from and through women.

Mercury. You're spilling over with moneymaking ideas, and seek out higher education as a means to increase your earning power. You keep detailed financial records and make shrewd investments. Your approach to money and finances is primarily mental and logical.

Venus (accidentally dignified). This fortunate placement for Venus indicates financial comfort, if not flat-out wealth. You spend extravagantly, but so what; you can afford it. Besides, it brings you pleasure to buy beautiful things. Unless aspects indicate otherwise, you probably benefit financially from marriage and partnerships.

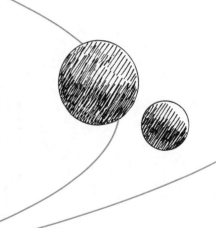

Mars. You pursue your financial goals with relentless drive and energy. But you may have trouble holding on to what you earn because you also love to spend. The best way to lick that is to follow the advice your father probably gave you: Save ten percent of everything you earn and put it someplace where you can't touch it!

Jupiter. This placement increases the opportunities for great wealth. Supported by other aspects in the chart, it can indicate the Midas touch; prosperity is drawn to you. On the downside, there may be an inclination to spend beyond your means. Since Jupiter's expansiveness works both ways, overspending may result in a huge debt.

Saturn. Delays and financial struggles are usually inherent with this placement. Saturn's discipline and careful work ethic can result in financial gain after the age of forty. The challenge here is to channel excessive frugality or greed into productive channels.

Saturn's lesson in the second house is to learn discipline and responsibility about finances.

Uranus. Sudden and unexpected changes in fortune. Just when things are going along smoothly, something happens that turns your financial prosperity around. But with Uranus's eccentric originality operating here, you find ways to make money that are unusual. Some of these methods may be so far ahead of their time they border on genius.

The challenge with this placement is to develop conservative saving and spending habits so that you have a financial base to see you through the lean times.

Neptune. Illusions can work two ways. You're either blind to your faults concerning finances or you're able to draw on deep intuitive resources to make money. On the negative side, you may be attracted to get-rich-quick schemes. The challenge with this placement is to develop a conscious awareness of your own weaknesses and strengths in this area.

Pluto. Given this planet's raw power for transformation, this placement can work for or against you. It may result in a bottomless pot of gold and prosperity or it may wipe you out. It may even do both. A lot depends on the state of your own consciousness and how you apply what you know. The challenge is not to allow the acquisition of money and material goods to become an end in themselves.

North Node. You grow through achieving financial prosperity by your own efforts. By not using other people's money to make your own money, you're able to use and develop the talents that help you attain prosperity.

South Node. Get rid of your old attitudes about money and making money. Formulate what you believe. Find your own value system.

Part of Fortune. You attract opportunities for making money and increasing your financial resources. The nature of the opportunities and people you attract depends on the sign.

The Third House

Planets in this house trigger mental activity, commuter travel, activities involving siblings, relatives, and neighbors, and the capacity to communicate.

Sun. You pride yourself on your intellectual prowess. You enjoy acquiring knowledge and you're good at it. You're an excellent, forceful speaker, able to communicate ideas clearly and succinctly. You're warm and generous with your siblings, relatives, and neighbors. The only downside to this placement is that it may lead to opinionated bragging.

Moon. Your reasoning left brain is constantly influenced by your intuition and imagination. Your memory is good, particularly when strong emotions back up your experiences. You have a tendency to daydream and benefit from frequent changes in your immediate environment.

Mercury (accidentally dignified). Your intellectual curiosity and hunger for knowledge give you an acute desire to learn and to communicate what you learn. You're so mentally restless, however, that you dart from one topic to another, rarely studying one particular thing in depth. Travel is highlighted in your life, perhaps commuting for your work or carpooling with neighbors. You maintain contact with siblings and neighbors.

Venus. Your intellectual interests revolve around literature, music, and the arts. You converse easily with people and bring harmony to all social situations in which you're involved. You take great pleasure in visiting your siblings, close relatives, and neighbors.

Mars. You think on your feet and make decisions quickly. Sometimes you're so aggressive about communicating your ideas

How do you see yourself?

_____
_____
_____
_____
_____
_____
_____
_____
_____
_____
_____
_____
_____
_____

that you become quarrelsome and create a lot of tension in your immediate environment. With this placement there can be considerable competition and tension with siblings and neighbors. The challenge is to think before you act.

Jupiter. You're a mental sponge, soaking up knowledge from a wide variety of sources to feed your broad intellectual interests. You travel frequently, visiting museums and other cultural niches that expand your knowledge. Your relationships with siblings, relatives, and neighbors are apt to be close unless Jupiter is afflicted.

Saturn. You funnel your intellectual interests through great discipline and ambition. Your travel is usually connected to business rather than pleasure. Education can sometimes be interrupted or delayed with this placement, if other aspects in the chart support it. Brother and sisters or other close relatives can impose responsibilities on you.

The lesson here is to approach all third house issues with discipline and responsibility. That means having Christmas dinner with your brother, even if you don't want to go!

Uranus. Intellectual freedom is paramount to your personal happiness. You chafe at traditional and mainstream thinking and aren't hesitant to expound your views on anything. Your entire mental framework is eccentric and original. Your brothers, sisters, and close relatives are intellectually stimulating, but you may experience sudden breaks in communication with them. You travel suddenly, unexpectedly, when the spirit moves you.

Neptune. If you're a poet or a filmmaker, this is a terrific placement for Neptune. It confers a mystical, highly intuitive mindset capable of delving deeply into the creative well. A photographic memory sometimes accompanies this placement, as well as a profound interest in the occult or metaphysical topics. On the other hand, Neptune here can indicate muddled ideas and an inability or unwillingness to communicate clearly. Contact with relatives is erratic.

Pluto. You regenerate and transform your environment through your intellectual efforts and your learning experiences. But because Pluto breaks down existing structures, mental instability is a possibility. The challenge is to channel the enormous power of Pluto into a constructive, creative framework.

North Node. You grow through what you learn and assimilate that knowledge into a wider belief system. Your brothers, sisters, relatives, and neighbors play a vital role in this process. Education is the key for you. You gain through the written word.

South Node. You need to release old thought patterns that inhibit your mental growth. Resist your tendency for mental laziness. Delve into something that interests you. Find your intellectual niche. Pursue higher education as your means to an end.

Part of Fortune. Educational and learning opportunities come easily to you. You gain through your relationships with close relatives, siblings, and neighbors and through daily travel in general.

The Fourth House

Planets in this house energize all affairs concerning the home, family, and one of the parents. The cusp of the fourth house is a critical point in a chart. Any planet within three degrees of the **IC** receives heavier emphasis in the chart.

Sun. Your self-expression focuses on your family and home. You have a deep need to establish roots and strive to make your home comfortable, warm, and a reflection of your own importance. You dominate your home and domestic affairs. You gain through one or both of your parents. Your early childhood was probably quite happy, energetic, and fun.

Moon (accidentally dignified). You either stick close to your birthplace or leave it when you're young. Many changes in residence are indicated, but you retain good memories and strong feelings for your birthplace. You benefit through your parents and from the opposite sex. Close emotional bonds exist with your parents. Since the Moon is dignified here, the latter part of life tends to be more stable.

Mercury. A lot of intellectual activity goes on in your home and you've probably got a tremendous library that reflects your varied intellectual interests. You move frequently, perhaps in connection

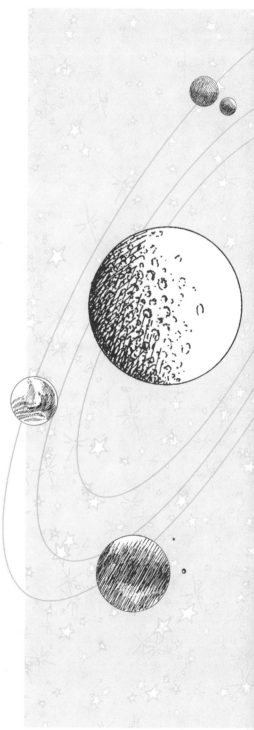

with business. Communication in your family is good and domestic disputes are settled through discussion.

Venus. You seek harmony in your home and go to great lengths to maintain it. You derive profound enjoyment from your family and home. The furnishings and decorations reflect your aesthetic tastes. You gain through inheritance and your parents, with whom you have a good rapport. You also gain through property, houses, and all things that concern the fourth house. Peaceful and comfortable conditions prevail for the last twenty years of your life.

Mars. Your family life is active, with an emphasis on the development of individuality, independence, and competition. Your urge to dominate the domestic scene can create an underlying tension and hostility. This Mars placement can also cause fires and accidental mishaps in the home.

Jupiter. This is about as good as it gets for a secure childhood and a good relationship with your parents. The domestic situation is generally peaceful and joyful, with a focus on pursuits unique to Jupiter—spiritual or religious ideals, foreign travel, and insights into other cultures and ways of life. The latter part of life is probably as secure as the first part.

Saturn. The traditional meaning for this placement indicates restrictions and heavy responsibilities in early childhood. Childhood discipline may be strict and emotional ties with the family may be strong due to a sense of obligation. In other words, the emphasis is placed on the early life, as obligations to parents and siblings.

While these characteristics are often true with this placement, they aren't the full story. Sometimes, Saturn here manifests in adulthood as a need to establish roots in a family structure. It can indicate that you're older than the norm when you start your family. While other people's kids have left for college and they're looking toward retirement, you're still enjoying your kids at home and working to support them.

The interpretation of Saturn in this house should be taken into consideration with the placement of the nodes and any planets that are conjunct Saturn. Also note the degree of the house cusp. Sometimes with this placement, the cusp is in a critical degree—29 or more. The Saturn lesson here is to learn responsibility and discipline toward your family and home.

Uranus. In this house, Uranus brings its eccentricities and originality to bear on domestic affairs. Many changes of residence are likely. The home life is atypical or unusual, with exceptional experiences often happening in or about the home. You may rebel against your parents. Disruptions occur from early childhood onward within a loosely knit and unusual family structure.

Neptune. Your family life may not be the neighborhood ideal, but it doesn't affect you adversely because you don't see it as it really exists. You idealize your parents and early childhood. You're very psychic when it comes to your home and family; your emotional bonds with them can be spiritual in nature. With this placement, there are frequent moves, journeys by water, and secrets regarding home life. On a more optimistic note, if Neptune is well-aspected here, you may delve deeply into profound cosmic mysteries.

Pluto. You transform your life and regenerate yourself through your domestic affairs, which are unusual in some way. Through your home and family, you break with tradition and create a constant source of renewal.

North Node. You gain through your family and home, which provide the greatest opportunity for your spiritual growth. You also benefit through real estate and property in general.

South Node. By overcoming deeply embedded, negative attitudes about family and home, you find great potential for growth. Your North Node position shows you the way to achieve this.

Part of Fortune. You gain through parents, property, and your home life. With this placement, you may work out of your home or with your family in some capacity. Inheritance may be indicated.

The Fifth House

Planets in this house stimulate all creative and artistic endeavors and romantic love affairs. The pursuit of pleasure is highlighted. Attention is focused on children, especially the first-born.

The Mars Effect

Michel Gauquelin, a French psychologist and statistician, and his wife, Francoise, actually set out to disprove astrology. Between 1949 and 1958, they analyzed the birth charts of 16,336 eminent professionals and 24,961 charts of ordinary professionals. They discovered that Mars tends to be near an angle in the charts of sports champions; that Jupiter is near an angle for actors; and that Saturn lies near an angle for scientists.

Their findings were statistically higher than chance. Twenty-two percent of the athletes, for example, were born with Mars near an angle; chance alone would put it at seventeen percent. But astrologer Robert Hand notes that one vital detail of the Gauquelin studies varies from astrological tradition. In traditional astrology, houses one, four, seven, and ten are the

Sun (accidentally dignified). Party time. Good times, friendly relationships and an active pursuit of romance and pleasure in general. You enjoy theater, the arts, sports, films. You're fond of animals and may have several pets of your own. Sometimes this Sun placement inclines toward gambling and speculative investments.

Even if you don't have kids of your own, you're fond of children. Your creative self-expression may manifest in some way through children—maybe you work with them, have kids of your own, or you write children's books. Look to the house cusp to determine if the Sun here is conducive to having children. If it's in Cancer, Scorpio, or Pisces, the chances for children are enhanced.

Moon. Unless the Moon is in a fixed sign, your affections go through phases. You're romantic and get along well with women. Your creative life fluctuates. When you're younger you may vacillate about having children, but at some point, the issue of children becomes more important. The Moon here inclines toward public success.

Mercury. You seek romantic partners who are mentally agile and as excited intellectually about the things that excite you. Your artistic talents may find expression in writing, the theater, or in entertainment. If Mercury is poorly aspected, your mental energy may be scattered; you start things that you don't finish.

Venus. This placement is great for happy love affairs, artistic projects, and beautiful children. Your children may have an unusual artistic or musical talent. You gain through romantic partners, offspring, and, if other aspects in the chart support it, through speculation and investments. You have a particular fondness for beautiful animals. Excessive pleasure may be your undoing.

Mars. Competitive sports, athletics, and workouts at the gym are highlighted. You enjoy strenuous activity and pursue it as aggressively as you pursue romance. Thanks to the impulsive nature of Mars, you may experience unfortunate romantic attractions. These affairs are filled with passion and sensuality but in the end go nowhere and only injure you emotionally.

Sometimes, if other factors in the chart support it, this Mars placement in a woman's horoscope indicates difficult childbirth.

Jupiter. This placement is naturally lucky. You expand tremendously through creative endeavors, romance, and children. Usually, Jupiter here indicates a number of children, who remain helpful to you throughout your life. You also benefit through speculation and investments. On the downside, there's an inclination for excessive gambling and speculation if Jupiter isn't well aspected.

Saturn. Wherever Saturn appears, you can expect delays, restrictions, limitations. In the fifth house, Saturn restricts creative self-expression or, at the very least, teaches strict discipline in creative expression. It may limit the number of children or can indicate a stillbirth, miscarriage, or termination of a pregnancy.

In romance, you may get involved with an older person or a sense of duty or responsibility may inhibit romantic involvement. The nature of Saturn's karmic lesson is creative self-expression.

Uranus. Your romantic affairs are totally unconventional and unpredictable. When one relationship collapses, you're on to the next one. Your sexual attitudes are as eccentric as you are. Your children are probably highly individualistic and perhaps brilliant.

If poorly aspected, there can be abrupt breaks with romantic partners, difficulty in childbirth, possible danger to the first-born child.

Neptune. The traditional meaning is disillusionment through romance and children and a penchant for secret intrigues and affairs. While this may be true, Neptune here can also bring deep psychic insight into the complexities of relationships and into the spiritual essence inherent in children. Your compassion extends to all living things.

The challenge is to make practical use of the insight and apply it to your own relationships and children.

Pluto. In this house, the great transformer brings revolution and evolution through romance, children, and creative self-expression. At the highest level, Pluto offers the chance to create unique and far-reaching works of art, spiritual love and compassion, and great spiritual growth through children. At its lowest level, Pluto can bring about the basest expression of all of the above.

One of the challenges with this placement is to avoid a dictatorial attitude toward children, which can destroy your relationship with them.

The Mars Effect

(continued)

angular houses and are thought to be the strongest placements for planets. "But Gauguelin's work showed the points of greatest strength to be a few degrees to the other side of the angles, in houses twelve, three, six, and nine."

CSI Cops has tried to debunk Gauguelin's findings, but never entirely succeeded. Then in the October 1981 issue of *Fate Magazine*, Dennis Rawlins, a Harvard-educated physicist and co-founder of CSICOPS (Committee for the Scientific Investigation of Claims of the Paranormal), blew the whistle on the group. He confirmed what critics of CSICOPS had long suspected: "that the organization is committed to perpetuating a position, not to determining the truth," wrote the *Fate* editors in a preface to the article.

North Node. Your deepest source of spiritual growth is through creative expression. This is how you develop your potential and enrich your life. Children are a blessing.

South Node. You need to release outdated attitudes concerning children, creativity, and romance. Get rid of your selfish attitudes. If Saturn is conjunct in this house, the lesson is reinforced.

Part of Fortune. You gain through children, the arts, and the pursuit of pleasure in its many and varied forms.

The Sixth House

Planets in this house trigger activity in the areas of health, work and work conditions, the services you perform, and associations with employees. Small pets may also be included in this house.

Sun. You need to be recognized in your workplace. After all, you're efficient, meticulous with details, and work hard and well at your job. Your concern about health and health issues is reflected in your intuitive understanding about how to keep yourself healthy. A conjunction or sextile with Mars strengthens your health and the affairs of this house; a poorly aspected Sun here can weaken your vitality.

Moon. Your physical health is directly connected to your emotional health. Once you're aware of this you can make sure that you vent your emotions when they need to be vented and that you don't block what you feel, positive or negative. Diet plays a vital part in your health.

You may feel a need to work with the public in a service capacity. Whatever your work conditions, the majority of your fellow workers are probably women. Your love of pets and small animals nurtures you emotionally.

Mercury (accidentally dignified). Routine work doesn't fit this placement and can result in many job changes. Your approach to work is practical and detailed. Your mind plays an important role in your health. By assimilating information and using it to consciously change your belief system, you can deal with or vanquish nagging physical ailments.

Venus. Your work brings you enormous pleasure. Your relationship with fellow employees and your working conditions in general are harmonious. You're a team player, cooperative and helpful. This placement favors good health but cautions against excess in eating and the use of alcohol and drugs.

Mars. A lot of your energy, skill, and precision goes into your work. You don't tolerate laziness in other people. You need to respect other people's work methods, otherwise there may be disruptions with fellow employees. With this placement, work may involve sharp tools or machinery. Surgeons often have Mars in the sixth house.

In terms of health, people with this placement often run high fevers when they're ill. The same energy that Mars brings to your work, however, can be brought to bear on any health problems.

Jupiter. You have an instinctive understanding that your physical health is connected to your mental and emotional health. This may lead you into the study of spiritual or psychic healing, massage, therapeutic touch, homeopathy, or other facets of alternative medicine.

Unless Jupiter is afflicted, this placement usually means your relationship with co-workers is congenial.

Saturn. You have a strong sense of responsibility toward your work and take your job seriously. At times you may feel overburdened and overworked, but you feel compelled to do the best that you can. Your approach to your work and your health is practical and specialized.

If Saturn is afflicted, chronic health problems may result, usually due to burnout and worry. An awareness of your limitations can mitigate health problems. The Saturn lesson with this placement is to learn responsibility toward work and health.

Uranus. Work and health conditions change suddenly and unpredictably. You need a lot of freedom in your job, detest routine, and enjoy trying out new ideas and techniques. Job opportunities seem to come out of nowhere, but you can also be terminated with little or no notice. With this placement of Uranus, there can be spontaneous remission from disease and chronic health problems.

If afflicted, nervous tension can play havoc with your health.

Neptune. You draw on intuitive resources in your work and have a deep interest in metaphysical matters. Neptune here makes you receptive to psychic energies, so try to associate with upbeat, positive people in your work environment and in health matters. There may be some self-deception with this placement concerning health, work, or both. A close scrutiny of aspects to the sixth house will clarify this issue.

Due to the psychic nature of Neptune, you benefit from a diet of fresh foods with little or no animal fat. A vegetarian diet would benefit you immensely.

Pluto. Unless Pluto is afflicted, its placement here indicates tremendous recuperative strength. You have the innate capacity to evolve through your work and service to others or to bring about chaos in this area of your life. Pluto's power is nearly always either/or, black or white. Look closely at other aspects to the sixth house.

North Node. This placement strengthens your health and your work conditions and opportunities. With this placement there can be spontaneous remissions. In such instances the belief system that led to the illness is torn down and a new belief system is built up. The North Node here can indicate natural healing talents that can be structured in new ways.

South Node. You release deeply embedded work and health attitudes through service to others. Even if you work alone or in seclusion, some aspect of your work finds its way into the public where it is judged on its merits. The challenge with this placement is to realize that everything—the state of your health and the conditions in your life—originates in your core beliefs.

Part of Fortune. You profit and benefit through your work and with small pets and animals. This placement strengthens health and confers a deep awareness of how to maintain good health. You gain through learning responsibility.

The Seventh House

Planets in this house address your interaction with society through marriage and partnerships. The cusp of this house is one of the four angles (descendant) in a horoscope. Any planet within three degrees of the cusp should be given more emphasis.

Sun. Your self-expression is directly linked to your most intimate relationships and to your partnerships with other people. Your achievements tend to come through joint work with others. Unless there are afflictions to the seventh house, you benefit tremendously through marriage or committed relationships and partnerships. Your significant other is apt to be generous and warm-hearted.

Moon. You're strongly intuitive about people you love, particularly marriage partners and significant others. Your own emotional health depends on the stability and happiness of your most intimate relationships. Marriage often happens early to someone who enjoys travel and who may be publicly prominent in some way.

If the Moon or the seventh house is poorly aspected, especially by Mars, your marriage may be marked by discord and disharmony.

Mercury. You either marry early in life or marry someone younger. Communication with your mate or significant other is of prime importance to you; you may meet this person while traveling, in connection with writing or education, or in some other pursuits governed by Mercury. You're at ease with people socially and are able to converse on any number of topics.

Venus (accidentally dignified). A happy marriage and profitable partnerships are indicated. This terrific placement for Venus confers ease in social situations. You act like a magnet in attracting what you need in terms of partnerships and financial benefits.

Mars. If well-aspected, this placement for Mars infuses energy into marriage and partnerships and acts as a source of inspiration. If Mars is afflicted here, it leads to strife and disharmony in partnerships, usually because of the impulsive beginnings of the relationship. It can indicate a fierce, sometimes violent temper. According to some astrologers, an afflicted Mars here can testify to the death of a partner. But death is never indicated by just one planet or aspect in a chart.

Jupiter. If well-aspected, this is a fortunate placement for Jupiter. You benefit financially and spiritually from all

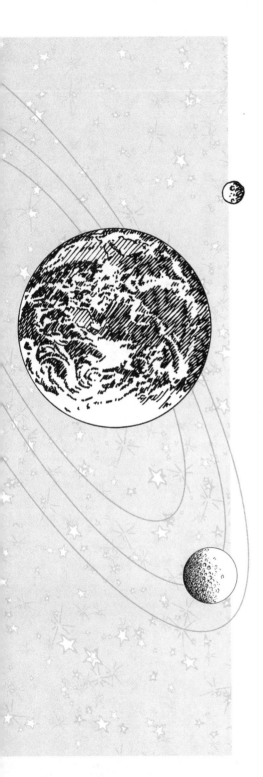

partnerships and from marriage in particular. Foreign travel or cultures are highlighted; you may meet your significant other in another country.

If Jupiter is afflicted in the seventh, it can result in selfishness, delayed marriage, or problems with litigation.

Saturn. This position tends to delay marriage until you're established. You may be attracted to someone older who is already established, and there can be burdens and heavy responsibilities with marriage. Since Saturn is the karmic planet, the lesson here is to learn about cooperation in partnerships.

Uranus. Sudden, unpredictable involvements and changes in partnership and marriage. The significant other can be unusual in some way, eccentric, or a genius. If your personal freedom is restricted at all, you end the marriage or relationship without a second thought.

When afflicted, Uranus here indicates unstable partnerships, an impulsive marriage that ends unhappily, and loss through partnerships.

Neptune. Marriage and partnerships are your blind spot. Your idealism in this area can lead to a marriage or partnerships that are either spiritual and psychic in nature or which ultimately disappoint and hurt.

Pluto. You evolve through marriage and partnerships. There's considerable intensity in any close relationship, but in marriage in particular. Your partner may be a source of your regeneration or may deplete your energy. It depends on aspects to the seventh house.

North Node. You benefit and evolve through marriage and partnerships. This placement is excellent for understanding public sentiment and opinion, which can be helpful in whatever you do.

South Node. Selfish attitudes lead to disharmony in marriage and partnerships. The lesson here is to learn through cooperation and tolerance of other people's viewpoints.

Part of Fortune. Partnerships and marriage are fortunate for you. You gain through them and win over any enemies you might have.

The Eighth House

Planets here focus energy on joint finances, inheritances, death, sexuality, and the occult.

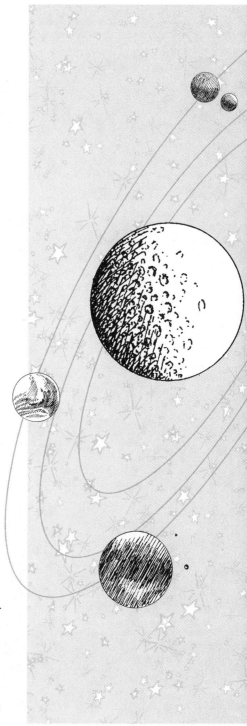

Sun. Your financial prosperity increases after marriage, through partnerships, and inheritances. You have a deep interest in metaphysics, specifically in life after death and reincarnation.

Some astrologers contend that the Sun in this house indicates that fame comes after death and that any afflictions or poor aspects enhance the possibility of premature, sudden, or violent death. But this smacks of predestination and fate.

We're endowed with a free will that acts on the *pattern* inherent in a chart and creates our experiences from the raw material of our core beliefs. On a deeper level, our free will allows us to choose our parents and the circumstances into which we're born and how and when we die. From the pattern intrinsic to the blueprint of our birth chart, free will creates the structure of our lives and our deaths.

Moon. Your joint finances go through many fluctuations and changes. You may inherit money, possibly from your mother or her side of the family, and gain in general through the affairs of the dead. Afflicted, this Moon placement mitigates all of the above.

Mercury. You may expend a lot of mental energy worrying about joint finances, inheritances, and matters pertaining to the dead. There's a strong possibility that you inherit money from a brother or sister or someone who is like kin to you. Metaphysical topics intrigue you. You may write about such topics.

Venus. You're lucky when it comes to other people's money, joint finances, inheritance, and everything associated with this house. You gain financially through marriage and partnerships, attracting the right people just when you need them. You're fortunate when it comes to inheritances, contracts, taxes.

Poorly aspected, you may have a tendency for sexual excess. Exert caution about excesses with sex, drugs, and alcohol.

Mars (accidentally dignified). You're actively involved in joint finances in any marriage and partnership. This can cause friction between you and your partner(s). There can be disputes over inheritances. A lot of energy goes into the management of joint finances. This can be a good placement for bookkeepers, trust and tax attorneys, and insurance adjusters.

Jupiter. You benefit from all affairs of the eighth house, particularly through partnerships and marriage. You're interested in spiritual or religious issues, and this may lead you into a penetrating study of life after death, reincarnation, and how you fit into the larger scheme of things. Your death is likely to be peaceful and natural. Jupiter in the eighth inclines toward long life.

Saturn. Benefits associated with the eighth house tend to come later in life, after forty, and are largely a result of your own efforts. Your spouse or business partners may be stingy, which may limit what you gain through joint finances. There could be tax trouble with this placement also. Check the placement of the North and South Nodes and aspects to this house and to Saturn for additional insight. Saturn here implies a long life.

Uranus. You benefit from a partner's sudden, unexpected windfall or legacy, or, if Uranus is afflicted, you experience sudden reversals in joint finances. Sexuality may manifest in eccentric ways. There's usually an interest in the occult with this placement. The partner usually earns money in a manner contrary to the mainstream.

Uranus here can also indicate an unusual and idiosyncratic approach in using other people's money and resources to augment your own income.

Neptune. You have the innate ability to enter higher realms through the harnessing of psychic energy. This placement can indicate precognitive dreams, astral experiences, a deep interest in spiritualism, and an attunement with metaphysical and mystical energy. In terms of the real world, your partners or significant other may handle your joint finances in a deceptive or fraudulent way. Mysterious circumstances may surround death.

Pluto (accidentally dignified). This powerful placement for such a powerful planet means that you can evolve through a piercing study of life after death, reincarnation, and spiritualism, and all affairs associated with this house. You can also evolve

through the development of joint resources with a partner. In people who are self-aware, this placement often indicates involvement in the psychic healing arts.

If poorly aspected, Pluto here can mean that you drain other people's resources, sucking them dry.

North Node. Increases prospects for good health and longevity. You evolve through your dealings with others and gain through joint finances, contracts with partners, and investigation of the occult.

South Node. You evolve through your involvement in joint financial affairs. If you rely on your partner to make all the decisions, your own development is stymied.

Part of Fortune. You gain through inheritances, marriage, partnerships, and all eighth house affairs.

The Ninth House

Planets that occupy this house spur activity in philosophy, religion or spirituality, higher education, foreign travel and cultures, in-laws, and the higher mind. The ninth house also represents publishing.

Sun. Foreign cultures and countries intrigue you. You either study about them or live or travel extensively in foreign countries. You may work in publishing or academia. Unless the Sun is poorly aspected, you find success abroad and honors through universities, law, or religion.

Moon. You enjoy travel, particularly to foreign countries, and benefit through the kinds of changes that travel abroad brings you. The ethical and religious values you learned as a child give you a sense of security. Your intuition is highly developed; sometimes you're outright psychic. Good relations with in-laws.

If poorly aspected, your religious or spiritual views may be totally unorthodox and travel abroad may be difficult in some respect.

Mercury. You have a quick, keen mind that easily grasps abstract concepts in philosophy, spirituality, law, and education. You enjoy lively intellectual discussions and debates. Your wanderlust may be

House Rulers

To fully understand house rulers, it's necessary to regress briefly to the signs and their rulers. In the natural order of the zodiac, the signs begin with Aries and progress through the months to Pisces. Why couldn't the signs start with January? Why April and Aries? And why end up in March and Pisces instead of in December and Sagittarius?

Part of the reason for this order in Western astrology is due to the nature of the signs themselves. In other words, Aries is the pioneer who goes out into the world first. Pisces swims through the waters of the imagination and his dreams eventually root in the physical world and become the reality of Aries.

temporarily sated by studying about foreign places and cultures. At some point, the need to get out and travel overpowers you. You may even live in a foreign country for awhile. If poorly aspected, this placement leads to a dispersion of energy and the inability to bring what you've started to completion.

Venus. This terrific placement for Venus brings you benefits through all ninth house pursuits and interests. Music and art with religious or spiritual themes fascinate you. Your literary interests may attract you to publishing or writing. Travel appeals to you, but not if you're alone. You want to share the adventure with someone! If you're uninvolved, you may meet your significant other overseas.

When Venus is the highest point in the chart (closest to the Midheaven), it indicates success and honors. Afflicted, it means high ideals that may not reach fruition.

Mars. Wanderlust is elevated to new heights with this place-ment. You hike the Inca trail, meditate inside the Great Pyramid, ride a dogsled across Antarctica. You aren't satisfied to simply debate your philosophical and spiritual beliefs; you must act on them. If Mars is adverse, the potential for danger and accidents exists while traveling abroad.

Jupiter (accidentally dignified). You gain through higher edu-cation, the pursuit of your ideals, and the affairs of the ninth house. You may be a university professor or lead workshops and seminars on esoteric topics. You may even lead spiritually-oriented trips to sacred power spots abroad. Your relationship with your in-laws is excellent.

Saturn. Your moral and spiritual beliefs find structure within higher education or within orthodox religion. Your travel tends to be associated with business and professional ambition. You enjoy investigating esoteric religious and ancient texts. After the age of forty, your religious and spiritual beliefs solidify and your careful, studious methods pay off.

Afflicted, you may encounter trouble abroad and with your in-laws.

Uranus. You have unusual and progressive ideas about higher education and religion and spirituality. Your beliefs probably don't gel with anyone else's, but your belief system works for you.

Foreign travel stimulates you and you often travel on the spur of the moment. Your intuition is sometimes prophetic; cultivate the art of listening to your inner voice.

Adverse, Uranus in this placement can indicate trouble overseas or an unexpected break or interruption in your education.

Neptune. This is a very psychic placement for Neptune. You probably have a deep interest in Eastern thought and belief systems, as well as spiritualism, reincarnation, and mysticism. Higher education probably isn't high on your list of priorities, unless aspects indicate otherwise. You travel in connection with spiritual beliefs, but you should take time to plan whatever trips you take. Otherwise, disorganization mitigates what you might glean from your travels.

Pluto. You evolve and regenerate yourself through the affairs of the ninth house. With this placement you can breathe new life into old ideas. Adverse, you should take great care traveling abroad.

North Node. The path of your greatest growth lies in the development of the higher mind and comes through higher education and foreign travel. Psychic ability is often finely developed with this placement.

South Node. To evolve and grow, you need to vastly expand your narrow views on life.

Part of Fortune. Luck with foreigners and in foreign cultures, through publishing, higher education, and all matters connected with the ninth house.

The Tenth House

Planets in this house activate energy dealing with career, status, worldly ambitions, and professional achievements. The Midheaven, or cusp of the tenth house, is a critical angle in a chart. Any planet that is within three degrees of the Midheaven should be given heavier consideration.

Sun. Even if it's poorly aspected, the Sun here is always beneficial in some respect. When it's well-aspected, it denotes success in the

How do you see yourself?

chosen profession, honors, authority, and independence. Your hunger to achieve may draw you into the public eye where you thrive on the authority and power you have. This placement is excellent for CEOs, political leaders, and people in prominent positions.

Moon. You experience fluctuations in your career, business, and employment. You're able to read the tide of public opinion, which gives you a terrific advantage in your work. Women and family are supportive of what you do and helpful in attaining what you desire. With good aspects to Jupiter, you're prosperous; adverse aspects to Mars can indicate public scandal.

Mercury. This is a good position for novelists, reporters, teachers, and metaphysical professions in general. Your diverse interests can turn into several separate and distinct careers. You can communicate with virtually anyone, so you tend to get along with employers and bosses. If poorly aspected, this placement indicates restlessness and impulsive speech.

Venus. Writers, artists, musicians, diplomats, actors, entertainers of all sorts are indicated by Venus in the tenth house. You're popular and well-liked and your social ease is an asset in whatever you do. Your professional ambitions incline toward the arts and finance.

Mars. When you want something, you go after it full steam. Your self-motivation drives you relentlessly and can make you reckless and extreme. With this placement it's best to occasionally kick back and evaluate where you are, where you're going, and what you want before you make major career decisions.

Jupiter. This is about as good as it gets! Jupiter's placement in the tenth indicates success in your career, with few if any setbacks. This is particularly true if Jupiter is the highest point in your chart. This placement attracts recognition and awards like a magnet. It's good for any profession where fair judgment and ethics are required.

Saturn (accidentally dignified). Your career ambition is probably one of the primary driving forces in your life. You may feel that you came in this time to accomplish something very specific. Even if you don't know what it is yet, you bring discipline and perseverance to your work, certain you will achieve whatever it is you came here to do. Success and recognition are important to you.

Even though Saturn in the tenth inclines toward success, it also imposes certain restrictions: success may come after the age of forty. But when it comes, it sticks around for the long run.

Poorly aspected, Saturn in the tenth can indicate a drive for success that is so relentless, you lose sight of the things that really matter. Your integrity gets swallowed up and in the end you lose big time.

Uranus. The traditional meaning for this placement relates to freedom from restrictions. Sudden and unpredictable change, in terms of your career, are possible. This is certainly true for many people with Uranus in the tenth, but it isn't the whole truth.

Uranus here brings a unique and eccentric slant on the way you make your living. You may become an overnight celebrity, then recede from the public eye for awhile. Your methods may smack of genius. You don't feel comfortable with issues like status; you may feel like a loner on a singular mission that no one else understands. But that's okay. Persevere. Believe in yourself and allow yourself plenty of freedom in terms of your work. This placement is excellent for astrologers, writers, hypnotists, and anyone who studies metaphysics.

Neptune. This mystical placement of Neptune indicates that you're capable of winning recognition for some unique achievement. The knowledge that allows you to do this comes through the higher self, almost as if you channel the material. An illusion of some sort surrounds your career, some element of self-deception. You may not get along with employers, and you may go through periods where your ambition is low. But by remaining true to your dream, whatever it is, you can overcome the challenges.

This placement is good for mediums, hypnotists, poets, musicians, artists, and anything to do with the sea.

Pluto. You evolve through your worldly ambitions. Depending on the aspects to Pluto in the tenth, you may reach the celestial heights of your profession or plunge into humiliation—or both. How it manifests depends on how well you've learned Plutonian lessons.

North Node. This node placement is the equivalent of Jupiter and Venus sharing space in your tenth house. You don't miss; it's as if you're divinely protected. Your timing in career matters is impeccable. You evolve through your career and profession.

South Node. A wakeup call. Get out of your shell and look around. What are other people doing? What're they reading and talking about? What films are they seeing? You need to become aware of the public pulse and use what you learn in your career.

Part of Fortune. This one is very lucky! You have a knack for being in the right place at the right time. Who you know and connect with is as important as what you know and do.

The Eleventh House

Friends. Support groups. Networks. Your ambitions. Planets in this house emphasize the importance of groups in your life and tell something about how your friends can help you realize your dreams.

Sun. Social success is indicated with the Sun here. Your friends are warm, generous, honest people. They reflect your own integrity and ideals and can be helpful in the achievement of your ambitions. You gain through any clubs or social organizations to which you belong.

Moon. You have a large circle of acquaintances, but only a few deep friendships with people whom you trust implicitly. Many of your friends may be unreliable. You probably have more female friends than male, and some of them may be celebrities or public figures. The groups you belong to may be connected in some way to family issues.

Your intuition, especially with the Moon in a water sign, is well-developed and can help you attain your wishes and dreams.

Spiritual Astrology

Most astrologers acknowledge a spiritual dimension in horoscope interpretation. But authors Jan Spiller and Karen McCoy took the idea to new heights in their book *Spiritual Astrology*.

Their premise is that solar and lunar eclipses that occurred prenatally are significant to the individual. In McCoy's analysis of four thousand charts, she discovered that ". . . for the vast majority of people, the sign of their solar eclipse indicated lessons they had come to teach their fellow beings, while the sign of the lunar eclipse guided them to the lessons they needed to learn in order to continue their own soul growth."

They provide an ephemeris in their book that lists the date of every solar and lunar eclipse since the turn of the century. You locate the eclipse that occurred immediately before your birthdate, then look in the text to determine what it means.

When I tried it, I found that the solar eclipse that occurred closest to my birthdate of June 7, 1947, was on May 20, 1947. It was in Taurus, at 28'42". The lunar eclipse closest to my birthdate occurred on June 3, 1947, in Sagittarius at 12'22". This would place the solar eclipse in my seventh house of partnerships and the lunar eclipse in my second house of material resources.

"Through you, your fellow beings can learn a proper prosperity consciousness," McCoy writes under the heading for solar eclipses in Taurus. "You are also here to teach the impor-tance of having strong spiritual values." Since this eclipse falls in my seventh house, it suggests this will happen in my intimate partnerships.

What I find particularly interesting about this description is that I'm married to a Taurus, who is also a writer. We are each other's first editors and have collaborated on metaphysical books.

Under the description for Sagittarius in lunar eclipses, the authors write: "You have come into his life to break all prejudices and to learn to understand the common thread that runs through all forms of philosophy, religion, and spirituality." These are themes that I often explore in my fiction and the general descrip-tion certainly resonates for me.

Much of the research into esoteric facets of astrology involves unconventional tools—like hypnotic regression, meditation, and intuition. These very tools often come under attack simply because they aren't the norm. As Spiller notes, "There are many nonmate-rial realities that have very definite physical effects. Gravity is not visible, yet its existence is self-evident. In the same way the final 'proof' of astrology's validity is whether or not it can be of prac-tical use in your life."

Mercury. Your circle of friends is quite large and always lively. You share ideas, debate on intellectual issues, and may even travel with groups. Friends help you to achieve whatever it is you're seeking, and through them you make valuable professional contacts.

Venus. Your friends are very important to you and often share your taste in art, music, and books. Friends help you achieve your dreams and ambitions.

Mars. In true Mars fashion, you take the initiative in forming friendships and in joining groups and associations. In your social circles, you're considered a veritable whirl of energy, able to initiate projects and get them off the ground. You're the one they pick to head up charities and entertainment events.

When afflicted, Mars here can create discord with your friends.

Jupiter. You have truly sincere and honest friends who support you in all your endeavors. If you run for political office, your friends are the ones who work on your campaign. If you write a novel or a screenplay, your friends are the first to critique it and offer their opinions. Your social connections are among prominent individuals—judges, attorneys, politicians, and physicians.

Saturn. Your friends tend to be older than you are and they're generally serious, disciplined people with clear goals and objectives. You may not have dozens of close friends, but the ones you do have are friends for life. You join groups that are associated with business or your professional ambitions.

Uranus (accidentally dignified). Your friends are varied, eccentric, colorful, and unusual. If Uranus is well-aspected, you gain in unexpected ways through them. They may be writers, inventors, psychics, or spiritualists, and all of them are progressive thinkers.

If poorly aspected, Uranus here can result in sudden estrangements, difficulties through friends, and peculiar experiences related to friendships.

Neptune. There's a terrific capacity with this placement to attract highly evolved friends and associates. Poets, musicians, mystics, and artists may be part of your social circles. You find inspiration and develop and grow spiritually through them. You prefer psychic or secret organizations.

If Neptune is poorly aspected, friends prove to be your blindspot. They may deceive and desert you.

Pluto. You evolve through your friendships and group activities. You wield powerful influence over your friends or they over you. The nature of this power, good or bad, depends on the aspects to the eleventh house.

North Node. Your friends help you achieve your dreams and wishes. Groups that you join further your growth and potential.

South Node. You need to expand your social circles. You must learn the strength of group associations, networking, and the spiritual communion that occurs in the best of friendships.

Part of Fortune. You derive great pleasure and benefit from your social circles and friends.

The Twelfth House

Any planets in this house activate or bring to light issues dealing with aspects of ourselves that we may have repressed or disowned. Planets here pertain to confinement, institutions, unconscious motivations. The way these energies manifest depends on aspects to the twelfth house.

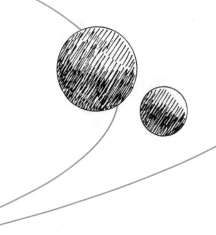

Sun. This placement can inhibit self-expression until later in life. This may be due to unconscious problems concerning the father or feelings of inferiority that aren't conquered until after the age of forty. You probably work in seclusion or behind the scenes and a lot of your energy goes into your inner life. You win over any enemies that you may have.

Moon. Your emotional expression is stymied. You're very psychic and through the development of this talent are able to reach out to others in a way that eludes you emotionally. Emotional problems may concern early childhood experiences with your mother. You benefit through solitary or behind-the-scenes work.

Mercury. You enjoy investigating hidden or esoteric topics and your intuition allows you to probe deeply into these matters. Your verbal and written expression, however, may be repressed in some way. There can be difficulties with close relatives.

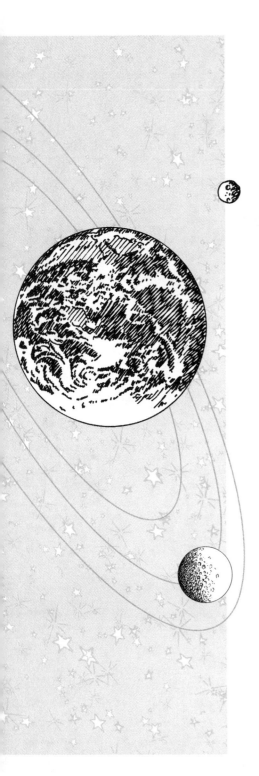

Venus. Secret love affairs and romantic intrigues are indicated. The end result of these intrigues can cause sorrow if Venus or the twelfth house are poorly aspected. You love mystery and adventure, although you can be sensually excessive in your pursuits of both. You enjoy horses and other large animals and may work with them in some capacity.

Mars. This usually isn't a good placement for Mars. If you've repressed your aggression, it can turn against you and create health problems. If you own up to your aggression, it needs to be tempered so that it doesn't become your greatest enemy. If Mars is poorly aspected in the twelfth, imprisonment, rape or sexual abuse, or assault are possible. Mars in Capricorn, however, strengthens this placement.

Jupiter. Unless Jupiter is poorly aspected, this placement gives you a built-in protection from all affairs of the twelfth house. You have a profound interest in spiritual issues. You find success in any behind-the-scenes setting and success usually comes around midlife.

Saturn. There's no way around it: this placement is difficult. Your penchant for solitude often results in loneliness and a quiet despair. You work hard for recognition in your chosen field but rarely receive the credit you're due. You may work in institutions or behind the scenes. If well aspected, this placement can lead to success through work done in seclusion.

Uranus. Your intuition is well-developed, but your personal freedom may be stifled in some way. Perhaps you have repressed your own freedom; maybe you hide your genius and originality out of fear of disapproval. A sudden illness or unexpected confinement is possible. A lot depends on the aspects to the twelfth house and the nature of what you've repressed.

Neptune (accidentally dignified). You possess deep spiritual compassion and may find success in any facet of metaphysics. You gain through mediumship, psychical research, and any type of solitary work or work carried on behind the scenes. This placement is great for the development of psychic ability. The attributes of Neptune here can manifest through the imagination in writing, acting, or a flair for the theater.

On the downside, however, you may have repressed the psychic side of your nature early in your life. Unless you release it by owning up to it, it's likely to affect your health in some way.

Pluto. You evolve through spiritual regeneration. If well aspected, this placement protects you from the negative influences of the twelfth house. You find inner reserves of fortitude to carry through on your ideas. If badly aspected, subversion seems to shadow you.

North Node. You're protected from people who work against you and may even win them over in the end. This protects you and gives you the ability to turn adverse conditions to your favor. You gain through work in metaphysics and anything carried out in solitude or behind the scenes.

South Node. Your selfishness hinders even your best efforts. Whatever you seek to achieve is thwarted if you place your own wants and needs above all else.

Part of Fortune. You gain through any work carried on behind the scenes or in secret. Even if the twelfth house is adversely aspected, this placement adds a measure of protection against the darker influences of this house. In other words, if you go into the hospital, the problem isn't life-threatening.

When interpreting a chart, the natural rulers of each sign must be taken into consideration. In Figure 6-1, Gemini (♊) is on the cusp of the second house. Mercury rules Gemini. In determining what this individual does or may do to earn a living, you should consider the nature of Mercury.

Mercury has to do with communication. In the broadest sense, this individual probably earns money through some profession that deals with communication, usually the written word: editor, journalist, novelist, writer, or columnist. Now look at the cusp of the tenth house of professions.

The Midheaven or **MC** is 26♑16—26 degrees and 16 minutes in Capricorn. This should immediately tell you the individual brings discipline and structure to his work because that's the nature of Saturn, which rules Capricorn.

To get you started, look at Aries (♈) on the cusp of the twelfth house. Aries is ruled by Mars, the planet of initiative, drive, and self-

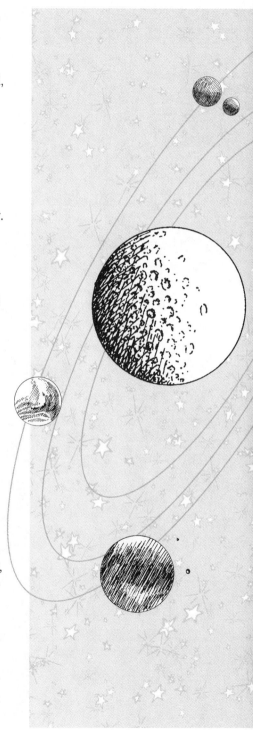

reliance. The North Node occupies this house, with the Sun close enough to affect the twelfth house. This should tell you that the individual probably works well in seclusion, that he's self-motivated and self-reliant, a person who seizes opportunity when he sees it or creates his own opportunities.

With his Sun in his first house, this guy is likable and probably projects a confident image. His Taurus ascendant and Taurus Sun, a fixed sign ruled by Venus, should tell you something about what he looks like and how he appears to other people. He's a double Taurus—that means double fixed, double earth, double stubborn. This guy doesn't buy into dogma of any kind and works hard and steadily at what he does.

We know quite a lot about this individual and we've only taken a look at several placements. In the practice exercise, carry your interpretation through the rest of the signs in the houses, jotting down a phrase that describes the planet's placement. Go through the same checklist for your own chart.

EXERCISE

Practice Exercise 1: Interpreting the Planets in the Houses

Using the chart in Figure 6-1, complete the following questions:

1. Mercury in Gemini 1st house _____

2. Uranus in Gemini 2nd house _____

3. Venus in Cancer 2nd house _____

4. **IC** Cancer _____

5. Pluto in Leo 4th house _____

6. Saturn in Leo 4th house _____

7. **PF/⊕** Leo 5th house _____

8. Mars Leo 5th house _____

9. Moon in Virgo 5th house _____

10. Neptune in Libra 6th house _____

11. Descendant, 7th house cusp Scorpio _____

12. Jupiter Sagittarius 8th house _____

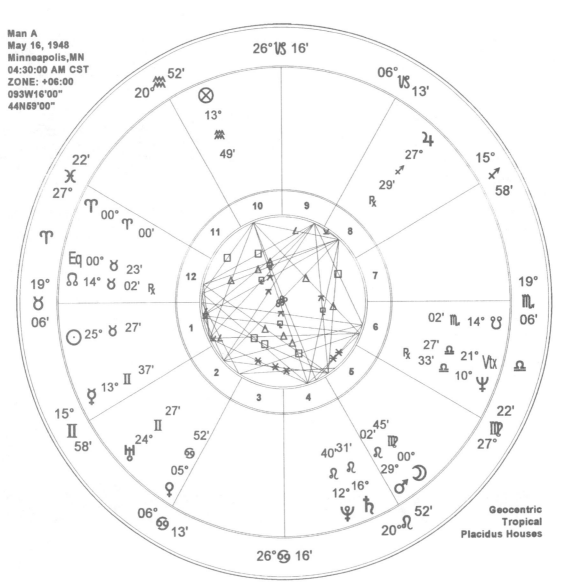

Man A
May 16, 1948
Minneapolis,MN
04:30:00 AM CST
ZONE: +06:00
093W16'00"
44N59'00"

26°♑16'

06°♑13'

20°♒52'

⊗ 13° ♒ 49'

22' ♓ 27°

♈ 00° ♈ 00'

Eq 00° ♉ 23'
☊ 14° ♉ 02' ℞

19° ♉ 06'

☉ 25° ♉ 27'

☿ 13° ♊ 37'

15° ♊ 58'

♅ 24° ♊ 27'

♀ 05° ♋ 52'

06° ♋ 13'

26° ♋ 16'

20° ♌ 52'

♆ 40° 31' ♌ 12° 16'

♄ 02° 45' ♍ 00° 29'

♂ ☽

22' ♍ 27'

02' ♏ 14° ☋

℞ 27° ♎ 33' 21° Vtx
10° ♆

19° ♏ 06'

♎

2♃ 27° ♐ 29' ℞

15° ♐ 58'

10 9 8 11 12 7 1 6 2 5 3 4

Geocentric
Tropical
Placidus Houses

©1994 Matrix Software Big Rapids, MI

Standard wheel

Figure 6-1

E X E R C I S E

Practice Exercise 2: Interpreting Your Own Chart

Use your own chart to complete the checklist.

The Big Guys

Sun sign: _____

Sun's house: _____

Moon: _____

Moon's house: _____

Ascendant: _____

1st house planets: _____

IC: _____

4th house planets: _____

Descendant, 7th house cusp: _____

MC or Midheaven: _____

10th house planets: _____

Natural Rulers

House 1: _____

House 2: _____

House 3: _____

House 4: _____

House 5: _____

House 6: _____

House 7: _____

House 8: _____

House 9: _____

House 10: _____

House 11: _____

House 12: _____

EXERCISE

Planets in Signs and Houses

Sun: _____

Moon: _____

Mercury: _____

Venus: _____

Mars: _____

Jupiter: _____

Saturn: _____

Uranus: _____

Neptune: _____

Pluto: _____

Nodes and Part of Fortune

North Node: _____

South Node: _____

Part of Fortune: _____

Critical Degrees

Which planets are in critical degrees?

_____

_____

Are any houses in critical degrees (29 degrees or more)?

_____

_____

EXERCISE

Jones's Patterns

What pattern fits your chart? _____

What does the pattern mean? _____

Planetary Distribution

Number of planets above the horizon: _____

Number of planets under the horizon: _____

Number of planets to the west: _____

Number of planets to the east: _____

Elements

Air: _____

Earth: _____

Fire: _____

Water: _____

What does this tell you? _____

Quadruplicities

Planets in cardinal signs: _____

Planets in mutable signs: _____

Planets in fixed signs: _____

What does this tell you? _____

Highest Planet (closest to Midheaven): _____

The closer this planet is to your Midheaven, the more impact it has. The planet's sign tells you what kind of influence it exerts over the tenth house. What does yours tell you?

_____

_____

_____

Saturn's Placement

Pay special attention to the sign and house placement of Saturn in your chart. If, for instance, it's in the first house, did you feel limited as a child? Did you suffer from lack of confidence? Were your parents divorced at an early age? Do you struggle against lack of confidence as an adult? Is the Saturn theme prevalent in terms of yourself as an adult?

A friend of mine has a Saturn placement in the first house and yet, to look at her, she seems to be everything this placement says she shouldn't. When I mentioned this apparent dichotomy to her, she told me that she was overweight as a child and suffered a terrible lack of confidence as a result.

She became a competitive swimmer as a way to control her weight and, ever since, an exercise program has been a daily part of her life. Now she's in her mid-forties, trim and fit and filled with confidence.

This is exactly the kind of structure Saturn seeks to impose.

Your notes

How does your chart mesh with what you know about yourself and about astrology?

_____

_____

_____

_____

_____

_____

...the horoscope seems to act as a schematic diagram of one's intentions in life. It only shows what one is going to experience because one intends to experience it. It is a description not of what is going to happen (that is, destiny), but of what one is and what shape one is going to give to one's life.

—ROBERT HAND
Horoscope Symbols

Solar and
Lunar Cycles

CHAPTER
7

Waxing and Waning

Walk outside tonight and glance up at the moon. Is it as bright and round as a quarter against the black skin of the sky? Is it a Cheshire cat's grin? Is it nearly full? Is it in the midst of an eclipse?

In astrology, the phases of the moon are significant. The phase you're born under influences your overall emotional responses and colors them in a particular way. A complete lunation cycle—the time between two New Moons—takes about twenty-nine days. During this time, the Moon waxes—becomes full—and wanes—shrinks.

At the beginning of the cycle, the Moon is conjunct the Sun, that is, in the same sign and degree as the Sun. As it pulls away from the Sun it becomes visible to us as a slivered crescent; it is waxing. The crescent leads into the first quarter, when the Moon looks half full to us. By the time it reaches the Three-quarter or Gibbous Moon, we know the full Moon is right around the corner. From the full moon back to the new Moon, the process reverses itself; the moon shrinks.

People born under a New Moon are the solar equivalent of an Aries: they act quickly, instinctively, often rashly and impulsively. They enjoy being challenged. Their responses are always colorful, bold, and sometimes irritating to others. Their responses are rarely *boring*. They seem to have an innate capacity to empathize with others.

Individuals born under a Crescent Moon are Sagittarian in nature. They look to the future and attempt to break away from tradition. They may try this on any number of levels—mental, physical, emotional, and spiritual—but one way or another they seek to extricate themselves from the habitual way of doing things.

The influence of the First Quarter Moon is an odd mix of Scorpio and Gemini. People born at this time meet crises head-on in a do-or-die fashion. They're survivors; they love the immediacy of the challenge. The struggle seems to infuse them with enormous energy and they tend to attract dynamic people. Sometimes they rush ahead, tripping over their own feet; their timing is off.

New Moon

Waxing Crescent

First Quarter

Half Moon

Waxing Gibbous

Waxing

People born during a Gibbous Moon share certain traits with Virgos. They analyze their every action and motive. They live with a therapist whispering in their ears. They seek to perfect themselves.

Ask any city cop about the influence of the Full Moon. If you don't believe what the cops say, watch your cat on the night when the Moon drifts up from the horizon in its fullest glory.

People born during a Full Moon focus on relationships—their relationships with others and their relationships with themselves. In this way, they're like Libra. But to the cop on the city beat, the Full Moon is aggressive Aries trying to get along with mystical Pisces and serious Capricorn. It's a horror show. These people seek structure. They crave structure. And when they don't find it, they create it, bulldozing through whatever stands in their way.

The Disseminating Moon is a mouthful. But its meaning is straightforward. Think Gemini and information. Think communication. People born under this phase of the Moon tend to cull and disseminate information.

The influence of the Last Quarter Moon is like a planet or the cusp of a house in a critical degree: crisis, eleventh hour, do it now and get it right. It's Scorpio at its most intense; its Pluto doing his usual number. Transformation. Regeneration. Pay special attention to the house and sign placement of this Moon in a birth chart.

The Balsamic Moon is a misnomer. Balsam means that which soothes or cools and the definition doesn't fit this phase of the Moon. People born under this influence may have a sense of destiny, an awareness that "larger" forces can operate through them if they allow it.

To find out what phase of the moon you were born under, check the *Farmer's Almanac* for the date of your birth. The child depicted in the chart in Figure 7-1 was born under a New Moon influence. The Moon in her chart is two degrees from the descendant, in the sixth house. This means that the characteristics of the New Moon manifest for her in the areas of health and work. Her seventh house is also influenced because the Moon is so close to the seventh house cusp.

Full Moon

Waning Gibbous

Half Moon

Last Quarter

Waning Crescent

Waning

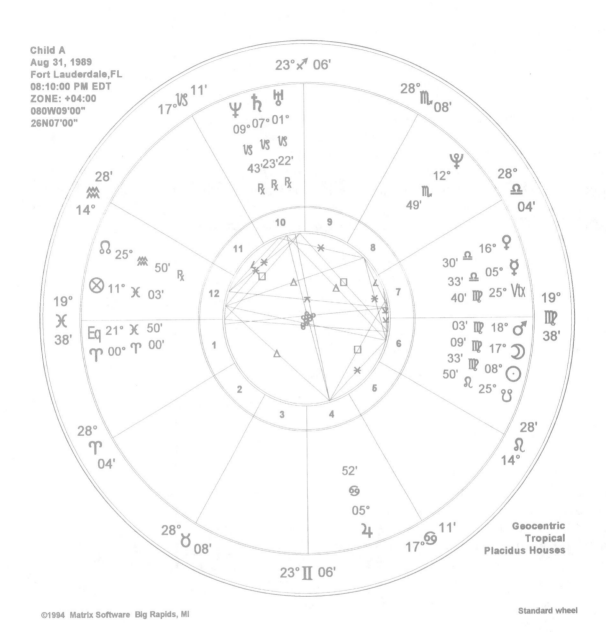

Child A
Aug 31, 1989
Fort Lauderdale,FL
08:10:00 PM EDT
ZONE: +04:00
080W09'00"
26N07'00"

23°♐06'

28°♏08'

17°♑11'

♆♄♅
09°07°01°
♑♑♑
43'23'22'
℞℞℞

28°♏♍
49'

12°

28°
♎
04'

28'
♒
14°

☊25°♒50'℞

⊗11°♓03'

Eq 21°♓50'
♈00°♈00'

19°
♓
38'

30'♎16°♀
33'♎05°☿
40'♍25°Vtx

03'♍18°♂
09'♍17°☽
33'♍08°☉
50'♌25°☊

19°
♍
38'

28°♈04'

28°
♌
14°

28'
♌
14°

52'
♋
05°
♃

28°♉08'

17°♋11'

23°♊06'

Geocentric
Tropical
Placidus Houses

©1994 Matrix Software Big Rapids, MI

Standard wheel

Figure 7-1

Lunar and Solar Eclipses

When I saw my first lunar eclipse, I was at an age where I knew the specifics of what happened. I understood that the Earth was passing between the Sun and the Moon and that the Moon darkened as Earth's shadow moved across the lunar surface. My rational mind felt fine about the whole thing.

But the rest of me didn't feel fine about it at all. As I stood outside watching the Moon darken, a kind of primal awe and fear swept through me. What if the Moon never reappeared? I suddenly realized how ancient people must have felt during lunar eclipses; I understood their acute terror, their superstitions. Even now, a lunar eclipse stirs something ancient in my blood.

Lunar eclipses can be partial or total. In a single year there can be a maximum of three lunar eclipses, which always precede or follow a solar eclipse within two weeks. Solar eclipses, when the Moon passes between the Earth and the Sun, however, aren't necessarily followed or preceded by a lunar eclipse; they can happen alone. A lunar eclipse can last as long as an hour and forty minutes.

The effect of a lunar eclipse in astrology is quite forthright. The Moon represents emotion; the dictionary meaning of eclipse is to obscure. So for people born during an eclipse, the emotions may be stunted somehow and the instincts dulled. The effects of this influence show up in the house the Moon occupies.

For example, if you were born during a lunar eclipse and have a Cancer Moon in the fourth house, then your emotional approach to everything represented by Cancer and the fourth house isn't as strong as it would be otherwise.

The Prenatal Eclipse

A solar or lunar eclipse that occurred closest to the time of your birth is significant. In a solar eclipse, the house that holds the eclipse (according to its sign and degree), is heightened, sensitized. That means that anything ruled by that particular house has a special influence in your life.

In a lunar eclipse, the affected house is also sensitized, but usually on an unconscious level, emotionally and psychically.

In *Spiritual Astrology*, authors Jan Spiller and Karen McCoy explore the spiritual implications of prenatal solar and lunar eclipses. They contend that the prenatal solar eclipse closest to your birthday indicates your universal destiny. It represents ". . . the energy the universe has invested in you and that you have promised to share during your travels on Earth." The prenatal lunar eclipse closest to your birth ". . . is what you need for your own soul growth pattern . . . ."

Astrology's Ancient Origins to Present Day

The origin of astrology is so intimately entwined with the genesis of astronomy that it's nearly impossible to separate the two. Think of them as Siamese twins born some 32,000 years before the birth of Christ, when Cro-Magnon man kept track of celestial happenings and the passage of seasons by carving notches into bones.

It's not known, of course, whether Cro-Magnon man related celestial events to his daily life. What *is* known, however, is that most scholars agree that astrology probably dates back to the Chaldeans of Mesopotamia, who lived 3000 years before Christ was born. These people built tremendous watch towers called ziggurats, from which their priests observed celestial movements. Many of the megaliths across Europe, of which Stonehenge is the best known, are also thought to have been celestial observatories.

Astrology was practiced among the ancient Egyptians, in ancient China around 2000 BC, and in ancient Greece. From Greece, its practice traveled to Rome, where Augustus, the first emperor, became an avid believer.

Modern astrology actually began about 200 A.D. when Claudius Ptolemaeus (Ptolemy), the most important astronomer of the time, wrote his four-volume book on the subject, *Tetrabiblos*. He regarded astrology and astronomy as adjuncts to each other. Much of astrological practice today is based on Ptolemy's material.

During astrology's long journey from Ptolemy to the close of the twentieth century, it has been ridiculed by scientists and condemned by Christians. Saint Augustine, a fourth-century bishop, contended that if you believed in astrology, then you were denying the power of God. This attitude prevailed with such force that the practice of astrology nearly vanished until the twelfth century, when scholars started translating Arabic texts on the subject.

It was during this time that the Arabic parts in astrology began to surface. These included thirty-two points in a chart that were believed to be significant in horoscope interpretation. They ranged from the part of fortune to the parts of life, death, sickness, and marriage.

In 1610, Galileo explained that he'd discovered new stars and four new planets, which ancient astrologers had not accounted for. The planets were later found to be four of Jupiter's moons, but the damage had been done. In 1660, Copernicus came along and said that Earth wasn't the center of the universe, that the Earth, in fact, revolved around the sun. With each successive scientific pronouncement—Newton, Darwin, Gregor Mendel—astrology was driven farther underground and into greater disrepute.

In today's world, astrology has been attacked virulently by fundamentalists and scientists. The former equate the practice of astrology with being in league with Satan. The latter consider astrology to be irrelevant.

One organization in particular, CSICOPS (Committee for the Scientific Investigation of Claims of the Paranormal) was formed specifically to disprove astrology. The article that set the stage for CSICOPS was called "Objections to Astrology" and was published in the organization's magazine *The Humanist*. It was signed by 186 scientists that included eighteen Nobel prize winners, all of them disturbed by the exploitation of a public that believed astrology and astronomy were synonymous.

The Moon Void of Course

You're having a rough day. The contract you expected in the mail hasn't arrived. Your teenaged son blew his math exam and may have to go to summer school. Your cat took a tumble from the roof and you had to rush her to the vet's office. Your significant other decided to take off for Cancun for a long weekend and didn't invite you along. You had an argument with your sister and said things you regret.

This is the kind of stuff that happens when the moon is void of course—making the transition from one sign to another. Little things go wrong that pluck at your emotions. The nature of the events depends on the sign and the house your natal Moon occupy. Even though the Moon doesn't turn retrograde, it's the equivalent of a retrograde.

Void of course (VC) can happen to any planet and is most important in terms of the Moon in horary astrology, but you should be aware of its influence on your birth chart.

A Personal Story

In December 1988, I discovered that I was pregnant. My gynecologist, who no longer delivered babies because he didn't carry malpractice insurance, referred me to his associate. From the second the associate walked into the examining room, I disliked him. He was cold, arrogant, and seemed to be offended by my age (41) and my many questions.

I promptly went home and began calling friends, hoping to find one who liked her OB. A friend of my sister's referred me to her obstetrician, whom I liked on sight. He was everything the first doctor wasn't. He gave me a delivery date of September 4, the Monday of Labor Day weekend, an irony we joked about. The only thing he said about my age was that I should have an amniocentesis.

Sixteen weeks into my pregnancy, I had the amnio and discovered my baby was a girl and that the due date was "about right." On August 30, 1989, around five a.m., I went into labor. Midmorning, I called my OB's office, only to discover that he'd left town for Labor Day weekend. I was, quite frankly, devastated. I'd spent nearly nine months building a relationship with this man and now, when I needed him, he wasn't around. I was referred to the OB who was covering for him, called the office, and was asked to come in.

He said I was only dilated a centimeter and didn't want to admit me to the hospital until I was dilated at least five centimeters. This disturbed me. I was in pain, I wanted the process to get moving. But I went home, figuring I could lay around there as well as a I could in the hospital.

But by mid-afternoon, my lower back pain was so acute I called the physician and told him that I was either in the next stage of labor or my kidneys were shutting down. About thirty minutes later, I was admitted to the hospital.

In my birth chart, Virgo is intercepted in my twelfth house—that is, it's contained completely in my twelfth house. The Sun was in Virgo, passing through my twelfth house, which represents, among other things, "karma" and hospitals. I had a pretty clear idea what the "karma" part meant, but I was very uneasy with the hospital part of the twelfth house.

My natal Neptune (retrograde) lies in the twelfth house at eight degrees and four seconds; I knew that the longer the labor took, the closer that transiting Virgo Sun—my daughter's Sun—would come by degree to my natal Neptune. Even though it wouldn't conjunct my natal Neptune because my Neptune is in Libra, the closeness in degrees bothered me.

The long hours of labor wore into the next day, August 31. My nagging worry about Neptune and my twelfth house and the transiting Sun were literally swallowed up by pain. At one point, a friend who is an astrologer spelled my husband so he could go home and get some sleep. She reminded me that a partial solar eclipse had occurred earlier that morning. I suddenly understood, astrologically speaking, why my labor was so prolonged. Since the eclipse occurred in my twelfth house, it intensified the birth process and weakened my vitality.

When the eclipse occurred, it was at 7 degrees 48 seconds in Virgo; my daughter's Sun is less than a minute later, at 8 degrees and 32 seconds. According to Colorado astrologer Renie Wiley, this is close enough to affect the birth chart. "After an eclipse, solar or lunar, you look for the affects within six months of the eclipse. You can progress the chart six months to see which houses are affected."

Although this book focuses on natal astrology, it's important to see how eclipses impact a chart beyond the moment of the eclipse. In this case, since my daughter's Sun is in her sixth house, the eclipse affected her health. She had more ear infections her first six to twelve months of life than she has had any time since.

Aspects

CHAPTER 8

Y our eight-year-old son, a Libra, comes home upset from his first week at a new school. He says the kids pick on him, make fun of him, and he doesn't want to go back. In a fit of emotion he makes it clear that he hates his new neighborhood and his new school, and that he wants to go back to his old life.

You meet a neighbor several blocks away who is in a similar situation. She just moved here with her husband and eight-year-old daughter, who's also a Libra. She's surprised your son dislikes school. Her daughter loves it and has already made new friends.

What makes these two youngsters so different? Gender? Their ascendants? Their Moons? Their temperament? Look at the aspects in their respective charts for vital clues.

Aspects are merely geometric angles between planets. They result from the division of the 360 degrees in the horoscope circle. In Figure 8-1, the North Node (☊) is separated from Pluto (♇) by about ninety degrees, a square. The square is an aspect.

Symbolically, angles are the network of arteries and veins that link energies between the houses and the planets. They indicate connections between our inner and outer worlds. The square between Pluto and the North Node creates tension, a springboard for growth.

Traditional astrology considers aspects, like planets and houses, in terms of good and bad, difficult or easy. The terminology is actually misleading. Aspects, like planets, are merely representations of certain types of energy and energy itself is neutral. What we do with the energy is either beneficial or not; again, it comes back to free will.

Aspects, Orbs, and Other Tricky Bits

The traditional aspects have been in use at least since the second century A.D. They're called "classical" or Ptolemaic, after the Greek astrologer Ptolemy (Claudius Ptolemaeus). These aspects are the conjunction, sextile, square, trine, and opposition. They are considered the major or hard aspects and are also the most powerful.

Glance at the chart in Figure 8-1 again. The North Node (☊) in 14♉02 in the twelfth house and Pluto (♇) at 12♌40 in the fourth

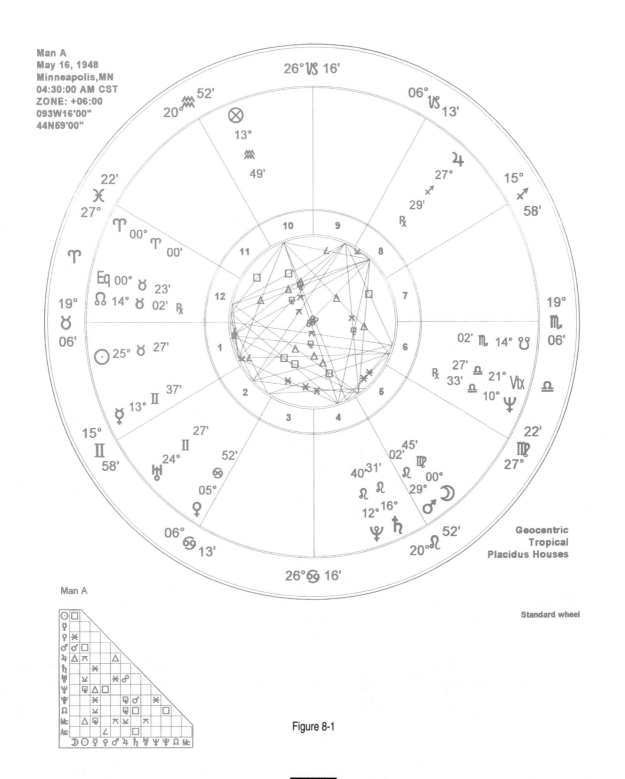

Man A
May 16, 1948
Minneapolis, MN
04:30:00 AM CST
ZONE: +06:00
093W16'00"
44N59'00"

26°♑16'

20°♒52'   ⊗
13°
♒
49'

06°♑13'

22'   ♃
♓   27°
27°   ♐   15°
                                                       29°   ♐
♈ 00°♈00'   ℞   58'

Eq 00°♉23'   10   9
♌ 14°♉02' ℞   11   8

19°   12   7   19°
♉   ♏
06'   ⊙ 25°♉27'   06'
                    1   6   02'♏14°☊

♂ 13°♊37'   2   5   ℞ 27'♎ 21°Vtx
                    3   4   33'♎ 10°♆
15°
♊   45'   22'
58'   24°♊   27'   02'♍   ♍
      ⛢   ♊52'   ♌ 00°   27'
            ♀   29°
                 40°31'   ☾ ♂
                 ♌ ♌
            12°16' ♆ ♄   20°♌52'

06°♋13'

26°♋16'

Geocentric
Tropical
Placidus Houses

Standard wheel

Man A

Figure 8-1

house are about 88 degrees apart; a square is 90 degrees. Does that mean they don't form a square? Not at all. Astrologers work with orbs of influence, which means there are several degrees of latitude allowed when the aspect isn't exact.

The problem with orbs is that astrologers don't generally agree on how many degrees should be allowed for each type of aspect. In *The Inner Sky*, astrologer Steven Forrest writes: "No orb can be defined rigidly. To attempt to nail them down is like trying to determine the exact day on which your kitten became a cat. It doesn't work."

Astrologer Robert Hand considers smaller orbs to generally be more accurate, but is rather philosophical about the whole issue. In *Horoscope Symbols*, he writes: "What the question boils down to is not how far out of orb an aspect can be and still have an effect, but rather how subtle a linkage one will accept as significant." In other words, with practice, you'll arrive at your own sense of how large or small an orb should be.

Hand tends to use relatively small orbs—five degrees for all major aspects. One of his exceptions to this rule is to use orbs wider than five degrees when a chart doesn't have many tight-orb aspects.

Rose Lineman and Jan Popelka, writing in *Compendium of Astrology*, use an eight-degree orb for conjunctions and oppositions and smaller orbs for other aspects. Steven Forrest favors orbs of up to five degrees. Although he feels that orbs of six and seven degrees should still be considered, he believes their impact is considerably less. In Forrest's opinion, orbs of eight or nine degrees hardly count. But if an aspect involves the Sun or the Moon, he recommends allowing a wider orb by one or two degrees.

In the past, astrologers assigned particular orbs for particular planets. A Jupiter aspect, for instance, was allowed an orb of ten degrees, which is very wide, considering that the ten degrees applies on either side of the actual degree. In this system, Mercury, Venus, Mars, Saturn, Uranus, Neptune, and Pluto were permitted an eight-degree orb. The Sun got twelve degrees for an orb and the Moon eight.

The astrology software program used in this book works with orbs between six and eight degrees. If there aren't any tight orbs in the chart, I usually allow orbs of five or six degrees for all aspects, including any to the nodes or Part of Fortune. Hand's orbs tend to

be smaller than the norm because he uses Midpoints in interpreting a chart.

A Midpoint is the halfway mark between any two planets. Hand, like many other astrologers, considers them nearly as important as the aspects themselves. He writes: "I use midpoints because they often give information that would not otherwise be available in the chart. Without them, I have seen important characteristics of a person and events in a life completely overlooked."

Imminent astrologer Grant Lewi, however, stuck to the broad strokes in horoscope interpretation. The Sun, Moon, and major aspects were enough for him.

The bottom line is that you can talk to ten different astrologers and get ten different answers on the issue of orbs. This is one of many gray areas in astrology which your own experience will determine for you.

Science or Art?

For decades, astrology has had an image problem. It was rather like the relative everyone in the family outwardly avoided, but with whom they met in secret.

As a result, many astrologers focused on its science, rather than its art, as though the scientific side of astrology would elevate the profession somehow. This is part of the reason why there are so many rules, parameters, and little details to look for. It also explains why, in the astrology section of most bookstores, you find entire books on a single planet.

Take Mars. Once you get through its influence in mythology, folklore, popular fiction, and the movies, the only thing left to explain is the meat: its influence in a chart. The rest is just filler to justify charging $19.95 for the book.

Unfortunately, this practice tends to make astrology seem about as exciting as the endless contemplation of your navel. Besides, it misses the point. What matters in the interpretation of a birth chart is the entire chart, the hologram. The whole is definitely greater than the sum of the parts. Also, by attempting to interpret increasingly smaller pieces of a chart, your intuitive voice may get lost. The science of astrology is left brain; its art is right brain. The interpretation should be a bridge between the two.

Aspects and Orbs

Major Hard Aspects: incite action and focus motivation. Major Soft Aspects: usually generate harmony and conditions of ease.

ASPECTS	SEPARATING DISTANCE	ORB
Conjunction ☌	0°	6°
Sextile ✶	60°	6°
Square ☐	90°	5–6°
Trine △	120°	6°
Opposition ☍	180°	6°

The Aspect Grid

Look at the chart in Figure 8-1. In the lower left-hand corner you'll see a graph with the planet symbols lined up along the bottom and the left side. The little squares contain the aspect symbols. This graph is called an aspect grid or Aspectarian. Most astrology software programs include them, so you can tell at a glance what aspects a chart contains.

Locate the Sun symbol (☉) along the bottom of the graph. Now locate the **MC** along the left side of the graph. To find out what aspect the Sun and the **MC** make, follow the Sun column up two squares until it's directly opposite the **MC**. You'll see a trine (△).

Aspects Defined

Conjunction, a Major Hard Aspect, O Degrees

This is the simplest aspect to identify, but one of the most complex because of the intensity and power involved. Whenever you see two or more planets piled on top of each other, usually but not always in the same house, their energies fuse and intensify. If the orb is exact or within one degree, the impact is considerable.

Let's say that Saturn and Pluto are conjunct in the tenth house, within six degrees of each other. Saturn seeks structure, Pluto seeks revolution and transformation; the purposes of the two planets are at odds. This conjunction can be disruptive because the structure of a person's career (tenth house) undergoes continual transformation.

It means that just when Saturn had found a structure that works (but which may also limit or restrict the individual in some way), Pluto comes along and blows it apart. Through this process, circumstances seem to force the individual to expand or change his or her professional approach.

Since the conjunction in this example is six degrees, the impact is considerably less than that of a precise conjunction.

In the child's chart in Figure 8-2, Mars (18♍03) and the Moon (17♍09) are conjunct within one degree. Since this conjunction involves the Moon (emotions) and is conjunct—within one and two degrees—of the descendant, it's particularly powerful. It influences both the sixth and seventh houses and energizes and intensifies the emotions.

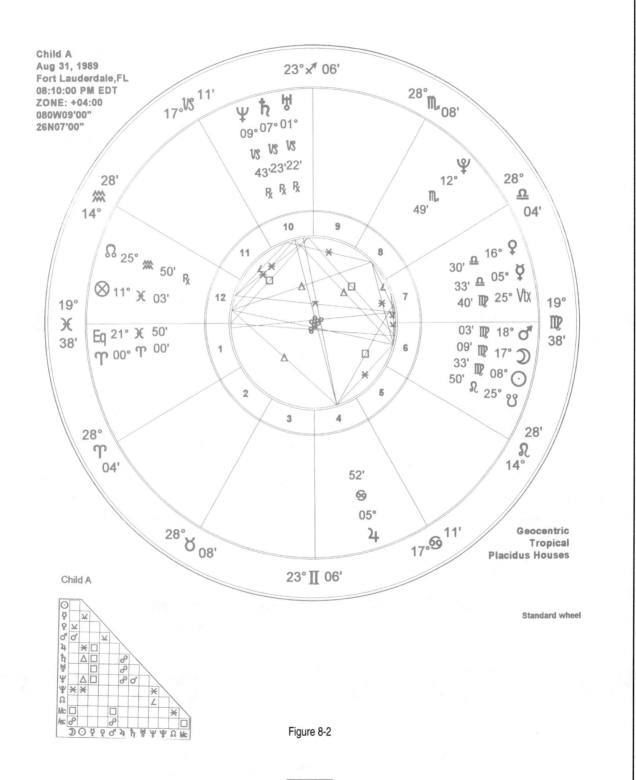

Child A
Aug 31, 1989
Fort Lauderdale, FL
08:10:00 PM EDT
ZONE: +04:00
080W09'00"
26N07'00"

Geocentric
Tropical
Placidus Houses

Child A

Standard wheel

Figure 8-2

Minor Aspects

There are numerous minor aspects to consider in a birth chart. But they exert far less influence and tend to get confusing when you're just starting out. I recommend that you don't use them until you've mastered the major aspects.

Minor Aspects	Separating Distance
Vigintile	18°
Quindecile	24°
Semi-Sextile	30°
Decile	36°
Semi-Square	45°
Septile	51°
Quintile	72°
Tredecile	108°
Sesquiquadrate	135°
Bi-quintile	144°
Quincunx	150°

A Sextile, a Major Soft Aspect, 60 Degrees

It usually represents a free flow of energy between the planets involved. It symbolizes ease and lack of tension, and provides a buffer against instability. But when there's an excess of sextiles in a chart, the individual may be too passive.

In the child's chart in Figure 8-2 there are sextiles to Pluto—the Sun, Moon, and Neptune. These aspects all have to do with the regeneration of energy through inner resources and the inherent potential to use Plutonian energies in a positive way.

Square, a Major Hard Aspect, 90 Degrees

The keyword with this aspect is friction. But the energy that accompanies the friction tends to be dynamic and forceful, galvanizing an individual to action. Squares force you to develop and evolve. They are expressed internally through the lens of our subjectivity.

Look at the chart in Figure 8-1 again. There's a square between the Sun (25♉27) and Mars (29♌02). The orb is about four degrees, certainly tight enough to have an impact. In this case, the ego represented by the Sun is never satisfied with personal achievements, so the Mars energy makes this person restless and sometimes argumentative. But if the Mars aggression is channeled constructively, the square can lead to success.

The important detail to remember about a square is that the tension can't be ignored or repressed. If you don't deal with it, the same pattern of friction repeats over and over again until you tackle it.

As Steven Forrest writes in *The Inner Sky*, ". . . the friction produced in a square exerts relentless developmental pressure on each of the planets."

Trine, a Major Soft Aspect, 120 Degrees

Like a sextile, the connected energies in this aspect work together harmoniously. The inner harmony related to trines often acts as a buffer against turmoil, just as sextiles do. But again, if there are too many trines in a chart, passivity may result.

When trines involve an event, it comes about on its own accord and not because the individual has taken action to make it happen. In the child's chart in Figure 8-2, the Sun in the sixth house

(08♍33) is trine to Saturn (07♑23R) and Neptune (09♑43R) in the tenth house. Both aspects are tight, within one degree of the Sun's eight degrees, so they exert considerable influence in the chart.

The aspect to Saturn allows the child to set realistic goals and to attain them. The aspect to Neptune gives her deep compassion for other people, as well as psychic ability. Taken together, the trine attracts the right opportunities for the advancement of her goals.

Opposition, a Major Hard Aspect, 180 Degrees

This aspect forces change through conflict. Sometimes this aspect represents traits that we project onto others because we haven't fully incorporated them into who we are.

Imagine an opposition as Siamese twins with different agendas. Twin A wants to stay home and read; Twin B wants to party. How can such different needs be resolved? The bottom line is that these differences may never be resolved. Or they may take a lifetime to resolve.

Oppositions often involve polarities: Gemini-Sagittarius, Taurus-Scorpio. This means their elements differ—air to fire, earth to water—but complement each other. They may also share qualities, as in the two earlier examples. Gemini and Sagittarius are both mutable signs; Taurus and Scorpio are both fixed. This gives some basis for compromise. One thing is for sure with oppositions: to resolve their differences ultimately enriches your life.

Special Aspect Patterns

Several aspects can combine to create particular patterns that change or enhance the original aspect. There are five such patterns you should look for when interpreting any birth chart.

Stellium

This is a cluster of stars within the same sign or house or within a certain orb in adjacent houses. Some astrologers contend that a stellium consists of three or more planets in the same house or sign; other astrologers say four or more planets. Astrologer Alan Oken allows a ten-degree orb for planets in adjacent signs.

My rule is to pay special attention to any sign or house that contains three or more planets. In Figure 8-3, note the stellium of five planets in the first house. Four of the planets—Sun (☉), Jupiter (♃), Venus (♀), and Mercury (☿)—are in Aquarius. Even though the Moon (☽) is in Pisces, it's conjunct the Sun at a five degree orb, so it should be considered in the overall impact of the stellium.

In the eighth house, there are three planets: Mars (♂), Neptune (♆), and Saturn (♄). The planets are in Libra and Virgo and aren't conjunct, unless you take into account a wide seven-degree orb between Mars and Neptune. But toss in the South Node (☋) and we find that eight out of the ten planets and two out of the three points fall within two houses. Now these three planets in the eighth house, even though they aren't conjunct by sign or degree, assume a vital importance.

At a glance, the stellium in the first house immediately tells us the individual's perception of the world is heavily colored by subjectivity. She probably has a clear sense of herself—who she is, where she's going. Her interaction with the world is expressed through the affairs of the eighth house. Not surprisingly, this woman was an attorney for many years and is now a family court judge.

T-Square

This pattern is formed when two or more planets are in opposition and square a third planet. The third planet becomes the center of tension and represents the challenge the individual faces. It's often found in the charts of prominent individuals.

In the horoscope in Figure 8-2, Jupiter in the fourth house opposes Saturn, Neptune, and Uranus in the tenth house at orbs of two to four degrees. These planets, in turn, square Mercury in the seventh house. This forms a T-square to Mercury.

Grand Square or Grand Cross

This pattern is an extension of the T-square. It's created by four squares and two oppositions and has at least one planet in each of the quadruplicities: fixed, cardinal, or mutable. This pattern is one of extreme tension and represents difficult challenges. But if the energies are used correctly, it leads to enormous strength.

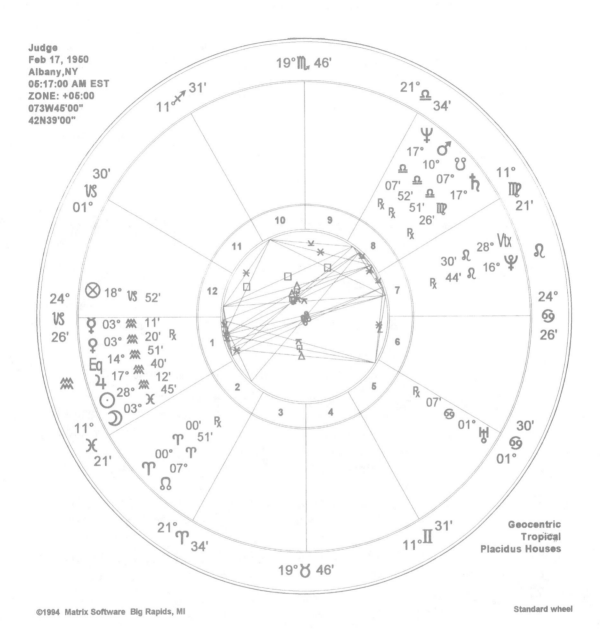

Judge
Feb 17, 1950
Albany, NY
05:17:00 AM EST
ZONE: +05:00
073W45'00"
42N39'00"

19° ♏ 46'

21° ♎ 34'

11° ♐ 31'

♆ 17°
♂ 10°
♎ 07' ♎ 51' ♏
Rx Rx 52' 26'
Rx

☋ 07'
♏ 17'

11° ♍ 21'

♄

30' ♌ 28° Vtx
44' ♌ 16° ♇
Rx

♌

24° ♋ 26'

30' ♋

♅ 07' ♋
01'

01° ♋
30'

19° ♉ 46'

11° ♊ 31'

21° ♈ 34'

11° ♓ 21'

☉ 28° ♓ 03'
☽

♃ 17° ♒ 12' 45'
Eq 14° ♒ 40'
♀ 03° ♒ 20' Rx
☿ 03° ♒ 11'
⊗ 18° ♈ 52'

24° ♈ 26'
♈ 01°
30' ♈
♈

00' ♈
♈ 51' Rx
00° ♈
07° ♈
☊

Geocentric
Tropical
Placidus Houses

©1994 Matrix Software Big Rapids, MI

Standard wheel

Figure 8-3

Grand Trine or Cosmic Cross

Look for three planets that occupy different signs of the same element at 120-degree angles. This auspicious aspect in a chart indicates tremendous creativity expressed through the element of the trine.

A water trine enhances psychic ability, receptivity, and compassion. A fire trine increases initiative and drive. An earth trine brings material abundance. An air trine intensifies intellectual ability and expression. Too many trines in a chart indicate that the individual may lack focus and ambition.

Kite

This pattern is an extension of the Grand Trine. A fourth planet forms an opposition to one corner of the triangle, thus sextiling the other two corners.

Applying versus Separating Aspects

Due to the different rates at which planets move, some aspects in a chart are applying or forming and others are separating or moving away from an exact aspect. Applying aspects have more impact than those which are separating.

When an aspect is forming, it means that conditions, events, circumstances, emotions or states of mind become evident as a person moves through life. Separating aspects pinpoint elements of an individual's experiences that are part of his nature at birth and may include karmic conditions and relationships.

In the chart in Figure 8-3, Mars (♂) is forming an aspect to Neptune (♀) because it is the faster-moving planet. In the chart in Figure 8-2, the Moon in the sixth house is forming an aspect with Mars because the Moon is the faster-moving planet.

In terms of their speed, from faster to slower, the planets line up with the Moon leading the procession, followed by Mercury, Venus, Sun, Mars, Jupiter, Saturn, Uranus, Neptune, and Pluto.

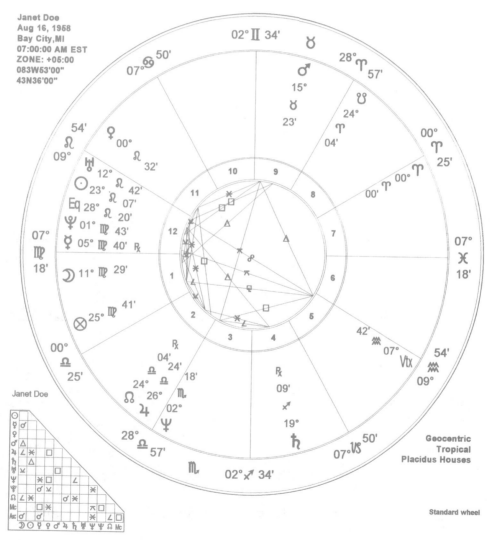

EXERCISE

Practice Exercise 1: Reading Aspects

The chart of Janet Doe in Figure 8-4 belongs to a well-known celebrity, whose name you'll find at the end of this exercise. Based on what you've learned to this point, study the chart, then jot down your immediate impressions. Don't get bogged down in detail; just take note of what is obvious. Use the questions below as guidelines and don't cheat!

Figure 8-4

E X E R C I S E

1. What is the focal area of this person's life?

2. How does this individual transform himself or herself?

3. In what area is this person most lucky?

4. What house has the greatest concentration of planets?

5. What do the conjunctions indicate?

6. Are there any stelliums?

7. In what area does this person find restrictions and need structure?

8. What do the Midheaven and **IC** signs tell you about this individual?

9. How many trines are there?

10. How many squares?

11. Are there any sextiles or oppositions?

Your Notes

_____

_____

_____

_____

_____

_____

_____

_____

The chart of Janet Doe in Figure 8-4 belongs to Madonna

Conjunctions:
0 Degrees

CHAPTER
9

C onjunctions are the easiest aspects to identify in a chart because the planets are clustered together. When interpreting conjunctions, remember that they fuse and intensify planetary energies. Relate the conjunctions to the houses in which they are found.

Conjunctions of the Sun

Conjunctions of the Sun act as a magnifying glass that intensifies and focuses solar energy. The essence of the conjuncting planet doesn't just blend with that of the Sun; it unites with it, enhancing and strengthening the solar energy.

If a planet lies within half a degree to four degrees from the Sun it's said to be *combust*. It means exactly what it sounds like: the planet's energy breaks down and is essentially absorbed by the solar energy. If a planet is less than half a degree from the Sun it's said to be *cazimi*.

There are at least two schools of thought on this type of conjunction. The first contends that the planet's energy is burned up by the Sun; the second theory is that the solar energy becomes a perfect vehicle for the manifestation of that planet's energy. Both theories can apply; it depends on the overall chart.

Sun Conjunct Moon

You get what you want through a perfect blend of will and ego. Your creative urges spring from deep instinctive levels. Your self-motivation can be impulsive, which may create problems for you. You have strong ties with your family, spouse, and home.

Sun Conjunct Mercury

Your will is focused through your intellect. You aren't the type who just sits around talking about ideas; you act on them, you make them happen. Mercury is never more than twenty-eight degrees from the Sun, so a conjunction is the only major aspect that occurs between these two planets.

Sun Conjunct Venus

You're definitely a lover. A lover of life, beauty, music, and art; a lover of love. You gain through speculation, unless the fifth and second houses are poorly aspected. In a man's chart, this conjunction can indicate an effeminate nature; in a woman's chart, she's the social butterfly. You have a terrific way with kids and possess the gift of bringing happiness to others. On the downside, you may have a tendency toward laziness and self-indulgence.

This is the only aspect Venus can make to the Sun because it's never more than forty-eight degrees from the Sun.

Sun Conjunct Mars

You charge through obstacles and meet challenges with all the subtlety of a T-Rex. You're aggressive, self-motivated, and bold. You're also outspoken and blunt, which sometimes proves to be an advantage, but usually gets you into trouble. You need to practice self-control so that your abundant energy can be channeled in more advantageous ways.

Sun Conjunct Jupiter

This aspect works like a magnet that attracts what you need exactly when you need it. Even in adverse times, you're naturally lucky. You're a lavish spender, but also generous and magnanimous to people you care about. Your self-confidence and self-reliance always bring you more than you need. You gain through your father.

Sun Conjunct Saturn

This aspect either provides the structure and discipline you need to achieve prominence or it oppresses you so deeply that you always feel a tinge of melancholy. Responsibility is thrust on you at an early age, which may cause you to withdraw into yourself. You may be the proverbial lone wolf, independent but often lonely. Your best bet is to turn your considerable intellect away from your own concerns and reach for whatever it is you most desire.

Sun Conjunct Uranus

Genius. Through flashes of insight and an instinctive understanding of divine laws, you have the ability to venture into unexplored realms and impact the world with what you find. You're high strung and probably try to get by on very little sleep, which only burns you out. You have the ability to succeed at virtually anything you set your mind to.

Sun Conjunct Neptune

People consider you somewhat mysterious. Your strong mystical bent, used constructively, can trigger enormous creativity. If the conjunction is in Taurus, your mystical side is grounded and you make the unreal real. The downside to this aspect is scattered mental and emotional energy, a fascination with or overindulgence in drugs or alcohol, and a tendency to daydream.

Sun Conjunct Pluto

Your powerful will regenerates and transforms everything it touches. Sexual and mental energy are usually your vehicles for transformation. In self-aware people, this conjunction may manifest as a pure channel for spiritual energy; in less evolved people there may be dictatorial tendencies.

Sun Conjunct North Node

With this aspect, the South Node is in opposition and should be considered in the interpretation. Your opportunities for self-expression are greatly enhanced and can manifest as leadership and power. The luck inherent to this aspect is something you've earned through past lives, in which your efforts were directed toward the world beyond yourself.

A solar or lunar eclipse usually occurred around the time of birth.

Sun Conjunct South Node

Circumstances in your life either deny or limit your chances for self-expression. The house placement tells which area is affected. This aspect usually indicates past lives in which you pursued your goals at the expense of other people.

Sun Conjunct Ascendant

Powerful. Imagine vitality at its peak, where illness is as rare as water in the Mojave Desert. Even when you do get sick, you recuperate quickly and completely. You possess an intuitive understanding of divine law and have a tremendous capacity for positive influence on the masses.

Sun Conjunct Midheaven

You seek fame, acclaim, and the realization of your professional abilities. Politics and public life may figure into the equation. However your fame manifests, it's sure to impact the masses.

Sun Conjunct IC

Family and home are paramount in your life. You have a deep appreciation of your early life, family roots, and values. You may do a lot of entertaining in your home and hobnob with famous people.

Sun Conjunct Part of Fortune

Your luck and success come through personal efforts, in the area represented by the house that the Part of Fortune occupies.

Conjunctions of the Moon

Conjunctions of the Moon heighten the emotions and unconscious mind. This aspect always involves women and relationships with women. It also governs instinctive reactions to events and situations indicated by sign and house placement.

Moon Conjunct Mercury

This aspect links the left and right brain, the conscious and unconscious mind. All your thoughts are heavily influenced by your emotions, but your emotions are your conduit to information stored in your unconscious. Your wit is sharp and often biting. If well-aspected, you have an excellent memory and heightened intuition. If poorly aspected, it creates restlessness and an excessive sensitivity to criticism.

Moon Conjunct Venus

Life is pretty easy for you, especially if you're a woman. You're physically attractive in a way that attracts other people's attention. You're successful in romance and friendships and with women in general. In a man's chart this aspect is all about the kind of sparkling personality that makes other people feel good when they're around you. You may be a little vain and self-indulgent, but so what. You deserve it, right?

How do you see yourself?

Moon Conjunct Mars

Your emotions are intense and you have a quick, expressive intellect. The combination can result in artistic or musical ability; combined with a Venus conjunction, you may develop into a great artist or musician. Generally, this aspect suggests fortunate financial affairs. In a woman's chart, it means a magnetic personality and a drive to achieve prominence or recognition that is commensurate with a man's.

Your aggression and intense emotions sometimes lead to disruptive relationships. Emotions have a strong impact on your health.

Moon Conjunct Jupiter

Your sympathetic and generous nature wins you friends among many different kinds of people. There's a certain nobility about you that people respect and gravitate toward. Women are especially helpful to you. Your health tends to be robust. You enjoy travel, particularly if it's with family members or people who are like kin to you.

Moon Conjunct Saturn

Your nature is rather serious and thoughtful. You're a plodder in whatever you undertake, moving carefully and efficiently through whatever steps are necessary to accomplish your goals. Your bluntness is sometimes hurtful to others, but you don't see it. You tend to be introverted, may be emotionally repressed, and sometimes act as if you're the center of the universe. On the other hand, Saturn here can lend structure to your emotions and channel them for a more constructive use.

Moon Conjunct Uranus

You're a complete original, eccentric, independent, and fearless. You often behave so unpredictably that people don't know what to expect from you. Your imagination and intuition are highly developed and erratic. Your home life is unusual in some way.

Moon Conjunct Neptune

You're psychically attuned to other people, to their emotional environments. In some instances, this trait can be so pronounced, you become a psychic sponge. Depending on other aspects in the chart, there can be mental and emotional confusion or heightened mediumistic tendencies that can provide spiritual insight.

Moon Conjunct Pluto

Clear the decks! Your emotions are so intense that other people may have trouble handling you for long periods of time. And yet others are drawn to your charisma. Your willingness to take emotional risks results in a periodic purging of your most intimate relationships. There may be sudden and drastic breaks with your family.

This aspect is psychically powerful and is often an indication of a true psychic. Edgar Cayce had this aspect in his birth chart. You have an abiding interest in life after death, reincarnation, and other metaphysical topics.

Moon Conjunct North Node

You've got your finger on the public pulse and use this to your advantage. Your relationships with women are generally good and beneficial to you in some way.

Moon Conjunct South Node

Your timing isn't good. You somehow miss being in the right place at the right time. This may lead to depression, bitterness, and, ultimately, isolation. But if you can get past your emotional reactions and learn to discipline your efforts, you succeed against the odds.

This aspect can be related to past lives in which you abused wealth and power.

Moon Conjunct Ascendant

You empathize with others. Your early childhood experiences are carried with you throughout your life and color your emotional responses as an adult. You have strong ties to your home and family.

Moon Conjunct Midheaven

If you're not living your life in the public eye now, you will at some point in your life. This aspect favors actors and politicians. Women are helpful in achieving your goals.

Moon Conjunct IC

The Moon rules here naturally, so this is an excellent aspect. Your strong family ties support you emotionally. Your intuition is well

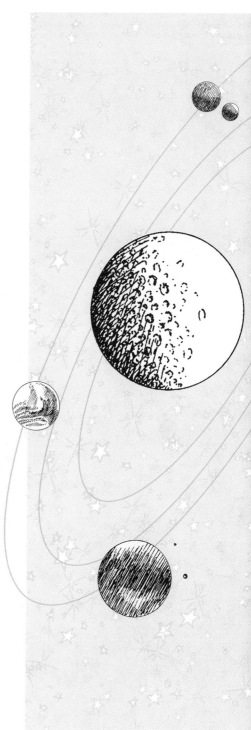

developed, particularly when it pertains to your children, parents, family, and home. You probably live or would like to live near water.

Moon Conjunct Part of Fortune

Listen to your intuition, heed your dreams, and pay attention to what your emotions tell you. Then act.

Conjunctions of Mercury

Mercury conjunctions energize the intellect, mental processes, and communication skills.

Mercury Conjunct Venus

You have literary talent and a deep appreciation of the arts in general. You're a soft spoken individual, with a facility for communicating your ideas. You never have to raise your voice to make your point. Your popularity is well deserved. On the other hand, this aspect can sometimes result in social airs.

Mercury Conjunct Mars

You want facts, not speculations. You speak your mind, act on your decisions, and enjoy debating about controversial issues. You may have a tendency to allow debate to collapse into heated arguments where you passionately defend your position, even if it's wrong. This aspect is a good one for investigative reporters.

Mercury Conjunct Jupiter

Your intellectual integrity may already be legendary in your workplace. You can't be pushed or coerced into doing something that isn't right. It's as if you were born knowing right from wrong; there are no gray areas for you. You have a deep interest in religion, spiritual issues, the law, and education. You enjoy the intellectual expansion that comes with foreign travel. You are recognized as an authority in your field.

Mercury Conjunct Saturn

Your innate understanding of structure and form gives you a powerful capacity for visualization. You can see something in its completed form when it's still an abstract idea. This aspect is good for engineers, architects, designers, and builders of all sorts. It may delay recognition in your profession, but your careful planning and foresight win in the end. You may be prone to excessive worry and occasional bouts of depressions.

Mercury Conjunct Uranus

Genius and originality are your birthright. Your mind moves so quickly that other people have trouble keeping up with you. Your intuitive flashes allow you to perceive things that other people miss. This inspiration provides you with original solutions to issues and problems. You never settle for the traditional route; you have to prove everything to yourself first. If this conjunction is poorly aspected, you may be conceited, stubborn, and hard to get along with.

Mercury Conjunct Neptune

Your imagination is an intimate and complex part of your life. Through it and your psychic receptivity to your immediate environment, you travel into realms that are closed to the rest of us. You may write poetry, music, or mystical fiction, a creatively beneficial outlet for this aspect. You need to express the beauty you see around you. But if you don't channel all this psychic input, then it may hurl you into a surreal world where you could eventually lose touch with reality.

Mercury Conjunct Pluto

You pierce the masks of other people's secrets. Your enormous willpower and resourcefulness allow you to penetrate to the truth of whatever it is you need and want to understand. You would make a terrific detective or scientist who works with classified or secret information. You seem to have an instinctive understanding of energy—what it is, how it works, and how you can use it. The danger with this aspect is misuse of power.

Mercury Conjunct North Node

You're in the flow, aware of what the public seeks. You can become an intellectual leader or spokesperson for a particular idea or set of ideals. You evolve through your communication skills.

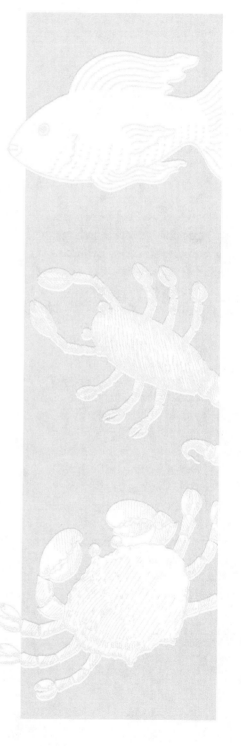

Mercury Conjunct South Node

Your timing is off. You're either behind the times or ahead of them. This can lead to deep frustration, but that's the easy way out. Persevere and your originality wins out.

Mercury Conjunct Ascendant

You're very bright, high strung, and maddeningly logical. You enjoy writing and are quite good at it. Once you apply your intellect to what you want, you succeed far beyond your own expectations.

Mercury Conjunct Midheaven

Career, business, and professional ambition are your areas of interest. Publishing, journalism, writing, any kind of communication profession would suit you.

Mercury Conjunct IC

You come from a well-educated family where intellectual achievements are recognized and honored. You love books and your home is probably filled with them. You may live with a brother or sister.

Mercury Conjunct Part of Fortune

Plan well, use your resources, and look to the house the Part of Fortune occupies to understand where to direct your energies.

Conjunctions of Venus

Any planet that conjuncts Venus influences your social behaviors, artistic expression, and romantic inclinations.

Venus Conjunct Mars

Yes, this may be your mother's nightmare. Your sexuality is a big issue for you. Your passionate nature gets you involved in many different types of relationships, not all of them good. If this conjunction is poorly aspected, promiscuity may be evident. In extreme cases, there may be involvement in violent crime.

But generally, this aspect indicates you're very attractive to the opposite sex. You're lucky in financial matters and you have a good time spending money. This is a good aspect for any kind of artistic endeavor; it adds fire, passion, and drive.

Venus Conjunct Jupiter

This aspect sounds like a carnival fortune teller's line: happiness and financial success. You're cheerful, optimistic, sociable, and kind toward other people. You probably support religious or spiritual causes and help people who are less fortunate than you. Artistic ability usually comes with this conjunction. In self-aware individuals, talent as a peacemaker may be indicated.

On the downside, this aspect can makes things too easy and lead to indolence, self-indulgence, and laziness. If Saturn is prominent in the chart, it adds structure and discipline to the overall horoscope and creates a channel for using this aspect positively.

Venus Conjunct Saturn

Romantic relationships are serious business for you. You don't love easily, but once your heart is won, your loyalty is unwavering. Your adherence to tradition, however, may compel you to stay in a relationship long after it no longer works. Divorce is rare with this aspect. Highly talented artists often have this conjunction; Saturn gives structure to creative expression.

If the conjunction is poorly aspected, you may marry for money alone.

Venus Conjunct Uranus

Your romantic relationships are unconventional and probably begin and end suddenly. The line between friendship and love can be quite blurred for you at times. Individuals with this aspect should never marry in haste. Your artistic tastes and ability are highly original and unconventional. Your earning and spending habits are marked by the same erratic tendencies as your love life.

Venus Conjunct Neptune

Your physical beauty reflects the mystical and spiritual traits inherent to this conjunction. People are drawn to your gentleness, sensitivity, and elusive spiritual nature. You love music and art that are mystically inspired. You tend to idealize your romantic partners.

Innate healing ability and transcendent knowledge are often evident with this aspect. But unless the individual is self-aware, a pattern of events and circumstances may develop that pushes the person toward a realization of this talent.

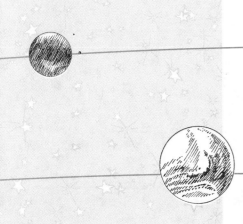

On the negative side, you may be disillusioned in love and romance by getting involved with deceitful people.

Venus Conjunct Pluto

Sexual magnetism and tremendous passion mark this aspect. Quite often, past-life attachments are indicated. In self-aware individuals, this aspect can lead to the height of spiritual love and compassion that transforms everyone who comes in contact with it.

As with all Venus conjunctions, artistic ability is indicated. But here it's likely to be expressed through drama and music or a combination of the two, like operas and musicals. As with all Pluto aspects, the risk is that the power of the conjunction can be used positively or negatively, to transform or destroy.

Venus Conjunct North Node

You have a knack for being in the right place at the right time. Through social contacts you develop in this way you attract what you need for personal fulfillment and success.

Venus Conjunct South Node

You feel emotionally isolated much of the time, but it's due to your own behavior patterns. Try to develop a more acute sense of timing in your social interactions; don't bug people when they're preoccupied with something else.

Venus Conjunct Ascendant

Physically you're a knockout, especially in a woman's chart. You can charm your way into virtually anything you want. If poorly aspected, however, there can be a tendency toward vanity and affected mannerisms.

Venus Conjunct Midheaven

Social ambition is what this aspect is about. It's a wonderful aspect for artists, publicists, and diplomats. You attract money and power through social contacts and relationships.

Venus Conjunct IC

Your life is about creating, maintaining, and enjoying domestic harmony. Your marriage and family are important to you, as are your

parents and early childhood. Your home is artistically decorated.
Chances are good that you enjoy gourmet food.

Venus Conjunct Part of Fortune

It doesn't get much better than this. You benefit financially
through marriage and partnerships in general. You gain through love.

Conjunctions of Mars

With Mars conjunctions, think activity, energy, aggressiveness, decisive
action.

Mars Conjunct Jupiter

You have few equals in terms of energy and enthusiasm, particularly when you're dealing with something you feel passionate about.
Whenever you're told that something can't be done or that you can't
do whatever it is that you want to do, you proceed to prove
everyone wrong. Your sex drive is as strong as your drive to succeed. Poorly aspected, there can be tendency to prove you're right
at any cost.

Mars Conjunct Saturn

Your physical endurance surpasses that of many of your contem-
poraries. You work hard and long to achieve what you desire. This
aspect is sometimes found in the charts of professional military
people. Your sex drive may often be channeled into your work.

Thanks to Saturn's restrictions, you may repress anger and other
hostile emotions until you explode, and your attitudes may be somewhat dictatorial. You may also be prone to broken bones.

Mars Conjunct Uranus

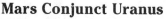

You despise boredom and are constantly looking for thrills
and chills. Your dare-devil attitude can lead into extremism and
rebellion against authority and any restrictions to your personal
freedom. In daily life, your strong personality may come across
as too impersonal to make you the popular kid on the block.
You're at your best when you follow your intellect rather than
your emotions.

Mars Conjunct Neptune

Astrologer Grant Lewi called this the "most powerful magnetic aspect in the horoscope." In self-aware people, it may well be exactly that because it unites physical and spiritual energy. In practical terms, this means that psychic healing ability may be evident and that you have the innate capacity to manifest what you desire.

On the darker side, however, this aspect may result in impractical goals, scattered energy, and peculiar romantic involvements. However it manifests in your life, you're advised to stay clear of drugs and alcohol and to maintain good health through diet and exercise.

Mars Conjunct Pluto

This aspect gives incredible physical strength and a powerful personal magnetism. How it manifests, however, depends on whether Mars or Pluto is the dominant planet in the horoscope. If Mars is more prominent, then the power is expressed through baser emotions: lust, greed, and achievement through the expense of others. With Pluto dominant, you have the capacity to transform and regenerate yourself in such a way that your voice becomes that of a spiritual leader.

If poorly aspected, Pluto does his usual shtick and turns everything around. The power may be expressed through cruelty, savage passions, and violence.

Mars Conjunct North Node

You're in step with the times and in harmony with your personal environment. Your drive to succeed (look to the house placement to find out which area is affected) allows you to overcome any restrictions imposed by the sign and house placement of the South Node.

Mars Conjunct South Node

You're a loner. You may object to the military values of the country in which you live and to many of the current trends. Your sense of timing if off, and because of it you may antagonize others.

Mars Conjunct Ascendant

You've got all the Mars traits: aggression, energy, initiative, and impulsiveness. On the downside, you may also be reckless and accident-prone. When you're ill, you probably run high fevers.

When Mars is in the opposition position (conjunct the descendant or seventh house cusp) there can also be high fevers because of its proximity to the sixth house. In this position it means your relationships and marriages are emotionally charged.

Mars Conjunct Midheaven

You're focused on your career and professional achievements and pour a lot of energy into attaining prominence. You're extremely competitive and don't wither up when confronted with setbacks. Good aspects from Jupiter, Saturn, and the planetary ruler of the sign on the tenth-house cusp help you achieve success.

Mars Conjunct IC

Disharmony in the home and family life is indicated unless Mars is well-aspected or unless you work out of your home.

Mars Conjunct Part of Fortune

You pour a lot of energy into your self-expression and individuality. Your greatest luck comes through being yourself.

Conjunctions of Jupiter

The influence of a Jupiter conjunction is felt mostly in the house where the conjunction falls. It's important to look at the aspects made to the conjunction. If they're good, then the terrific, expansive qualities of Jupiter dominate. If the conjunction is badly aspected, then look for extravagance and excess.

Jupiter Conjunct Saturn

This aspect, which comes around about once every twenty years, means you probably have to overcome major obstacles to expand the affairs of the house where the conjunction falls. The two planets are basically in conflict; Jupiter wants to expand, Saturn wants to restrict.

Jupiter Conjunct Uranus

This one rolls around every fourteen years or so. It means that you experience sudden and unexpected opportunities to expand in whatever area the house placement rules. You may travel suddenly. You gain through friends, occult groups, and through progressive, original ideas and methods.

Jupiter Conjunct Neptune

Look for this aspect every thirteen years. You're imaginative, have a distinct spiritual or mystical bent, and possess some sort of psychic talent that you should develop. There can be extreme idealism with this aspect, which must be channeled constructively to be put to practical use.

Jupiter Conjunct Pluto

This powerful aspect can work constructively or destructively. You either seek to achieve goals that benefit not only you but others as well, or you're a power monger. In self-aware people there's an involvement with yoga, meditation, metaphysical studies, and spiritual healing.

Jupiter Conjunct North Node

A terrific aspect, particularly if you're involved with the public. Your beliefs are in tune with current trends.

Jupiter Conjunct South Node

You feel blocked much of the time—restricted or limited—just as you would with a Jupiter-Saturn conjunction. Be careful while traveling abroad. Look to the house placement of the North Node to understand how to overcome the challenges of this aspect.

Jupiter Conjunct Ascendant

Your optimism inspires others, who may look to you as an authority of some kind. Your main passions revolve around education, legal, or spiritual concerns. You enjoy travel, particularly overseas. There's a tendency with this aspect to gain weight.

Jupiter Conjunct Midheaven

This is a fine aspect for achieving professional recognition and success. It's often found in the horoscopes of politicians, attorneys, educators, anyone in the public eye.

Jupiter Conjunct IC

You're a builder—either literally or figuratively. This aspect is good for real estate brokers and anyone in the home construction, improvement, or decoration business. Your early childhood was probably great, with many people coming and going. You have a solid relationship with your parents. In the latter half of your life you can expect prosperity and material comfort.

Jupiter Conjunct Part of Fortune

You profit and find luck through all affairs associated with Jupiter.

Conjunctions of Saturn

Saturn conjunctions can restrict and limit the flow of energy between planets or can discipline and structure the energies to create a single-minded purpose or goal. Definitely scrutinize the house that holds the conjunction to find out which area of life is affected.

Saturn Conjunct Uranus

This aspect happens every ninety-one years. In evolved individuals, it suggests the ability to funnel original and unconventional ideas into practical use and application. You're able to build on the experiences of past lives to enrich your creativity in this life. This conjunction can be found in the charts of astrologers, mathematicians, and scientists.

On the darker side, however, this conjunction means muddled thinking, a temper that flares periodically, and a lack of distinction between the real and the imagined.

Saturn Conjunct Neptune

You're clairvoyant and possess tremendous spiritual insight. You may practice meditation or yoga or study music or art. Your compassion extends to all living things. This is a lucky aspect, which usu-

ally indicates financial fortune. In strong charts, this conjunction often leads to fame and prominence.

Saturn Conjunct Pluto

With this powerful aspect the intense Plutonian energy is structured through Saturn. This gives concrete expression to your ambitions, for which you're willing to work long, hard, and patiently. If well-aspected, the conjunction can result in truly great accomplishments. This conjunction can be compared to John Fowles's masterpiece *The Magus* because it allows you to work with occult powers and to do so constructively.

Saturn Conjunct North Node

You thrive in a conservative environment and follow protocol to the letter. With the South Node opposing, you must work to overcome your prejudices.

Saturn Conjunct South Node

You're too rigid for your own good. It holds you back professionally and personally. Loosen up or decide what it is you want and go after it!

Saturn Conjunct Ascendant

Generally, this aspect makes for a tough childhood. It may mean that at an early age you were forced to face harsh realities and to assume responsibility. Or it may mean you suffered from self-consciousness or lack of confidence at an early age. Life for you is serious business. You're responsible, a hard worker, and conscientious in all you do.

Saturn Conjunct Midheaven

You're headed for the big time, but only through hard work and perseverance. Recognition is likely to come after the age of forty. If poorly aspected, this aspect may indicate a fall from power.

Saturn Conjunct IC

Saturn here usually indicates an emotionally detached relationship with your parents. You could become a caretaker to one of them later in life. You feel conflicted and torn between your professional ambitions and your duty to your parents and/or family.

Saturn Conjunct Part of Fortune

These two are at odds. Saturn here delays the benefits of the Part of Fortune, but doesn't negate them. You have to work harder for what you want.

Conjunctions of Uranus

Like conjunctions of Saturn, Neptune, and Pluto, conjunctions of Uranus have broad effects on generations of people because they're such slow-moving planets. This aspect of Uranus brings uniqueness and humanitarian ideals to the planets it conjuncts.

Uranus, Neptune, and Pluto are considered higher octave planets. As such, they represent how the soul's individual choices merge and meld with the shaping of nations, cultures, and the family of man.

Uranus Conjunct Neptune

Look for this one every 171 years or so. It occurred most recently in 1994, so children born under this conjunction will make incredible strides in psychic and spiritual development. They may be the ones who take computer technology light years from where it presently is. They will certainly impact life in the twenty-first century.

Uranus Conjunct Pluto

Blame this aspect for revolution. It's responsible for the overthrow of governments and the collapse of outdated belief paradigms. It comes along about every 115 years. It affects people born in 1965-1966. If you're self-aware, this conjunction brings unimagined occult talent; if you're not, it brings all the negative Pluto power to bear.

Uranus Conjunct North Node

You're quick to spot new trends in science and technology, the arts, films, and any endeavor that deals with the masses. Your best bet is not to resist the flow; if you do, the negative tendencies of your South Node mow you down.

Uranus Conjunct South Node

Your life is disrupted by changing mores, beliefs, and trends. Unless you roll with the punches, you're in for a tough ride.

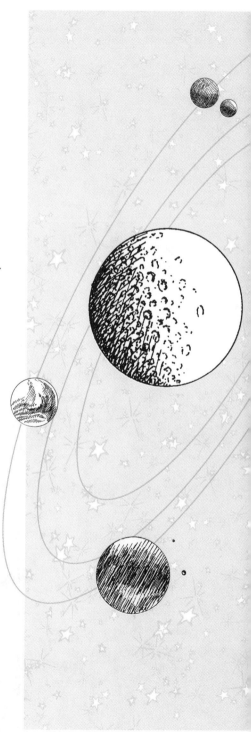

Uranus Conjunct Ascendant

You're exceptionally bright. Your IQ may even shoot into the genius range. You're also incredibly eccentric, with unusual tastes. Your early childhood was marked by independence, freedom, and sudden and unexpected changes. You may have moved a great deal.

You're tolerant of others, unless they try to restrict you in any way. If badly aspected, you may be intellectually arrogant.

Uranus Conjunct Midheaven

This aspect is good for astrologers, scientists, and occultists, and is marked by unusual work conditions. You do best as your own boss. If well-aspected, overnight success may result. But this can be followed just as quickly by obscurity. Play your cards wisely, carefully, and nurture your intuitive voice.

Uranus Conjunct IC

This conjunction is like working for IBM: the initials stand for "I've been moved." Your parents and/or home are peculiar in some way, and there are a lot of odd people coming and going. Electronic gadgets and cutting edge computer technology may be present.

Uranus Conjunct Part of Fortune

Your luck often comes in spurts, at unexpected moments, and probably when you need it most. If you learn to recognize synchronicities and attempt to understand what they're telling you, you'll stay ahead of the surprise game.

Conjunctions of Neptune

Neptune conjunctions, like those of Saturn, Uranus and Pluto, affect generations of people. They enhance psychic and spiritual development, imagination, and intuition. They bolster artistic ability and compassion. These conjunctions are akin to Luke Skywalker's quest in the *Star Wars* trilogy. On the negative side, they bear an unsettling similarity to the darkness of Darth Vader. In other words, Neptune conjunctions can reach mythic proportions.

Neptune Conjunct Pluto

Somewhere in the twenty-fourth century, this conjunction will roll around again. It usually means spiritual revolution and rebirth with

Pluto's capacity for constructive or destructive tendencies. It usually coincides with the rise and fall of cultures and nations.

On a personal basis, this aspect is sometimes found in the charts of people who are conflicted about their sexuality.

Neptune Conjunct North Node

Relax and follow your intuitive urges. If you do, you'll always be in the right place at the right time and make the right contacts. The challenge with the South Node is to resist the pull of the crowd. Don't get swept along with the mass hysteria, whatever it concerns.

Neptune Conjunct South Node

The road with this aspect isn't always easy. You say the wrong things at the wrong times. You have trouble getting your act together. Put one step in front of the other, maintain your individualism, and never forget that you create your reality.

Neptune Conjunct Ascendant

In a woman's chart, she's probably a knockout. In a man's chart, he's a charmer through and through; he'll seduce you and spin your head around. You've got a lot of psychic talent, but unless you develop and work with it, the talent lies latent. Guard against drug and alcohol abuse.

Neptune Conjunct Midheaven

Your career ambitions may be impractical and unrealistic. If you've got a degree in veterinary medicine, for instance, then at the age of fifty it would be impractical to go take up acting. Impractical, but not impossible. And that's the point with this conjunction. Listen to your intuitive voice. Heed its guidance.

Neptune Conjunct IC

On the plus side, your spiritual passions enter your home. You're mystically inclined, with the heart of a pagan who feels a kindred link with the planet and cosmos. On the minus side, your psychic energy can be misdirected and result in hauntings, paranoia, and an obsession with seances and the black arts. You probably live near a body of water, and the larger it is the better.

How do you see yourself?

Neptune Conjunct Part of Fortune

Wake up, take stock, and be aware. Use Neptune's energy to enhance your life.

Conjunctions of Pluto

All aspects of Pluto bear a disturbing similarity to marriage vows: "for better or worse, until death do us part." The conjunction is no different. With the slowly moving planets, conjunctions tend to affect mass movements, nations, cultures, and the planet. With the rapidly moving planets, Pluto intensifies the energy.

One of the popular notions among astrologers is that Pluto aspects don't affect you personally unless Pluto is strong in your chart. This is not a hard and fast rule.

When Pluto moved into Sagittarius at the end of 1995, many people went through monumental changes in their lives. Health crisis. Financial crisis. Marriage crisis. Professional crisis. Divorce, bankruptcy, psychological or physical breakdown. Other people sailed through the transition with hardly a ripple in their lives.

Pluto's impact depends to a large degree on how consciously aware you are. The planetary energy tends to hit us in the area of our lives where we most need to change so that we can grow and evolve as spiritual beings.

Pluto Conjunct North Node

You think you've got it all figured out? Think again. Look deeper. Take nothing for granted. Scrutinize the hidden elements in your life. Seek to understand what isn't obvious, then you're way ahead of the game.

Pluto Conjunct South Node

You work alone to transform your life. You may be a part of mass events that wipe your security slate utterly clean, forcing you to start over again and again. And when you finally figure out the pattern, you break it and evolve.

Pluto Conjunct Ascendant

Each of us possesses the capacity for good and evil. The manifestation of one or the other depends entirely on our free will and that's what this aspect is about. Free will. The development of clarity and the conscious, deliberate use of intuition to manipulate energy and the image you project into the world. Many people simply can't do what it takes to master the challenges of this conjunction. They give up too soon.

Pluto Conjunct Midheaven

You reinvent yourself professionally and publicly, time and again, until you get the message. This powerful aspect leads to fame or notoriety, either/or, black or white, that's how Pluto works.

Pluto Conjunct IC

It's not easy and it's not fun. But one way or another you learn to deal with change and transformation in your home life or you repeat the pattern again.

Pluto Conjunct Part of Fortune

If you embrace drastic change, you prosper from it; if you resist change, you hurt only yourself.

Conjunctions of the Nodes

North Node Conjunct Ascendant

Your cheerful optimism makes you popular with others. You need to cultivate your own beliefs and opinions and act on them rather than acting out of what is socially acceptable.

North Node Conjunct Midheaven

Fortune in general is indicated by this conjunction. You meet the right people at the right time and they help you professionally. The risk with the South Node opposition is that you may take on more than you can handle.

North Node Conjunct IC

Your family life is successful and brings you a lot of happiness and security. You gain and benefit through your parents and the solid foundation of your early childhood.

North Node Conjunct Part of Fortune

You find success and advantage in the house where the conjunction occurs.

South Node Conjunct Ascendant

You're very individualistic and this sometimes works against you because people don't understand you. You often feel inhibited socially.

South Node Conjunct Midheaven

Your timing is never quite right in professional matters. You don't get the recognition you deserve, which can lead to bitterness.

South Node Conjunct IC

Your responsibilities to your family are apt to be considerable. You may become a caretaker for your parents in later years.

South Node Conjunct Part of Fortune

The pot of gold in this aspect is fool's gold, indicating lessons to be learned according to the house in which the conjunction occurs.

Conjunctions of the Part of Fortune

Part of Fortune Conjunct Ascendant

This one reads like a fortune cookie: success, happiness, and many personal advantages.

Part of Fortune Conjunct Midheaven

Terrific professional opportunities come your way. Recognition and success are indicated.

Part of Fortune Conjunct IC

Success and happiness in early childhood and home life are the usual hallmarks of this placement.

Squares: 90 Degrees

CHAPTER 10

S quares tell a great deal about the challenges a soul chose before it was born into physical reality. They spur us to action because the points of friction they create are difficult to ignore. They create a kind of terrible itch in certain areas of our lives that compel us *to do something* to change the status quo.

Look at your own chart. What planets and houses are involved in the squares? What do these particular planets and houses tell you about yourself? How can you work with the *friction* to alleviate it? There can never be a Sun square Mercury or Venus.

Sun Squares

Sun Square Moon

Your conscious mind constantly battles with your emotions over what you want and how you should achieve your goals. To meet the challenge, you must bring old behavioral patterns to light that originated during your childhood.

Sun Square Mars

You're hot-tempered. It may take a lot to make you mad, but when you reach that flash point, you explode. You're also argumentative, passionate, and energetic. If well-aspected by Saturn, this square gives you terrific drive to achieve. Cultivate patience and learn to think before you act.

Sun Square Jupiter

You make a comfortable living, but spend money as fast as it comes in. You overindulge in everything and have great fun doing it. Your excesses may cause you problems of all sorts, particularly through ill health in later years. Your humanity, however, remains constant; you always help people in need. Learn moderation and you'll overcome the challenges of this aspect.

Sun Square Saturn

You struggle to succeed and at every turn, your efforts seem to be thwarted. But your ambition, pierced by inner friction, drives you forward. You seize on every mishap and somehow turn it to your advantage. The challenge is to recognize the difference between pride and principal. Cultivate optimism and flexibility.

Sun Square Uranus

Your powerful creative urge often frustrates you because it comes in spurts. You must develop perseverance and discipline so you can structure the urge and work with it regularly. Your creative urges propel you into erratic love affairs, which usually end because they restrict your freedom in some way.

Sun Square Neptune

Self-delusion may be your undoing. Guard against mystical feelings of grandeur, avoid cults of any type, and seek to cultivate your reasoning, left-brain faculties. Secret love affairs often accompany this aspect.

Sun Square Pluto

This one is difficult. Pluto creates so much inner friction, your need to achieve overwhelms nearly everything else in your life. But if the friction is turned inward, toward transforming the Self, the darker elements in this square are greatly mitigated.

Sun Square Nodes

Remember the T-square? That's what this aspect forms. It can be a dynamic aspect, one that propels you forward. But until you understand it, it makes you feel obstructed by circumstances in your life and in society in general. To overcome this, you need to nurture the part of your life described by the house your Sun occupies.

Sun Square Ascendant

You're conflicted about projecting yourself as you really are. It creates problems in your closest relationships because no one understands you. To overcome this, cultivate the area of your life described by the house the Sun occupies.

Sun Square Midheaven

You don't get along with the authority figures in your life. Your professional ambitions may be stymied somehow by your family obligations. Look to the house the Sun occupies to understand how to overcome this challenge.

Sun Square Part of Fortune

The benefits of your pot of gold are mitigated somewhat. Look to the house the Sun occupies to conquer the obstacle.

Moon Squares

Moon squares often indicate unconscious blocks, prejudices, and habits that impede your emotional expression. This can affect your health, particularly in a woman's chart.

Moon

Moon Square Mercury

You talk too much. But you're so witty and glib that people usually enjoy your company anyway. The problem, though, is that you may talk about things that should be better kept to yourself and at times your nervous chatter gets on people's nerves. Overcome this challenge by being more circumspect in your speech.

Moon Square Venus

You feel inferior to others and this prompts you to indulge in all sorts of detrimental habits. You spend your money foolishly, allow yourself to be taken advantage of, and aren't very sociable. With this square, there can be difficulties or delay in marriage. Think before you act and strive to overcome your feelings of inferiority.

Moon Square Mars

You take things much too personally, which fuels your emotionally volatile nature. Your independence often runs to the extreme, creating problems with your parents when you were younger and with your own family later. Avoid alcohol and drugs. If you need to relieve stress, follow an exercise regimen.

According to astrologer Grant Lewi, this aspect often manifests as precociousness in early childhood.

Moon Square Jupiter

You're a sucker for a sob story. You go overboard with everyone you love and even with people you don't know. But you can afford your extravagances because you believe you'll always have more than you need. The challenge here is to overcome your appetites and excesses.

Moon Square Saturn

Astrologers generally view this aspect unfavorably, saying that it leads to depression, melancholy, and emotional coldness. But Grant Lewi has a different take on it. "This is perhaps the most powerful single aspect you can have in a horoscope. It gives both ambition and the ability to concentrate on it."

He acknowledges that it's accompanied by bouts of moodiness and depression. But he believes the aspect is so powerful that if it's bolstered by any other favorable aspect, "it will produce success along some line or other."

No single aspect makes or breaks a chart. With this square, you need to look at how it fits with the rest of the horoscope. In one person it may very well lead to depression and ill health. But in someone else, it can be the trigger that galvanizes the individual to great professional heights.

Moon Square Uranus

You're emotionally restless, flitting from one thing to another in search of the ultimate. The problem is that you haven't defined what the ultimate is for you. Your talents are exceptional and reflect your individualism. External circumstances sometimes toss you a curve ball: a sudden accident or illness or involvement in some natural disaster. These events are your signposts. Once you understand what they're trying to tell you about yourself and your life, you break the pattern.

Moon Square Neptune

You're a daydreamer who spins wonderful tales and fantasies. But you're so impractical you don't know how to make these flights of fancy concrete. You feel emotionally confused much of the time. You need to ground yourself, set goals, and get moving with your life. Don't surrender your imagination; channel it in constructive ways.

Moon Square Pluto

Chill out. Slow down. Don't be so intense. Life isn't always an either/or proposition. You don't have to burn your bridges with your family and intimates just to make a point. Use your psychic abilities and intense emotions to bring about a more gradual change in your life.

Moon Square Nodes

This T-square configuration urges you to overcome emotional or unconscious habits and prejudices. Until you do, you run into problems with women and can't fulfill your ambitions.

Moon Square Ascendant

You have trouble expressing yourself emotionally. As a result, you experience difficulties in partnerships, marriages, and with your family. If you can become aware of your habitual attitudes and patterns of behavior, you're on your way to breaking them and freeing yourself.

Moon Square Midheaven and IC

Domestic problems seem to get in the way of your professional ambitions. This leads to frustration, which only compounds the original problems. The source of the trouble isn't external. It lies somewhere in your unconscious behavioral patterns; this is what other people respond to.

Moon Square Part of Fortune

Your emotional frustration detracts from the areas of life in which you're lucky. Dig deep within yourself to find the habitual patterns that are holding you back.

Mercury Squares

These squares create friction intellectually through all types of communication. They also create friction with siblings and neighbors. Look to the houses and signs to understand where the intellectual abilities aren't being developed to their fullest. Mercury and Venus can form only a conjunction and sextile because they are never 47° away from each other

Mercury Square Mars

Your sharp tongue often borders on outright rudeness. It tends to alienate the very people whose support you need. Your mind is equally sharp but as undisciplined as your way of speaking. Take time to cull all the facts and plan what you're going to say before you say it. And really, do you have to be so argumentative? What does it get you?

Mercury Square Jupiter

You would make a terrific fiction writer or tribal storyteller. Your mind is rich and imaginative, but your judgment is often flawed because you either misinterpret or don't have all the facts. The best way to overcome the challenges of this aspect is through education, books, and any kind of mental training.

Mercury

Mercury Square Saturn

You're a thinker with a profound mind able to grasp complex issues. But you think and worry too much, dwelling on past injustices and injuries. This may create negative and prejudicial attitudes that ultimately hold you back. You're selfish—not always, not consistently—but the tendency exists. If it's perpetuated, you may become one of those people who believes the end justifies the means.

To overcome the challenge of this square, you need to break with your habitual patterns. Release the past. Forgive people who have injured you. Strive to consider other people's feelings before you act.

Mercury Square Uranus

Mentally, you're way ahead of the pack. Your insight can be brilliant and original. Your entire thought process is radical and independent but sometimes so unfocused that your energy ends up scattered and wasted. At times you can be so obstinate about your opinions that it borders on intellectual conceit. You can be tactless, which alienates others. You're always in a hurry to get things done.

To overcome this challenge, slow down, think before you act and speak, and try to see the issue the way the other guy does. Don't jump to conclusions.

Mercury Square Neptune

This aspect favors fiction writing, particularly of the mystical variety. It also gives insight into the motives and behaviors of other people, which is helpful in creating interesting fictional characters. Writing or art are constructive ways to channel the challenges of this square, which lends itself to confused thinking and unreliability. Psychic talent is usually evident with this aspect, but it needs to be developed and funneled constructively.

Mercury Square Pluto

You're able to assess a given situation swiftly and accurately. No one pulls anything over on you. You're secretive, but when you've got something to say, you don't mince words. Your willpower is well-developed, and you may try to force your ideas on others. You don't take anything anyone says at face value; you need to prove the truth to yourself. To conquer this aspect, you need to be less suspicious of others, to speak your mind more gently, and to turn your willpower to improving yourself.

Mercury Square Nodes

Think before you speak, otherwise, you speak at the wrong time and are misunderstood. Take a deeper interest in the world you inhabit; an awareness of current trends improves your professional ambitions.

Mercury Square Ascendant

It's difficult for you to express yourself verbally or in writing. It's not that you lack talent or don't know what you want to say; it's the way you go about it. You benefit from training in speech and writing, through education, workshops, and anything that provides a structure. This, in turn, improves your relationships with the important people in your life.

Mercury Square Midheaven

Your communications skills are flawed and it creates disharmony at home and on the job. The misunderstandings that result make you miserable. Seek educational training in these areas. Apply your natural talent. The change in your life may shock you!

Mercury Square Part of Fortune

Most of the squares to the Part of Fortune conflict with the benefits of this Arabic part and this one is no different. But if you set goals and plan ahead, you reap the benefits despite the square.

Mercury Squares: An Applied Lesson

In the chart in Figure 10-1, note the Mercury/Uranus square in the Aspectarian. This alone tells you that the person probably has an unusual and original way of communicating. She feels pressured to communicate, to find her particular voice; you might even say she feels compelled to find that voice.

But if you read the descriptions for this square in several different astrology books, you'll find differences of opinion about what it means. This is precisely what's wrong with what some astrologers refer to as "cookbook astrology." These contradictions are also found in astrology software programs that provide interpretations. You can't interpret a chart just in bits and pieces; you have to look at it as an organic whole.

The point with the square in Figure 10-1 is that it's a Mercury square, which means the mind and communication are involved. Up against Uranus, it indicates a humanitarian bent, originality, an unusual perception. Always break aspects down into their simplest components.

The chart belongs to a woman writer, a novelist whose series character is in charge of a charitable organization in New England. The character is an amateur sleuth married to a cop, an idiosyncratic woman with her own ideas about how things work. The character fits the Mercury/Uranus square.

Venus Squares

These squares create friction in relationships generally. They also affect finances and artistic ability.

Venus Square Mars

Your strong passions are attracted to the wrong kinds of people. You often find yourself in stormy romantic relationships that go nowhere. You use other people for sexual gratification or you yourself are used. Your spending habits and extravagances lead you into financial troubles. To overcome the challenge of this square, you must cultivate temperance and balance.

Venus

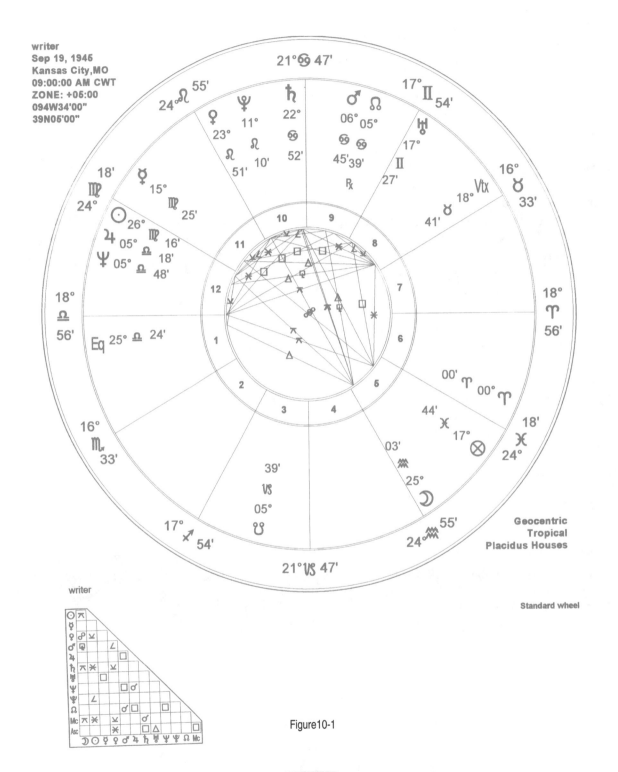

writer
Sep 19, 1945
Kansas City, MO
09:00:00 AM CWT
ZONE: +05:00
094W34'00"
39N05'00"

Geocentric
Tropical
Placidus Houses

writer

Standard wheel

Figure10-1

Venus Square Jupiter

You're seduced by the pleasures in life and tend to be extravagant in everything you do. Your emotions may lack depth, but people are drawn to your expansive, affectionate nature. In a woman's chart, this square spells vanity and expenses in maintaining her physical appearance. In a man's chart, there's a certain egotism about physical appearance. To overcome the challenge of this square, you need to pull back from your life and scrutinize it with detachment.

Venus Square Saturn

Your fear of poverty may be related to past lives in which you had nothing. This fear colors everything you do and feel. Your basic nature alternates between seriousness and a certain melancholy, particularly when you're intimately involved with someone. The bottom line is that you're probably at your best when you're alone. You desperately want a place of your own—a house, land, or a sanctuary. To overcome this challenge, bring your fears to the surface and deal with them.

Venus Square Uranus

Your love life is marked by sudden changes, abrupt beginnings and endings, and unusual, sudden attractions. You're constantly seeking the excitement of new romances, but the second the relationship infringes on your freedom, you split. This square may indicate homosexuality if the fifth house is also aspected or some sort of unusual marriage arrangement.

You need to honestly assess what you're looking for in life and pursue it diligently with forethought.

Venus Square Neptune

Your artistic abilities are excellent and can provide you with a creative outlet for much of the friction caused by this square. Your imagination is fueled by the forbidden and, as a result, you may get involved in secret love affairs. Bisexuality is a possibility with this aspect, if other factors in the horoscope support it. You need to come to terms with what you need emotionally, then try to create it in your life.

Venus Square Pluto

Your sexual passions nearly swallow up the rest of your life. You attract people who may be involved in illegal activities. In extreme cases, this aspect indicates prostitution, criminal tendencies, and sex-related crimes. This square doesn't favor harmonious marriages or partnerships.

Venus Square Nodes

In social situations, your emotional reactions are inappropriate. You're the proverbial fish swimming upstream against social norms.

Venus Square Ascendant

You're rarely satisfied with your close relationships or your marriage partner. You need to develop insight into your own motives and needs and strive to communicate those needs.

Venus Square Midheaven

Somehow, your career and home life always seem to conflict with your social and artistic needs and desires. Get rid of the chip on your shoulder and strive to improve your behavioral patterns.

Venus Square Part of Fortune

Your romantic inclinations and financial habits cause setbacks in your life.

Mars Squares

This aspect creates friction due to rash and impulsive speech and behavior. It also triggers intense and often focused activity and ambition as well as some sexual concerns. By seizing the energy of Mars and using it constructively, this square can be conquered. It's often found in the horoscopes of successful people.

Mars

Mars Square Jupiter

Moderation will take you much farther than the financial and emotional gambles you take now. Slow down and don't count so heavily on your luck, because when it runs out, you'll be up against the consequences of your actions. Your life is screaming for moderation. This aspect, incidentally, is often found in the charts of people who support war.

Mars Square Saturn

Your judgment is flawed. You either overestimate your abilities, your luck, or both. Grant Lewi calls this square ". . . the aspect of fortunes made and lost . . ." Emotionally, your aloofness translates as outright coldness to others. You're seen as austere, even harsh. Lighten up on yourself, control your temper. Go out and have some fun!

Mars Square Uranus

Your temper can be so explosive and fierce that it threatens to overtake your entire personality. Sudden, unpredictable events disrupt your plans. There's a thrill-seeking element to this square that manifests in dangerous sports and in taking physical risks. If other factors in the horoscope support it, this square suggests a sudden, possibly violent death.

Mars Square Neptune

This aspect is often found in the charts of astrologers and psychologists because it allows insight into deep, unconscious patterns. Your active imagination seeks expression through art, music, and dance, all of which are excellent vehicles for the mystical and psychic inclinations of this aspect. On a darker note, escapism can be prevalent. Avoid, alcohol, drugs, and cults. Control and direct your imagination.

Mars Square Pluto

This aspect is a double punch because both planets are associated with Scorpio. Your sex drive and aggression are pronounced. When something pushes one of your buttons, your temper can be explosive. When you refuse to acknowledge the friction of this square, it finds expression in some other area of your life, thus forcing you to change. In self-aware individuals, however, this square provides the impetus for great accomplishments.

Mars Square Nodes

If you control your anger and get rid of your resentment, you're able to use the energy of Mars more constructively.

Mars Square Ascendant

You can't bully your way through life and expect to be viewed as a paragon of gentleness and diplomacy. You need to learn tact and cooperation, otherwise your partnerships and marriage will be filled with discord.

Mars Square Midheaven

You bring your work problems home with you, which creates disputes and arguments with your family. Stop being an agitator. Think before you speak.

Mars Square Part of Fortune

To achieve the benefits of the Part of Fortune, you have to control your impulsiveness.

Jupiter Squares

These squares are similar to those with the Part of Fortune. They tend to hinder the beneficial aspects of the planet. This aspect can also indicate legal problems, obstacles or difficulties in higher education, and all things associated with Jupiter.

Jupiter Square Saturn

Aim higher. Your goals are too limited, narrow, and restrictive. Part of the problem is that you don't imagine yourself achieving more than what you already have. You get discouraged too easily by setbacks and obstacles that you run into. You would certainly benefit from workshops in self-confidence, visualization, and using your imagination to succeed.

Jupiter Square Uranus

Your ideas and imagination are impressive but impractical. You love to gamble in a big way with investments, real estate, or business deals. You would be better off curbing this impulse because you may lose your shirt. You're too impulsive. You may be drawn to eccentric religions or spiritual belief systems. Your restlessness sends you off on countless travels and adventures.

Jupiter Square Neptune

Your wanderlust propels you into foreign countries, the more exotic the better. If you were born into money, you won't hold onto it for long. You usually promise more than you can deliver, but people like you in spite of it because your nature is generous and kind. To overcome the challenge of this square, you need to cultivate pragmatism.

Jupiter Square Pluto

You're dogmatic about religious and spiritual issues. Your beliefs are so inflexible that you have no tolerance for people who don't believe as you do. Power is vital to your well-being and how it manifests depends on the house placement.

Jupiter Square Nodes

Your religious beliefs and educational experiences aren't in step with the prevalent societal trends. Take steps to correct this and your life in general will be much simpler and easier.

Jupiter Square Ascendant

You don't know when to keep quiet. People perceive you as bombastic and perhaps intellectually arrogant. You try to do too much at once and, consequently, end up doing few things well. Learn to focus on one thing at a time and cultivate humility.

Jupiter Square Midheaven and IC

You have a large family and a large home, both of which place heavy financial burdens on you. Strive to be realistic about your abilities.

Jupiter Square Part of Fortune

You rely too heavily on luck. You need to evaluate situations before acting.

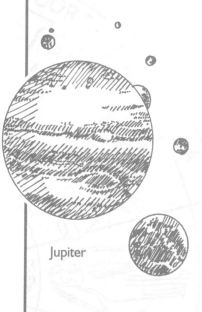

Jupiter

Saturn Squares

Discipline, patience, and perseverance are the cornerstones of Saturn squares. The friction created isn't easy to deal with, but if you learn the lessons, tremendous inner strength and resilience results.

Saturn Square Uranus

Talk about dichotomy! Saturn imposes discipline, while Uranus screams for freedom. You're constantly confronted with situations that require thought and consideration, but the Uranian influence chafes at the restraints. Your inventiveness and originality need limitations and discipline to flourish. Find a balance. Control your hot temper.

Saturn Square Neptune

Lack of ambition characterizes this square. It's not that you can't do what you set your mind to; it's simply that you don't feel like exerting yourself. You may try to escape the uglier realities of life through drugs or alcohol or some other form of escapism. Your best bet in overcoming this square is to find something that stirs your passions, plan how you'll attain it and go after it.

Saturn Square Pluto

Your hunger for power may be acute. You may be involved in schemes, plots, intrigues, the stuff of spy novels. Maybe you need the drama; maybe you simply don't know anything else. To conquer the friction of this square, you need to be brutally honest with yourself and attempt to change.

Saturn Square Nodes

Your selfishness and outdated prejudices hold back your development. Honest self-appraisal helps overcome the challenges of this square.

Saturn Square Ascendant

Others probably see you as somewhat aloof, maybe even cold. This is certainly true when strangers intrude on your time or people make unreasonable demands. It may also be why you choose to

Saturn

limit your close friendships. Learn to structure your time so that your life is more balanced.

Saturn Square Midheaven

Your home life as a child was rigid and overly disciplined. As an adult, your responsibilities to your own family and parents may block or delay your career ambitions.

Saturn Square Part of Fortune

Use the discipline of Saturn to gain the benefits of your pot of gold.

Uranus Squares

These squares affect generations of people. Their impact on personal horoscopes depends on whether Uranus is prevalent in the chart.

Uranus Square Neptune

Rebellion. Pioneers. Idealism. Psychic talent. The generation born under this aspect (1950s) face tremendous social upheaval and emotional confusion. Their lives are disrupted by wars, catastrophes, and major disasters. On a personal level, peculiar circumstances seem to plague your life. Your thinking can be muddled and confused.

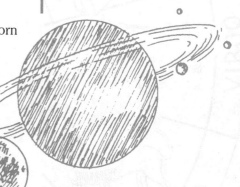

Uranus

Uranus Square Pluto

Worldwide, this suggests upheaval, fanaticism, and massive destruction. Hardly the kind of stuff you want to write home about. The generations born under this aspect (1930s) are now in their sixties and seventies and have faced drastic social upheaval in their lives.

On a personal level, there can be a need to reform the established order of things in general. Even if you're born into money, you never feel completely secure.

Uranus Square Nodes

You don't think much of traditions. You're a nonconformist at heart, but at times you take it so far you alienate the very people who could be helpful.

Uranus Square Ascendant

You want to be unpredictable and rebellious, but don't expect other people to love you for it. Your personal life would improve immeasurably if you learned to be cooperative with the people you care about. If you don't change, your intimate relationships aren't going to improve at all.

Uranus Square Midheaven and IC

You bounce around a lot by changing jobs and moving frequently. You're forever seeking the elusive job or relationship that won't restrict your personal freedom. Step back, detach, and honestly evaluate what you're doing and why.

Uranus Square Part of Fortune

The general instability of your life impedes whatever benefits you might derive from the pot of gold.

Neptune Squares

Like the squares of the other slower-moving planets, Neptune squares affect generations and impact a personal chart primarily if Neptune figures prominently in the chart.

Neptune Square Pluto

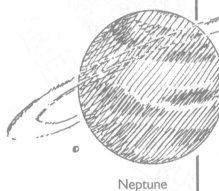

This is an ugly aspect, there's no other way to put it. It last occurred in the early 1800s and will roll around again in the twenty-first century. It indicates the breakdown of society and the general collapse of the old paradigms and belief systems. Spiritual bankruptcy and moral depravity are in the cards with this one.

Neptune Square Nodes

Cultivate practicality and bring your mystical daydreams back to Earth. Stop drifting and dig in your heels. Set goals. Forget drugs.

Neptune Square Ascendant

You don't mean to be deceptive or unreliable, but you often are. As a result, you attract people who reflect these traits in yourself. Be

Neptune

more aware of what you say, what you promise, and how you act. Cultivate honesty in yourself. Don't take criticism so personally.

Neptune Square Midheaven and IC

Your professional and home life are in a state of confusion and turmoil. You need to set goals, which is often the case with these squares. Find your passions and try to channel them constructively.

Neptune Square Part of Fortune

Once you stop deceiving others and yourself, the benefits of your pot of gold begin to manifest in your life.

Pluto Squares

Expect the usual heavy Pluto stuff with this aspect. With any Pluto aspect, go back to the root meaning of the planet: transformation, the death and collapse of the old, regeneration, and tough lessons.

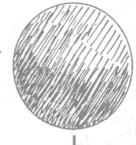

Pluto

Pluto Square Nodes

By adjusting to the nuances of pop culture and current trends, you overcome the darker aspects of this square. Everything doesn't have to be a life or death issue.

Pluto Square Ascendant

You're too aggressive and demanding in your personal relationships. You would do better trying persuasion instead of coercion and force to get what you want. This lesson may hit home when you're not very high on the corporate pecking order and have to take orders from others.

Pluto Square Midheaven and IC

You rebel against all authority figures: parents, cops, employers, the government. You want to reinvent everything, to transform existing institutions, and you probably want to do it out of some lust for power. You need to reassess your life and where you're going.

Pluto Square Part of Fortune

Intense and baffling experiences inhibit the benefits of this aspect.

Node Squares

These squares act as distractions in whatever areas they affect. They often offer penetrating insights into issues we would rather avoid.

Nodes Square Ascendant

You're continually distracted from whatever it is you're trying to accomplish. You tend to blame other people for the things that go wrong in your life. As soon as you understand that you create your own reality, that you, in fact, are completely responsible for yourself, you'll be on the way toward vanquishing your distractions.

Nodes Square Midheaven and IC

Your frustrations manifest in the two areas of your life that you value most: your career and your home. Once you realize how intimately the two are connected, you overcome the obstacles that have stood in your way.

Nodes Square Part of Fortune

You feel that you aren't deserving of success or achievement. As a result, you continually undermine your own efforts. Get to the source of your feelings and work with the emotion to turn things around.

Sextiles and Trines:
60 and 120 Degrees

CHAPTER
11

Sextiles, 60 degree angles, symbolize ease and provide a buffer against instability. Trines, angles of 120 degrees, are similar but relate more to inner harmony, a state of equilibrium. Sextiles and trines to the Nodes, Ascendant, Midheaven, **IC**, and Part of Fortune are so similar that they are lumped together.

Sun Sextiles and Trines

Sextiles to the Sun pinpoint areas in which your abilities can be expressed positively; they often represent opportunities. Trines to the Sun enhance self-expression and generally indicate harmony in the affairs associated with the planets that form the sextile and trines. Venus and Mercury are too close to the Sun for a sextile or trine.

Sun Sextile Moon

You get along well with people, try to help them when you can, and they in turn do the same for you. You're successful working with the public and have the communication skills to do it well.

Sun Trine Moon

You attempt to create the kind of harmony in your home that you knew in your childhood. The smooth flow between your unconscious and conscious desires helps you to achieve what you want and need.

If there's any drawback to these aspects at all, it's that at times your life is so pleasant and generally happy that you're apathetic about doing something when you should be asserting yourself.

Sun Sextile Mars

You're one of those individuals with seemingly endless reserves of energy. Your creative ideas usually find expression in some form because you're forceful about achieving them. But you don't step on anyone else's toes to accomplish what you want. You respect other people for their talents and abilities.

Sun Trine Mars

Your physical vitality keeps you moving long after your competitors have gone to bed for the night. Your magnetic personality and decisiveness draw people to you. You may follow some sort of exercise program that maintains your stamina and bolsters your already

considerable physical strength. Good leadership abilities come with this trine.

Sun Sextile Jupiter

If we still lived in villages, you would be the village philosopher. You have high ideals, lofty aspirations, and numerous opportunities throughout your life to manifest what you want. Your self-expression usually comes through the house that Jupiter occupies.

Sun Trine Jupiter

Luck, optimism, and financial prosperity usually accompany this trine. You have tremendous creative potential, but you may not do much with it unless squares and oppositions in your chart create sufficient friction and tension. Your personal integrity is probably without equal.

Astrologer Grant Lewi made a classic remark about this aspect: "No poet with this aspect ever starved in a garret or anywhere else, for that matter."

Sun Sextile Saturn

Your ambition won't ever exclude everything else in your life. You plan carefully, take your work seriously, and structure your life so that everything is judiciously balanced. You achieve through your own efforts.

Sun Trine Saturn

You have great self-confidence, abundant talent, and luck. Your parents or the people responsible for you are probably older than the norm and have shielded you from hardships.

Opportunities often come to you. Combined with a Moon/Mars conjunction, those opportunities either drop into your lap out of nowhere or you create them.

Sun Sextile Uranus

Your personality is charismatic, magnetic, and often forceful. You're deeply intuitive, which gives you valuable insight into other people. You don't pay much attention to traditions. You prefer going your own way, even if others consider it eccentric. This aspect is often found in the charts of people who are interested in or practice astrology.

Astrology Software

If you're in the market for an astrology software program, by all means search the web before you buy. Many software companies offer free demos that you can download or view online. I found this particular feature extremely helpful when I was looking for an astrology software program. I knew what I needed, what I could afford, and found it.

Astrology software covers a vast spectrum in prices. At Office Max, you can pick up Xpert's astrology software program for about $10. It's very basic, with a limited atlas, and planet degrees and configurations that are sometimes inaccurate. But it's a good place to start because it's simple to use.

For years, I used an Astro program that did the job well and efficiently, but wasn't user friendly. I supplemented this with Xpert's software, which did transits quickly, but couldn't do progressions.

At the other end of the spectrum lies Solar Fire, touted by some astrologers and damned by others. It costs about $200. WinStar's program runs about the same price, but their demo on the web is far superior to Solar Fire's. I finally settled on WinStar Plus, which features database capabilities, an astrology tutor, and midpoint dials, and computes virtually any kind of chart you can think of.

Sun Trine Uranus

You're an original and progressive thinker whom other people want to know simply because you're so different. Things happen around you. Your perception of reality is broad and profound; you never lose sight of the larger picture.

Sun Sextile Neptune

Much of your inspiration rises from the deeper levels of your psyche and flows easily into your conscious thought. It's as if a conduit exists between the psychic activity in your unconscious and the you who participates daily in the world. Your creativity is considerable and, with a little effort on your part, can flourish and bloom.

Sun Trine Neptune

If you aren't self-employed now, then you should take steps in that direction because you don't work well under others. You need to create and express yourself in some artistic way, and you have profound creative talent that needs to be expressed. If your talent doesn't find expression, the block can create health problems.

You're very psychic. In fact, much of your knowledge comes to you that way even if you don't realize it. Your sleeping mind is psychically active, with vivid, colorful dreams that bubble up from the deeper levels of your psyche. Work with your dreams and strive to understand them. They will provide you with an endless supply of answers and guidance.

Sun Sextile Pluto

Deep inside yourself, answers and information are available to you. Once you're able to access this deeper level, you'll understand why your will is so powerful and how you can use it to achieve what you want. You need to communicate what you know and sense. You evolve through creative expression.

Sun Trine Pluto

You're the person who brings their friends and loved ones back from the brink of chaos. You help restore order to their lives. You would excel at any profession where you can do this for other people. Your willpower is considerable; you're a natural leader. Always listen to your intuition before you act.

Sun Sextile or Trine Nodes

You do just fine in most circumstances, with most people. Conditions overall in your life are helpful to you. With very little effort, you overcome whatever holds you back.

Sun Sextile or Trine Ascendant

You don't have much of a problem expressing who you are. You're honest in your dealings with other people and won't tolerate dishonesty from others. You're a natural optimist, which helps bring about the many opportunities you experience in life. Your personal relationships are harmonious and because you cooperate with others, you're able to achieve what you want.

Sun Sextile or Trine Midheaven and IC

Your family is helpful to your professional ambitions and success. They support your efforts completely, which is part of why both your professional and domestic lives are so harmonious.

Sun Sextile or Trine Part of Fortune

These aspects feel so good that you're sure you've been blessed in the areas indicated by the houses. This aspect denotes the kind of luck where you win the lottery or suddenly inherit a large sum of money. Big luck.

Moon Sextiles and Trines

These aspects deal with the expression of emotion, early childhood, and your relationship with your mother and women in general. They also focus on the harmony within your own home, certain qualities of memory, and intuition.

Moon Sextile Mercury

Your memory is excellent. Your emotions and mind operate together in complete harmony. Your communication skills are highly developed and you can use them in virtually any profession you choose. This aspect favors writers or others who use communications skills professionally and may also work out of their homes.

Children and Astrology

Robert Hand wrote what is probably the best book on kids and the stars. *Planets in Youth: Patterns in Early Development* takes the reader through every possible facet of natal astrology but applies it to children. In his introduction, he explains his concept of what children are and how he tailored his book to coincide with his perceptions.

"I prefer to assume, and my observations as a parent and teacher confirm this, that children have exactly the same needs and drives as adults, that they are neither virtuous nor bestial and that they do whatever will allow them to survive, both as biological entities and as personalities."

The ultimate test with any astrology book is to test the content with someone you know well. I read the portions of Hand's book that apply to my daughter's chart and found his observations to be quite

Moon Trine Mercury

You have a lot of common sense and you're a quick learner. Your ability to recall past events is nothing short of remarkable, but you're not hung up in the past. You communicate well, especially with members of your family. A good aspect for people who work with their hands.

Moon Sextile Venus

You have abundant charm and a generous nature. Your artistic interests and inclinations are considerable. In a man's chart, you get along well with women and benefit from your partnerships with them. In a woman's chart, you are sociable and affectionate. This also indicates fertility and a fulfilling, happy marriage.

Moon Trine Venus

Financial prosperity and an element of luck go along with this aspect. It indicates that you're charming, refined, and physically attractive. You enjoy being surrounded by beautiful things. You're an optimist, love children, and want or have kids of your own. Harmonious marriage is indicated.

Moon Sextile Mars

You're an emotionally charged individual whose energy and vitality propel you through whatever needs to be done. You may flare up occasionally, particularly if you're provoked, but you generally don't hold grudges. You're known as a person who gets things done.

Moon Trine Mars

You have good control over your emotions and passions and a quick, sharp intellect. Your emotions and your mind are rarely at odds. Your self-confidence and ease with the public is impressive and helps you to achieve your ambitions.

Moon Sextile Jupiter

Your hunches and gut feelings about situations and people are usually right on target. You have an enormous storehouse of experiential knowledge and an excellent memory. You nearly always recognize the good in people.

Moon Trine Jupiter

Unconscious urges may prompt you toward foreign travel where you seek evidence of ancient cultures or your own past-life connections with these places. Your spiritual leanings, whether orthodox or unconventional, form an intricate part of your inner life. Your optimistic outlook and charitable nature inspire others. This aspect usually indicates a happy, satisfying family life and financial prosperity.

Moon Sextile Saturn

Your patience and insight allow you to understand the inner workings of personal relationships. You're able to structure your unconscious feelings so that you work with them consciously, with awareness. You have excellent business sense.

Moon Trine Saturn

You're reserved and cautious by nature, but you don't allow this to hold you back. You change when it's time to change. You're loyal to your family and friends, who return that loyalty to you. You're able to structure your creative impulses into practical projects.

Moon Sextile Uranus

You embrace change and use it to your advantage. Your heightened intuition allows you to quickly grasp the intricate workings of any situation. You're different from other people, but that has never bothered you.

Moon Trine Uranus

Your magnetic personality attracts stimulating people. You're a progressive thinker whose timing is usually so acute that you know instinctively when to seize an opportunity. The past holds meaning for you only in terms of what you learned from it; the future interests you far more. This aspect often indicates involvement with metaphysical groups. An interest in astrology often shows up with this trine.

Moon Sextile Neptune

Your imagination and psychic ability are equally strong and fuel each other. This is as an excellent aspect for fiction writers, physicians, and psychic healers. Your memory may be photographic.

Moon Trine Neptune

Expression in dance, art, music, theater, acting, and writing are particularly strong with this aspect. Your nature is fundamentally spiritual, imaginative, gentle, and compassionate.

Moon Sextile Pluto

Somehow, you're always able to regenerate yourself through your emotions. You draw on the deepest levels of your psyche to find the answers or create the opportunities you need whenever you need them. Great purpose and a sense of destiny is suggested by this aspect.

Moon Trine Pluto

Your emotional intensity is well-controlled and channeled constructively. You use it, consciously or unconsciously, to evolve spiritually. Others recognize this quality in you and gravitate toward you because of it.

Moon Sextile or Trine Nodes

Although you remember the injuries and losses of the past, they don't hold you back. You learned from them and embrace your future. Your instincts rarely fail. Listen to them. Cultivate your inner voice.

Moon Sextile or Trine Ascendant

You're sensitive to criticism, but as you get older you begin to understand why. You have a good sense of the public pulse and take advantage of it. Your sensitivity to other people's feelings helps you to get along with just about anyone. Your family and intimate partnerships are vital to your emotional and physical well-being.

Moon Sextile or Trine Midheaven and IC

Pay attention to the synchronicities in your life; they'll guide you to the path of your greatest fulfillment. Women and family members are helpful to your career and support your professional ambitions. The trine usually strengthens the chances for professional success.

Moon Sextile or Trine Part of Fortune

Look to the house the Part of Fortune occupies; this is where you'll find the advantages that ultimately put you on the most fulfilling path.

Mercury Sextiles and Trines

These aspects provide opportunities for intellectual development and communication skills. They're excellent for professional writers, speakers, and people in public relationships or politics.

Mercury Sextile or Trine Venus

You're gifted in both speech and writing and have refined artistic tastes. Your lively intellect and gentle nature instill your life and relationships with harmony. Mercury and Venus are never far enough away from each other to form a trine.

Mercury Sextile or Trine Mars

Mental energy is what you're about. You're decisive, intellectually quick and agile, and able to finish what you start. This aspect favors professional writers, sports strategists, and professional speakers or politicians. It's good for anyone involved in organizations. These people usually follow some sort of exercise program.

Mercury Sextile or Trine Jupiter

You respect the truth, whatever its guise. You're an unbiased individual with broad intellectual interests. You teach and are involved in publishing, writing, universities, or religious/spiritual organizations. You enjoy foreign travel because it expands your understanding of the world.

Mercury Sextile or Trine Saturn

You're intuitive but practical. Your mind is finely balanced, your thought processes are structured, and you have the discipline to create whatever it is you want out of life. So go for it.

Mercury Sextile or Trine Uranus

When supported by other factors in the horoscope, these aspects suggest brilliance. Your thinking is well beyond the scope of the present, but you're somehow able to bring your advanced ideas into the here and now and communicate them. Your intuition and psychic awareness are well-developed.

Mercury Sextile or Trine Neptune

Your psychic ability fuses seamlessly with your imagination, allowing you access to deep spiritual realms. Poets sometimes have this aspect as do novelists, shamans, mystics, composers, and spiritual speakers.

Mercury Sextile or Trine Pluto

Words are your gift. You transform and regenerate yourself through your intellectual resources and communication skills. Your profound insight into the nature of reality allows you to achieve luminous success.

Mercury Sextile or Trine Nodes

You've earned an intellectual ease through efforts in other lives. In this life, you use these gifts to overcome any limitations or restrictions that hold you back.

Mercury Sextile or Trine Ascendant

Your wit and self-confidence attract friends and allies who reflect your intellectual interests. You work hard at expressing your creativity and it's likely that if you persevere, you'll make money at it.

Mercury Sextile or Trine Midheaven and IC

The people you care about most understand exactly who you are and what you're trying to do. They support your professional ambitions and urge you to follow and achieve your dreams.

Mercury Sextile or Trine Part of Fortune

You achieve your greatest success by evolving intellectually.

Venus Sextiles and Trines

These aspects signify opportunities related to social, financial, artistic, and romantic issues. They also indicate expression in these areas, as well as artistic ability.

Venus Sextile or Trine Mars

You get along well with the opposite sex. Your romantic relationships, partnerships, and marriage are harmonious and satisfying. A lot of energy goes into your creative pursuits. You may even work with your spouse or significant other in some sort of artistic endeavor or business. You enjoy spending the considerable money that you earn and should probably start stashing some of it away.

Venus Sextile or Trine Jupiter

This lucky financial aspect allows you to attract wealth and ample opportunities for making money. It indicates a happy marriage and prosperous partnerships. You're admired by your peers and recognized in some way for your artistic ability.

Venus Sextile or Trine Saturn

Your social activities revolve around your business concerns. You're thrifty about money, but not penurious, and have numerous business opportunities to increase your financial base. You don't jump into partnerships, especially romantic relationships. But when you do commit, the marriage is stable though not particularly demonstrative.

Venus Sextile or Trine Uranus

You're very attractive to the opposite sex and get involved in a variety of stimulating romantic affairs. You fall in love quickly, but your affairs end just as abruptly, usually without rancor on either side. You benefit through involvement in groups, which may include e-mail news groups and chat groups you meet online. Unusual people are attracted to you.

Venus Sextile or Trine Neptune

Compassion, artistic ability, and spiritual depth are indicated by this aspect. There are usually karmic ties with the marriage partner, who is apt to be gentle and refined. This aspect quite often suggests great wealth, especially when combined with any Venus or Mars conjunctions with Jupiter. There's usually considerable clairvoyant ability with this aspect.

Venus Sextile or Trine Pluto

Love is your vehicle for transformation and regeneration. You listen to your intuition and follow its guidance, particularly in romantic issues. When you do commit to someone, it's because you share a mutual depth of love and have many interests in common. There may be a sense of destiny connected to the relationship that you're both aware of. You have a strong sex drive. This aspect is often indicative of an inheritance and of material benefits in general.

Venus Sextile or Trine Nodes

Through your social contacts, you find the opportunities you need when you need them. You're very conscious of proper social conduct and protocol, which allows you to overcome the restriction of the South Node.

Venus Sextile or Trine Ascendant

Your physical beauty is enhanced by innate grace and charm, particularly in a woman's horoscope. You probably have considerable musical or artistic talent.

Venus Sextile or Trine Midheaven and IC

Through your physical graces and social contacts, you further your ambitions. Your home reflects your personal harmony and beauty and is often a social meeting place. For artists, this aspect usually indicates professional recognition.

Venus Sextile or Trine Part of Fortune

Financial prosperity and recognition of some sort comes through your social contacts.

Mars Sextiles and Trines

These aspects help channel energy and drive in positive, constructive directions. The planets and houses that are aspected indicate the areas of development that are enhanced.

Mars Sextile or Trine Jupiter

Physical strength, a muscular body, and integrity are indicated by this aspect. Your optimism and enthusiasm infuse your ambitions and provide you with many opportunities to realize your dreams. These aspects usually suggest eminent achievements in your chosen field.

Mars Sextile or Trine Saturn

You're a relentless worker, particularly in the pursuit of your ambitions and dreams. You're able to structure your considerable energy and creative ability to achieve what you want. Your sex drive is strong, but more controlled than in most Mars aspects.

Mars Sextile or Trine Uranus

Your courage and daring extend to all areas of your life. In your profession, you don't hesitate to try progressive but unproved methods to attain results. Once you reach one goal, you embark on a new journey with new goals. In your personal life, you're sexually uninhibited and enjoy exotic travel off the beaten path. You're an explorer in the truest sense of the word.

Mars Sextile or Trine Neptune

You're compassionate, gentle, and blessed with spiritual insight. You would benefit from meditation, yoga, body building, and a vegetarian lifestyle. Your acute psychic ability alerts you to opportunities in finances and the arts that enhance your professional ambitions.

Arabian Parts

Hundreds of Arabian parts exist in astrology and Hindu astrology still uses many of them. But in the West, the only part used with any frequency is the Part of Fortune, which most astrology software programs calculate. Astrologers Marion D. March and Joan McEvers, authors of an excellent series on all facets of astrology, also routinely use the Part of Spirit.

Nearly all the Arabian parts begin with the Ascendant, then add and subtract the degrees and signs of various planets. When computing the parts, it's essential that you have an accurate birth time to know the exact degree and sign on the Ascendant. The actual math for computing the parts is found in the text of the book. Some of the Arabian parts are listed below:

Part	Formula
Children (female)	Ascendant + Venus - Moon
Children (male)	Ascendant + Jupiter - Moon
Death	Ascendant + 8th cusp - Moon
Friends	Ascendant + Moon - Uranus
Honor	Ascendant + 19°Aries - Sun
Marriage	Ascendant + Moon - Venus
Karma	Ascendant + Saturn - Sun
Sudden Advancement	Ascendant + Part of Fortune - Saturn

You're secretive but honest. Your creativity may manifest in dance, music, or competitive sports.

Mars Sextile or Trine Pluto

With this aspect, the house ruled by Pluto in the chart will pinpoint the area of life most likely to be affected. Your enormously powerful will can bring about immense and drastic change in your life through which you evolve spiritually. Your insight into deeper mysteries about the nature of reality is keen and profound. In self-aware individuals, these aspects indicate metaphysical knowledge that can be used to benefit humanity.

Mars Sextile or Trine Nodes

Your timing is usually on target. This aspect favors politicians and celebrities whose lives are public. Your dynamic personality attracts people who aid you in your endeavors.

Mars Sextile or Trine Ascendant

Your directness impresses other people and makes them willing to help you. You're physically strong and your health is good.

Mars Sextile or Trine Midheaven and IC

You have numerous opportunities to advance yourself professionally. Your career is solid and dynamic and so is your home life. You may work out of your home.

Mars Sextile or Trine Part of Fortune

Your drive to achieve pays off because your ambitions are directed, funneled, singular. Your physical stamina and health are generally strengthened with this aspect.

Jupiter Sextiles and Trines

These aspects usually imply success and prosperity in the areas governed by Jupiter: law, publishing, religion and spiritual issues, higher education, foreign travel and cultures. The trines in particular are like built-in safeguards that mitigate other less fortunate aspects to Jupiter.

Jupiter Sextile or Trine Saturn

Business success is practically assured with this aspect, unless there are indications to the contrary in other parts of the horoscope. You may work in the legal or jurisprudence field, higher education, the clergy, or as a public servant. Your integrity is beyond reproach.

Jupiter Sextile or Trine Uranus

This is a karmic aspect in that you receive unexpected windfalls of money or opportunities. Your insight is highly developed and alerts you when to seize opportunities that other people miss. You travel suddenly and unexpectedly and have unusual experiences abroad that expand your perceptions of what is possible. Your political beliefs are liberal. Your spiritual inclinations lean toward the unconventional and metaphysical rather than the orthodox.

Jupiter Sextile or Trine Neptune

This mystical aspect often finds expression in spiritual studies and attainment. The knowledge, thanks to the expansive nature of Jupiter, is usually shared with others. Spiritual practices like yoga and meditation may be practiced. In evolved people, this aspect can indicate a benevolence that approaches that of a Mother Theresa.

Jupiter Sextile or Trine Pluto

This is one instance in which the darker attributes of Pluto are absent. Your tremendous willpower and finely honed psychic ability indicate that you can emerge as a spiritual leader. You act on your spiritual convictions and are capable of instigating the kind of change that affects the masses.

Jupiter Sextile or Trine Nodes

Whatever direction your life takes is in keeping with your soul's intent. You have opportunities to correct the excesses or mistakes in past lives.

Jupiter Sextile or Trine Ascendant

This aspect attracts the things we all seek: good luck and health, happy marriages, and prosperous partnerships. Your optimism and humor attract loyal friends and supporters.

Jupiter Sextile or Trine Midheaven and IC

This is another one of those incredible aspects that indicates outstanding professional success and a happy domestic life. If you've got this aspect, consider yourself blessed.

Jupiter Sextile or Trine Part of Fortune

This aspect suggests material benefits, spiritual insight, and happiness according to the sign and house placements.

Saturn Sextiles and Trines

Considering the nature of Saturn, these aspects to the planet are always welcome. They enable you to structure your energy around realistic and practical goals, bring stability to your life, and often result in tangible rewards.

Saturn Sextile or Trine Uranus

Due to the conflicting natures of these two planets, most aspects between them create a tug-of-war. This struggle for power is absent with a sextile and trine between the two. The unique inventiveness and brilliance of Uranus is molded into practical expression by Saturn. You respect conventional thought, but aren't limited by it. You have an acute sense of timing.

Saturn Sextile or Trine Neptune

The dreamy, imaginative, and spiritual qualities of Neptune are brought down to earth with this aspect. You're able to put your spiritual knowledge into action through humanitarian efforts on a small or large scale. You believe that every species, regardless of its order on the food chain, lives to realize its greatest potential. Even the lowly black snake in the garden deserves its freedom.

Saturn Sextile or Trine Pluto

This aspect funnels all that Plutonian power into a positive, practical structure that you can use. Your ambitions are tempered by your innate understanding that if you're to effect change, you must do it through careful planning. It's quite likely that if you adhere to your path you'll achieve a prominent and powerful position in your life.

Saturn Sextile or Trine Nodes

Your efforts are rarely without purpose. You find the proper vehicle for their most practical expression and, in doing so, overcome the limitations of your South Node.

Saturn Sextile or Trine Ascendant

You possess a quiet dignity that impresses everyone you meet. Even though you may marry later in life, you marry for keeps. Any partnership you enter is usually beneficial to your long-range goals.

Saturn Sextile or Trine Midheaven and IC

You attain professional success through hard work and careful planning. Your home life is satisfying and orderly.

Saturn Sextile or Trine Part of Fortune

This aspect brings status, success, and good fortune.

Uranus Sextiles and Trines

If you're quick, if you're prepared, you'll be able to take advantage of the opportunities that show up with this aspect. Think of them as psychic gifts, things you've earned from previous lives: a glimmering insight, a flash of inspiration, a psychic hunch that pays off big time.

Uranus Sextile or Trine Neptune

On a broad basis, this signals a fertile time for psychic and spiritual development and humanitarian reforms. If Uranus or Neptune is prominent in your horoscope, then you're most likely spiritually aware. You're probably very psychic, with a mystical imagination that connects you to the deeper levels of reality.

Uranus Sextile or Trine Pluto

Under this aspect, great forces are harnessed and channeled. Atomic and nuclear power, space exploration, quantum physics, and the nature of reality all come into play. On a personal level, you abhor social injustices and strive to live your own life free of bias with your sight on the future.

Uranus Sextile or Trine Nodes

By following your path of humanitarian ideals and progressive thought, you evolve spiritually.

Uranus Sextile or Trine Ascendant

You're one of those magnetic personalities who attracts the unusual and often bizarre. You set trends and are constantly moving forward. You probably marry quite suddenly and your significant other is as unusual as you are.

Uranus Sextile or Trine Midheaven and IC

You're not interested in following the crowd; instead, people tend to follow you because of your uniqueness. Unusual career opportunities come your way when you least expect it. Sudden fame is possible. Your home is unusual in some way, with many interesting people coming and going.

Uranus Sextile or Trine Part of Fortune

Look for unexpected bonuses and rewards with these aspects. The house placement tells you what areas are affected.

Neptune Sextiles and Trines

These aspects emphasize imagination, artistic and psychic ability, and spiritual evolution. They affect large numbers of people.

Neptune Sextile or Trine Pluto

The personal importance of this aspect depends on the prominence of Neptune or Pluto in the horoscope. If either planet is placed in the first house, rules the Ascendant, or displaces the ruler of the chart, the Sun, or the Moon, then this aspect suggests intense spiritual evolvement is possible.

Neptune Sextile or Trine Nodes

Your uncanny instincts about social trends put you in the professional driver's seat. Your spiritual pursuits allow you to evolve and overcome the limitations of the South Node.

Neptune Sextile or Trine Ascendant

This aspect favors marriages and partnerships. You're compassionate, sympathetic, and idealistic and have a mysterious allure that attracts the good will of others. You feel psychically attuned and connected to your mate.

Neptune Sextile or Trine Midheaven and IC

If you're in the arts, then your chance for public recognition is greatly enhanced by this aspect. You use your intuition in your profession to alert you to opportunities. You share a psychic connection with your parents, a significant other, and close family members.

Neptune Sextile or Trine Part of Fortune

Intuition is a major factor in your life. Use it to recognize opportunities and to manifest what you desire.

Pluto Sextiles and Trines

If Pluto is strong or prominent in your chart, then these aspects are definitely good ones to have on your side.

Pluto Sextile or Trine Nodes

Your intuition is well-developed and one of your most valuable assets. It allows you to see past appearances to the truth of a situation. You have the ability to influence how others think on a broad scale. These aspects favor people in public life.

Pluto Sextile or Trine Ascendant

Your willpower and natural clairvoyance give you a decided edge on your competition. You're able to raise the level of consciousness in other people and are presented with many opportunities to increase your personal power.

Pluto Sextile or Trine Midheaven and IC

Your career opportunities are many and varied. Through them you gain professional prominence and power. Your intuition helps you to direct your career and overcome any obstacles or challenges in your domestic life.

Pluto Sextile or Trine Part of Fortune

The capacity to transform and regenerate your life comes through lucky opportunities and events. Look to the sign and house placement to see which areas of your life are affected.

Node Sextiles and Trines

Nodes Sextile or Trine Ascendant

This is a "feel good" aspect. Most of the time you feel comfortable with yourself and who you are. This buoyancy and self-confidence is communicated to others who invariably prove helpful in your career. These aspects usually indicate good marriages and partnerships.

Nodes Sextile or Trine Midheaven and IC

Your career and home life seem to be blessed with luck. You realize your ambitions professionally, and your domestic life is involved somehow in your career.

Nodes Sextile or Trine Part of Fortune

Your luck often seems to come out of nowhere. By cultivating an awareness of synchronicities you can capitalize on this aspect and learn to create your own luck.

Oppositions:
180 Degrees

CHAPTER
12

O ppositions are as easy to spot in a chart as conjunctions. They lie directly across from each other. Planets in the first house, for example, are in opposition to planets in the seventh house.

Oppositions involve conflict and tension. They often represent attributes in ourselves that we project onto others.

Sun Oppositions

Remember the example about the Siamese twins? Twin A wants to go left, Twin B wants to go right. This is the nature of an opposition: tension. To overcome it, you have to reach a compromise. With Sun oppositions, the tensions manifest as a conflict of wills. No opposition exists between the Sun and Mercury and the Sun and Venus.

Sun Opposed Moon

Your emotions are pitted against your ego. The stress may show up in your relationships with the opposite sex. It can also affect your health, especially in a woman's horoscope. You're forced to be more objective about everything in your life, which often results in a sense that you constantly have to choose between your affairs and those of someone else. By understanding the nature of the aspect, you go a long way toward overcoming it.

Sun Opposed Mars

When people disagree or oppose you, take a dozen deep breaths and remove yourself temporarily from the situation. This will ultimately get more results than your usual hostile reactions. Even though you're physically strong, never use physical force to make your point; that only creates an enemy.

Sun Opposed Jupiter

Your inflated ego and grandiose schemes don't exactly endear you to others. You waste energy on excess of all kinds and if you don't cut back, it may affect your health. Stop pontificating. Learn to listen sincerely to other people and you can mitigate the influence of this opposition.

Sun Opposed Saturn

Your conflicts usually boil down to one salient factor: you chafe and rebel against the restrictions imposed on you by others. These restrictions may come from heavy responsibilities you take on for a spouse, parent, or child. With this aspect, children are sometimes denied or born later in life. But marriage generally happens later in life, too. This aspect asks that you attempt to take all things in stride. Cultivate optimism. Lighten up.

Sun Opposed Uranus

The bottom line is that you can't have everything your way all the time. Your insistence on this, coupled with your extreme independence, makes it difficult for you to get along with other people. The very freedom you insist upon for yourself is not something that you allow others. Until you clear up this dichotomy in your life, expect a lot of tension with friends and partners.

Sun Opposed Neptune

Meeting the challenge of this aspect requires strength of will and great focus. You're easily deceived by other people and confused about your religious beliefs and personal relationships. Strive for objectivity.

Sun Opposed Pluto

Your overbearing nature can get on other people's nerves. You need to step back, relax, and stop trying to control everything around you. Many people are intimidated by the forcefulness of your personality, so you tend to lose support you might have otherwise.

Sun Opposed North Node, Conjunct South Node

Vanquish your selfishness and learn to cooperate with other people. Look to the houses occupied by the Sun and the Nodes to determine which areas will be affected.

Sun Opposed Ascendant

This aspect means the Sun is also conjunct the seventh house cusp. This focuses energy on marriages and partnerships. These intimate relationships fulfill and ground you. They provide you with the self-confidence to assume leaderships roles.

How do you see yourself?

Sun Opposed Midheaven, Conjunct IC

Your professional achievements are largely dependent on the harmony of your domestic life. You need a fulfilling home life to be able to function well in the larger world.

Sun Opposed Part of Fortune

Selfishness has to be overcome to receive the benefits of the pot of gold.

Moon Oppositions

This aspect creates tension and conflict in your emotional nature. You may have trouble relating to others on an emotional level and are always very aware that you need to develop in the areas influenced by the Moon opposition.

Moon Opposed Mercury

You talk too much about nothing, have trouble finding the proper words to express your opinions and thoughts, and have difficulty relating to people emotionally. As a result, you're indecisive and frustrated. Trines or sextiles to this opposition mitigate its influence.

Moon Opposed Venus

You sometimes erect emotional walls to protect yourself. This creates distance between you and the people you love and causes unnecessary problems. Your emotional vulnerability may go back to your early childhood when you felt unloved by your mother or a mother-like figure. Your extravagance may be directly related to these early childhood feelings.

Moon Opposed Mars

You're wired too tightly emotionally. It causes impulsiveness and makes you impatient, restless, and volatile. There can be some dislike for women in general. In men, this can manifest as abusiveness toward women; in women, it may show up as an overbearing attitude toward other women.

Moon Opposed Jupiter

You're much too emotional. You waste a lot of energy fretting about small things in your life. You're very rigid about your religious and spiritual beliefs, defend them emotionally, and tend to get involved in emotional causes. Step back from your emotions.

Moon Opposed Saturn

You withdraw emotionally to protect yourself from other people. You're the proverbial turtle, ducking back into its shell. This creates problems with other people, who may see you as somewhat inhibited, even cold. Your professional ambitions drive you.

Moon Opposed Uranus

The emotional connection with this aspect often originates in an insecure childhood. You shy away from restrictive emotional ties of any sort, move frequently, and your relationships with others begin and end abruptly. Parents with this aspect tend to be irresponsible, easily bored with child-raising duties.

Moon Opposed Neptune

You're a psychic sponge who absorbs the emotions and attitudes of the people around you. Be careful not to hang out with people who exude negativity. You tend to project your own emotional confusion onto other people, which makes it difficult in your relationships to determine who is feeling what. Any health problems you have may stem from early childhood experiences and belief patterns.

Moon Opposed Pluto

Your conflicts with others revolve around joint finances and inheritances. You also keep trying to re-invent the people around you. Step back and honestly assess where you are in your life and where you would like to be five years from now. Then implement a plan to get there. A creative outlet for your emotional energy would be most beneficial.

Moon Opposed North Node, Conjunct South Node

The belief patterns that hold you back originated in early childhood and are deeply immersed in your psychological makeup. If you work at breaking these patterns, do so gently. The house the North Node occupies will tell you which area of your life you should work with in overcoming these patterns.

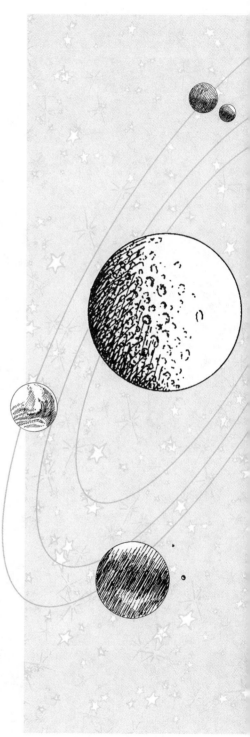

Moon Opposed Ascendant

You have excellent insight into the needs and wants of the public, which benefits you professionally. Most of the time, you prefer the company of others to solitude; you find emotional fulfillment through others. Be aware that this tendency can make you dependent on your spouse or on other people you're close to.

Moon Opposed Midheaven, Conjunct IC

You're close to your parents and have warm memories of your early childhood. The death of a parent can result in deep shock. You don't like being away from your family and may not take jobs that cause you to be away from them for any length of time. This can inhibit your career opportunities if you allow it to.

Moon Opposed Part of Fortune

You feel dissatisfied with the luck and success that your pot of luck brings you. To break this pattern, you need to cultivate gratitude.

Mercury Oppositions

This aspect creates enormous tension in the way you communicate with others. Heated disagreements often occur, usually because of intellectual beliefs you hold.

Mercury Opposed Mars

You're intolerant of other people's ideas that differ from your own. You argue about everything and when you can't win an argument, you resort to shouting. Your behavior is often crude and hostile. Get rid of the chip on your shoulder and detach from your emotions when dealing with others. Cultivate the ability to listen to others.

Mercury Opposed Jupiter

You tend to blame others for your own failures. But the truth is that your grand plans and ideas lack practicality and you usually promise more than you can deliver. Religious and spiritual ideas interest you and you may pursue them educationally at the expense of everything else in your life. You need to cultivate responsibility for yourself and your own actions.

Mercury Opposed Saturn

You're bright, you have ability, and you're an excellent listener. But you fret too much over inconsequential details and throw up blocks that impede the natural flow of ideas. Your overall nature leans toward pessimism and a somber demeanor. Lighten up on yourself and be more patient.

Mercury Opposed Uranus

In all probability, you're a genius. But your ideas may be too eccentric to be practical. Your complete indifference to other people's opinions often results in bad timing: You say or do things that offend others. Good aspects to either planet mitigate the influence of the opposition. You should nurture an interest in other people and try to bring your genius down to earth.

Mercury Opposed Neptune

You're very sensitive to other people's feelings, but sometimes you can't seem to help what you do or say to them. You hate being pinned down in any way, so instead of saying yes or no to something you simply refuse to commit. This produces chaos in the areas of your life influenced by the opposition. You would be better off being direct with others and attempting to focus your considerable psychic ability on improving yourself.

Mercury Opposed Pluto

This aspect can be found among spies, diplomats, researchers, and people involved in secretive pursuits. It may also be found among novelists who write books that deal with these themes. You're very good at organizing secretive or sensitive information and have an innate understanding of opposing views. Your language, however, sometimes borders on the obscene, which offends others.

Mercury Opposed North Node, Conjunct South Node

You need to keep learning and not settle with the knowledge that you already have. There's a tendency toward mental laziness with this aspect. Through education and intellectual growth, you overcome the limitations of the South Node.

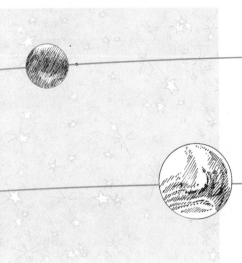

Mercury Opposed Ascendant

Since this aspect means that Mercury is conjunct the seventh house cusp, it indicates a solid mental rapport with significant others. You may attract a younger lover or spouse.

Mercury Opposed Midheaven, Conjunct IC

Your home is loaded with books and other intellectual materials. You have a good rapport with your family, even though they may not always support your professional ambitions.

Mercury Opposed Part of Fortune

This aspect restricts the benefits of the Part of Fortune. You simply don't have any intellectual interest in the area indicated by house placement of your pot of gold.

Venus Oppositions

This aspect usually suggests conflict in the romantic and social arena. This can mean challenges in marriages and partnerships, artistic expression, and financial matters.

Venus Opposed Mars

This isn't a particularly happy aspect for marriage. For a woman with Venus more dominant in the horoscope, it implies that you may leave yourself open for abusive relationships. If Mars is dominant, you may be sexually aggressive and act without consideration for anyone else's feelings. Your jealousy and generally contentious personality create problems in your relationships.

Venus Opposed Jupiter

Your insincerity toward others shows up as grandiose gestures toward strangers and people you barely know. As a result, most of your relationships are superficial. You're an extravagant spender and probably live well beyond your means. You need to cultivate balance.

Venus Opposed Saturn

It's difficult for you to reach out to others emotionally. You may be shy and withdrawn with the opposite sex. When you do marry, your partner may be emotionally cold and possibly older than you.

Your finances suffer setbacks. To overcome this challenge, you need to get in touch with your emotions.

Venus Opposed Uranus

You're attracted to eccentric people who provide excitement and unusual romance. Your relationships tend to begin and end abruptly. Emotionally, your need for personal freedom is constantly at odds with your need for companionship and stimulation. This aspect can suggest homosexuality. You need to find balance in your relationships and within yourself.

Venus Opposed Neptune

Your idealized notions about love, romance, and money prevent you from seeing things as they are. This aspect doesn't favor a harmonious marriage because your blind spots gradually undermine the relationship. Your expectations are unrealistic. This aspect may also indicate homosexual tendencies.

Venus Opposed Pluto

You need to be more aware of the motives for your actions. Are you trying to remake your significant other rather than working on yourself or your own beliefs? Why do you feel such a hunger for power over other people? What parts of yourself are you projecting onto others? Shed your dictatorial attitudes, control your passions, and stay clear of anyone involved in illegal activities. Ultimately, this will take you farther.

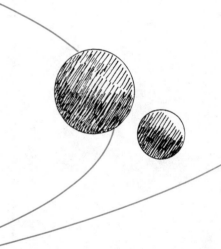

Venus Opposed North Node, Conjunct South Node

The problem in overcoming this aspect is that you get pleasure out of your habitual patterns regarding relationships and finances. Unless you seriously scrutinize these patterns and attempt to change them, it will be very difficult to overcome the restrictions of the South Node.

Venus Opposed Ascendant

Since this aspect means that Venus is conjunct the seventh-house cusp, it indicates happiness and success in marriage and partnerships. You derive much pleasure and happiness through your personal relationships, which allows you to relate well to society.

Venus Opposed Midheaven, Conjunct IC

Your deepest pleasure comes through your home life. Look for aspects to the tenth house that may create harmony or conflict with ambition goals because of your attachment to home and family.

Venus Opposed Part of Fortune

This one detracts from the benefits that would usually come through the Part of Fortune.

Mars Oppositions

This aspect infuses a horoscope with aggression, energy, and anger. Your reaction to sensitive issues is likely to be rash, impulsive, and hostile. You've got a short fuse. If other adverse aspects to Mars are present, you may experience physical danger.

Mars Opposed Jupiter

Forget gambling and financial speculation if this aspect is in your chart. To engage in either is to invite financial disaster. Scrutinize your own motives in the way you treat other people. Are you being friendly or gracious just to get something out of them? Your restlessness and thirst for adventure send you off on trips to foreign countries. These trips are exciting, but don't mitigate your restlessness.

Mars Opposed Saturn

These two planets are really at odds. Mars wants to rush ahead impulsively; Saturn wants to plan. You're frustrated and angry much of the time and resent others whose lives seem to be clicking along smoothly. Try to go out of your way to help others. This cooperative spirit will trigger more positive responses from other people toward you.

Mars Opposed Uranus

Your life is literally screaming for balance. You either work to the point of exhaustion or are consumed by laziness. Your explosions of temper are followed by remorse. You make sweeping changes in your life without taking the possible consequences into account. Step back, chill out, seek balance.

Mars Opposed Neptune

This one reads like a manual of things to avoid in your life. You're better off avoiding alcohol, drugs, sexual excesses, and clandestine activities of any sort. Make great efforts not to lie, cheat, or act in an underhanded way with anyone. Above all, examine your own motives.

Mars Opposed Pluto

The conflict here is rather like the struggle between Darth Vader and Luke Skywalker. Your personal desires are at war with your higher or spiritual self. In the charts of self-aware people, this aspect tests what you're made of: Do you bow to your personal desires or do you follow a higher path?

Mars Opposed North Node, Conjunct South Node

If you learn to control your flagrant disregard for social conventions and traditions, you'll break the restrictions and limitations that hold you back.

Mars Opposed Ascendant

This aspect means that Mars conjuncts the seventh-house cusp. A lot of energy goes into your close partnerships. Your confidence attracts dynamic partners whose ambitions match your own. Friction that arises may have to do with who calls the shots.

Mars Opposed Midheaven, Conjunct IC

Your home life may be riddled with arguments and disagreements. Your responsibilities toward your family may interfere with your career ambitions. Balance is key. Cultivate it.

Mars Opposed Part of Fortune

This indicates that you're accident prone and waste a lot of energy that would be better used defining what you want and then going after it.

Jupiter Oppositions

This aspect creates conflict in terms of expansion, religious and spiritual issues, higher education, the law, and any of the other affairs ruled by Jupiter.

Using Astrology with Other Divinatory Tools

As a divinatory tool, astrology is sometimes used in conjunction with tarot spreads—the way the tarot cards are laid out in a reading. Twelve cards are selected that represent an astrological house or area of your life.

The first card would relate to everything that concerns you personally; it would be analogous to the ascendant. The second card relates to your material resources and money. The third house relates to your siblings, friends, neighbors, the way you communicate, and short journeys.

If the cards are laid out in two straight lines, with six in the first row and six in the second, it's easy to spot certain aspects. Oppositions, for instance, would be seen in cards one and seven, two and eight, and so on through the houses. A trine, for instance, would be cards four, eight, and twelve.

The astrological spread is excellent for a yearly reading.

Jupiter Opposed Saturn

Professional success may be gradual with this aspect, but your perseverance and dedication make it happen. You may feel somewhat conflicted about your religious and spiritual beliefs. However, you benefit by working with your beliefs in a constructive, positive way. After all, your core beliefs determine your reality; the patterns in your horoscope merely reflect what is possible. If you cultivate and maintain optimism even when faced with enormous challenges, you stay well ahead of the game.

The negative parts of this aspect are greatly mitigated by trines, sextiles, and conjunctions to Saturn.

Jupiter Opposed Uranus

This aspect usually manifests in one of two ways. In a chart that lacks direction and focus, it may lead to involvement with revolutionary groups who do little more than make trouble and break rules. There can be involvement in religious cults and get-rich-quick scams. You may be prone to a purposeless wanderlust and flights of imagination that have no grounding in reality.

In a strong horoscope, this opposition can lead to great humanitarian efforts that instigate progressive change which affects large numbers of people. With this kind of characteristic in your birth chart, why would you even be tempted to follow a less evolved path?

Jupiter Opposed Neptune

Spiritual conflicts sometimes come up with this aspect. Illusory thinking and utopian ideals fail to find practical outlets unless there are positive aspects to Saturn. You may be too trusting of smooth talkers with devious plans. To overcome this aspect, ground yourself through physical and spiritual practices like yoga, meditation, or some sort of exercise program. Also cultivate pragmatism and look beyond the mask that other people present to the world.

Jupiter Opposed Pluto

Your religious and spiritual convictions are an intrinsic part of your life. Unfortunately, you try to convert everyone to your way of thinking about these issues and create considerable animosity. In extreme cases, this aspect indicates a complete disregard for laws and conventions.

Jupiter Opposed North Node, Conjunct South Node

You get a lot of pleasure out of your excesses, even though they're actually impeding your development. You would be better off trying to break your habits, whatever they are. Work to develop yourself through the house placement of the North Node.

Jupiter Opposed Ascendant

Since this means that Jupiter is conjunct the seventh-house cusp, it indicates good fortune generally in marriage and partnerships. Your significant other supports your ambitions and you benefit through the cooperation of others.

Jupiter Opposed Midheaven, Conjunct IC

Your family's generosity embraces all areas of your life. They fully support your professional and personal endeavors. Your spiritual beliefs are strongly influenced by your parents.

Jupiter Opposed Part of Fortune

To take full of advantage of your pot of gold, get an education. Always act with scrupulous integrity in your dealings with others.

Saturn Oppositions

With this aspect, look for conflicts concerning tradition, authority, discipline, structure, and anything that Saturn stands for.

Saturn Opposed Uranus

These two planets are locked in combat. They represent totally opposite traits. Discipline and structure are pitted against freedom and reform. Even though you demand total freedom from others, you tend to be dictatorial toward other people.

Saturn Opposed Neptune

Your sense of reality may be seriously flawed. You need to step back from your life and take a long, hard look at what you're doing and where you're going. Are you being deceitful or dishonest? Instead

of using subterfuge to deal with people, attempt to cultivate directness. The results may astonish you.

Saturn Opposed Pluto

If you're up to the task of personal evolvement, this aspect helps you do it, but only through hard work and discipline. It's a good idea to study this aspect in light of the rest of the chart. If criminal tendencies appear elsewhere, this aspect can confirm it.

Saturn Opposed North Node, Conjunct South Node

To evolve, you need to break with tradition and convention. Try the new, seek out the unconventional.

Saturn Opposed Ascendant

Since Saturn is conjunct the seventh-house cusp, this aspect indicates a solid marriage and partnerships. You may marry later in life or to someone older than you. You definitely shoulder your part of the overall responsibility.

Saturn Opposed Midheaven, Conjunct IC

Your childhood was probably far too strict and your early life, too rigid. You feel a heavy duty to your parents and/or family, which inhibits and frustrates your career ambitions.

Saturn Opposed Part of Fortune

To achieve what you want, you need to cultivate discipline and patience and be willing to work very hard. On the surface, it hardly looks like a pot of gold. But if you follow Saturn work ethics, your success will be beyond anything you dared imagine.

Uranus Oppositions

This is a tough aspect. It tends to bring about traumatic experiences that cause shattering disruptions and irresolute change. Once the pieces fall, you have to rebuild. The success or failure of your transition is entirely up to you. If you rise to the challenge, you succeed. If you don't, you fail.

Uranus Opposed Neptune

On a broad, societal scale, this aspect causes major disasters, upheaval, and turmoil. On a personal level, if either planet rules or is prominent in your chart, it creates deception and delusion related to the houses Uranus and Neptune occupy.

Uranus Opposed Pluto

In a generational sense, this aspect causes sweeping and destructive change in society: mobs, riots, the collective madness of people out of control. If Uranus or Pluto prevail in your chart, this aspect indicates sweeping and often violent changes in your life.

Uranus Opposed North Node, Conjunct South Node

You should temper your eccentric attitudes and try to go with the prevailing social flow. Even if it seems to block your personal freedom, it will do more for your freedom in the long run.

Uranus Opposed Ascendant

This aspect means that Uranus is conjunct the seventh-house cusp, so hold onto your hat! Your partnerships, romantic and otherwise, tend to happen suddenly. The partners you attract are exciting and unusual. Even if the relationships don't last long, it's a great adventure. When you're ready for stability in a relationship, try not to worry so much about your personal freedom. You may discover that love can be incredibly liberating.

Uranus Opposed Midheaven, Conjunct IC

This aspect means frequent moves and a disruptive home life. You need to be your own boss and call your own shots. Your hunger for personal freedom seems to interfere with everything else in your life.

Uranus Opposed Part of Fortune

The Uranus influence here nearly swallows up the benefits of the pot of gold. Your need for personal freedom creates so much tension that your headway is, at best, intermittent.

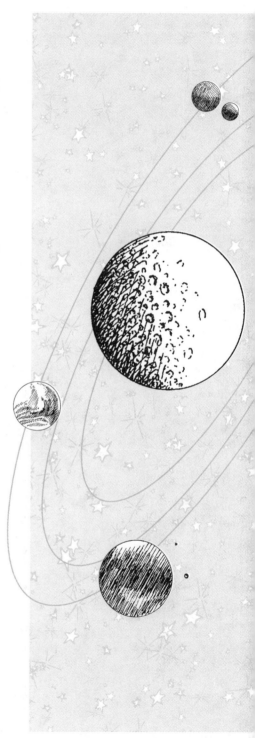

Neptune Oppositions

Even when Neptune is badly aspected, it's not all bad. Its better attributes—psychic ability, imagination, artistic talent—remain. The problem with the oppositions is that they create enormous tension and conflict between ideals and the reality.

Neptune Opposed Pluto

This one reads like a Shakespearean play. It comes down to the archetypal struggle between good and evil, destruction and regeneration. It last occurred in the early 1800s and will come around again in the twenty-first century. At its worst, it suggests an era of psychic and spiritual depravity, when sexual perversion and debauchery are the norm.

On the other hand, in the rubble of old belief systems, a spiritual alignment can take place that revolutionizes the way we perceive reality.

Neptune Opposed North Node, Conjunct South Node

Your habits are so ingrained that you may not even recognize them as habits. But unless you break them, you fail to evolve to your potential.

Neptune Opposed Ascendant

This aspect means Neptune is conjunct the seventh-house cusp and the news is far from good. Relationships are your blind spot, but you can be just as deceptive as the people you get involved with. Your intuitive ability is so finely tuned it can literally give you the inside track on whatever you focus on.

Neptune Opposed Midheaven, Conjunct IC

Your illusions about your career can work to your advantage once you recognize them. You may have an unstable home life where psychic abilities are the norm rather than the exception. Good. Take it for its worth, then head out into the world on your own and satisfy your spiritual hunger.

Neptune Opposed Part of Fortune

Usually, this indicates secrecy, treachery, and subterfuge associated with the benefits due you from your pot of gold.

Pluto Oppositions

Remember the marriage vow: for better or for worse. That's the nature of all aspects to Pluto, but is particularly true for oppositions.

Pluto Opposed North Node, Conjunct South Node

Even though I dislike the word karma, that's what this aspect is about. Old debts need to be repaid before you can progress or evolve through the area indicated by the house placement of the North Node. On some level, you'll recognize the debts when they enter your life and circumstances will force you to deal with them one way or another.

Pluto Opposed Ascendant

As an opposition here, Pluto conjuncts the seventh-house cusp. Relationships and partnerships may not be entirely pleasant for you. Get rid of your need to dominate, keep your spiritual self uplifted, and the influence will be diminished considerably.

Pluto Opposed Midheaven, Conjunct IC

There are easier ways to evolve as a spiritual being. But one thing is certain with this aspect: Much of your inner life will wrestle with the issue of spiritual evolvement. You may have to overcome an early childhood that was the equivalent of living under Hitler. You may get sidetracked. One way or another, the events and conditions in your life bring you back to the bottom line: Get it right this time around or you'll be back to try again.

Node and Part of Fortune Oppositions

North Node Opposite Ascendant

You gain advantages and benefits through your interactions in society. But you may feel blocked or challenged somehow by your most intimate relationships.

North Node Oppose Midheaven, Conjunct IC

You find support and strength through your family and home life; they are your refuge. Thanks to your problems with bosses and employers, you do best when self-employed.

North Node Opposed Part of Fortune

It's who you know that counts. You gain through social interactions, even though your soul cries out for solitude.

Part of Fortune Opposed Midheaven, Conjunct IC

Your greatest luck and success come through your family and domestic life, real estate, and all fourth-house affairs. Using this as your base, you can create advantages in your career through your own efforts.

Part of Fortune Opposed Ascendant

Since it's also conjunct the seventh-house cusp here, look to marriages and partnerships as your strengths.

Putting It All Together

CHAPTER
13

The Puzzle

Now that you have the astrological pieces, it's simply a matter of putting them together to create the holographic whole. With any chart, the interpretation should be a blend of your right and left brain, with logic and intuition working as partners.

To bolster that partnership, I recommend a simple breathing exercise that aids in shifting your awareness. Sit with your feet flat against the floor, take several deep breaths, then press your left nostril shut and breathe in through your right nostril. Hold the air to the count of eight, then slowly exhale through your left nostril. Repeat this process with your left nostril, then alternate three or four times.

Another technique that works is to use a three-dimensional image from one of the *Magical Eye* books. Once you perceive the image, your right and left brain are synchronized.

Now you're ready for your interpretation. Use the chart in Figure 13-1, which has appeared before in this book. Begin with the broad strokes, then gradually narrow your focus to include the aspects. Use the checklist to facilitate the interpretation.

Birth Chart Checklist

The Immediately Apparent
Jot down a word or phrase for each item in the checklist.

1. The Jones's pattern
2. Sun sign and house placement
3. Sun sign element and quadruplicity
4. Moon sign and house placement
5. Moon sign element and quadruplicity
6. Rising sign
7. Fourth house cusp (**IC**)
8. Seventh house cusp (descendant)
9. Tenth house cusp (**MC** or Midheaven)
10. What do the signs and degrees of the four angles tell you about this individual?

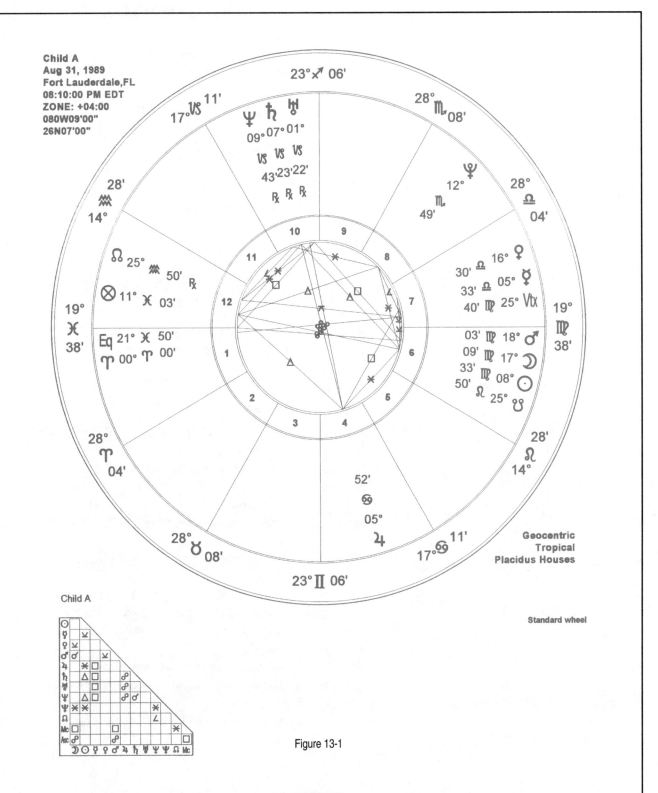

Child A
Aug 31, 1989
Fort Lauderdale, FL
08:10:00 PM EDT
ZONE: +04:00
080W09'00"
26N07'00"

Geocentric
Tropical
Placidus Houses

Standard wheel

Child A

Figure 13-1

11. Do any of the houses contain three or more planets? If so, which planets and which houses? What do these planets and houses tell you about the individual?
12. Are there exact conjunctions to any of the four angles? If so, which planets and angles? What does this tell you?
13. Your interpretation of these

The Next Layer

1. Sign and house placement of individual planets
2. Conjunctions
3. Squares
4. Trines
5. Sextiles
6. Does one planet or house have an unusual number of aspects to it?
7. House and sign placement of Nodes
8. House and sign placement of Part of Fortune
9. Oppositions

Questions to Consider

1. What does the ascendant tell you about the person's physical appearance and general health?
2. How does this individual handle money?
3. What kind of relationship exists with siblings?
4. What kind of relationship exists with the parents?
5. How does this person function creatively? What's the likelihood for children?
6. What kind of work might the individual do? What are his or her working conditions?
7. How does the person interact socially? What is the general quality of the person's intimate relationships and partnerships?
8. Does the chart show problems or benefits through inheritances? Taxes? Sexuality?
9. How is the individual's career likely to develop?
10. What kinds of friends and social groups does the person have?
11. What parts of himself or herself have been repressed?

Interpretation of the Sample Birth Chart

The chart fits the bowl pattern, that of a self-contained individual. The hemisphere emphasis, with six planets above the horizon, indicates an outgoing individual. Her primary contributions in life will be through the sixth and tenth houses, which contain six of the ten planets. She faces challenges from the unoccupied section of the chart—houses three through eleven.

The influence of Jupiter is vital in overcoming these challenges because it's the leading planet moving clockwise through the chart. The child will benefit through expansion of her mind, education, exposure to foreign countries and cultures, benevolence to others, and through all issues related to Jupiter.

As a double Virgo (both Sun and Moon), this child's mental faculties are finely honed. Since both are Mercury ruled, it's likely that she'll be involved in some form of communication. The double whammy from Virgo makes her fretful about small details related to her relentless pursuit of perfection in all she undertakes.

Her Pisces rising can create ambivalence in her decision-making if she allows it to. But it also gives her artistic interests and a deeply intuitive approach to life. As her intuition develops, so will her psychic ability. The Pisces Ascendant also gives her compassion, the capacity to step into someone else's shoes and feel what that person feels. It connects her to animals and to the sea.

Her Part of Fortune in the twelfth house insulates her against any enemies she might make. She benefits through illuminating her own unconscious.

Her home life and early childhood are generally harmonious. She shares a good relationship with her parents, in particular the nurturing parent. A lot of intellectual activity goes on in her home, both as a child and as an adult. Education and spiritual issues are important, as are all affairs related to Jupiter.

Jupiter is directly opposed to Saturn, Neptune, and Uranus, which creates tremendous tension in everything to do with her tenth house of careers and professions and her home life. This opposition also places additional pressure on the conjunctions of these three planets. She'll feel a deep need to clarify and structure her career goals, spiritual beliefs, and psychic impulses.

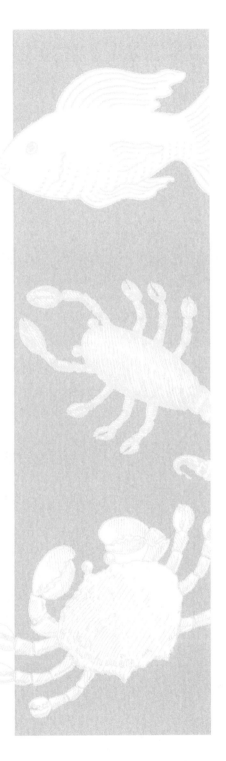

She may have to find a way to combine the three, which could be expressed through the opposition to Uranus. Of the three planets, it's the closest to her Midheaven. Because of Uranus she may create something completely unique and different that results in sudden, unexpected fame. Since these three planets are focused through Capricorn, this could benefit large numbers of people.

The conjunction of the Moon and Mars in her sixth house of health and work suggests that her emotions play a major role in her health. She feels everything intensely and when emotions are blocked, the blockage manifests somewhere in her body. If she doesn't learn to control her temper, then as a youngster it disrupts her friendships, and as an adult it strains her partnerships and intimate relationships.

Even though her Sun is conjunct the Moon at a wide nine degree orb, the influence should still be considered. She may be somewhat impulsive, which can be problematic in her work and in her relationships. It also means that her will is focused through her mind; once she brings her intellect to bear against something, watch out!

The South Node placement in the sixth house, with the North Node in the twelfth, suggests an unconscious bias concerning outdated work and health methods. These methods may have worked for her in past lives, but she needs to move beyond them this time around. Perhaps this is part of the reason why she has three planets in the sixth house.

The fact that the North and South Nodes are either trine or sextile to her **MC** and **IC** is good; both aspects strengthen career opportunities and the stability of her home life.

She should open herself to the natural rhythm and flow of life, rather than trying to compartmentalize her experiences. She tends to analyze and nitpick every little thing, and it would be better for her health if she released this tendency. Her work will probably be behind the scenes, but it could quite possibly become public or bring her public recognition. The sextile between her Sun and Jupiter helps her to expand her horizons and take advantage of opportunities that come her way.

With Venus and Mercury in Libra in the seventh house, her attraction to friends—and later, to partners—is likely to happen on

two levels. She's attracted to people with whom she feels a mental connection and also to people who share her artistic interests. It's possible that she will work closely with her spouse or a partner with whom she's romantically involved. The Libra means she tends to seek balance in her relationships.

Mercury in her seventh house is squared to four planets: Jupiter, Saturn, Uranus, and Neptune. This forms a T-square, with Mercury as the planet in the hot seat. This puts tremendous pressure on her to achieve in her career, either through her communication skills or her intellect.

She also has oppositions to her Ascendant from the Moon and Mars in Virgo. As a child, the Moon opposition makes her sensitive to other people's needs, moods, and motives. This sensitivity won't vanish in adulthood, but may become more finely tuned to the public pulse. It also strengthens the intuitive abilities in her chart.

In addition, the three planets in her tenth house are all in Capricorn, ruled by Saturn. This suggests that the eccentric genius of Uranus and the imagination of Neptune will somehow find structure, form, and practicality. Her Midheaven, however, is in Sagittarius and is ruled by Jupiter, which brings luck and expansion to the profession and career.

Pluto in Scorpio in the eighth house is powerfully placed. It suggests this child's life is transformed and regenerated through all the affairs governed by the eighth house: inheritances, joint finances, taxes, metaphysics, and the collective unconscious. This placement also gives her the ability to remember dreams and to use them to enhance the quality of her life.

By using the energy of Pluto here in a positive way, she'll transform not only her own life for the better but the lives of the people around her as well.

The sextiles to Pluto are vehicles she can use to harness all this Pluto energy. In fact, when you look at the aspect grid for her chart, the sextiles line up in a vertical row as tidy as the horizontal row of Mercury squares. Both of these aspects struck me immediately the first time I looked at her chart. It's as if her soul wanted to be absolutely sure that she didn't miss the point this time around.

She has six planets in earth signs in her chart divided equally between Virgo (mutable) and Capricorn (cardinal). The two air signs

Clinton and the Void-of-Course Moon

President Bill Clinton was elected under a void-of-course moon. The term, which can apply to any planet, means that no major aspect is made before the moon changes signs. In horary astrology, this suggests a lack of action. Many astrologers believe that it means Clinton will not complete his term in office.

While it remains to be seen if scandal spells the waning of the Clinton presidency, it's interesting to note that Clinton's popularity appears to be soaring. It's always wise to remember that all of astrology is ultimately subject to an individual's free will.

are both in Libra (cardinal), with a North Node in Aquarius (fixed). The two planets in water signs are in Scorpio (fixed) and Cancer (cardinal). Her Ascendant is also in a water sign, Pisces (mutable). Fire is conspicuously absent from her chart except for the lone South Node in Leo. Its partner in Aquarius is the only other fixed sign in the horoscope.

The earth planets ground her in reality and infuse her nature with practicality. They also help balance the mystical qualities of Pisces and mitigate some of the Piscean tendencies toward ambivalence and indecisiveness.

The concentration of Virgo in her sixth house of health and work creates a lot of nervous tension. This can manifest in the digestive tract because Virgo rules the intestines. As an infant, this can indicate colic; as an adult, it could mean stomach upsets— viruses, colitis, or diverticulitis—anything that affects the digestive system. Diet and nutrition are as important in the maintenance of her health as her emotions are.

Her only air planets both lie in the seventh house, which reinforce the mental and communication qualities of her partnerships and intimate relationships. These qualities are reinforced by Virgo on the seventh house cusp because Virgo is ruled by Mercury. Her challenge with partnerships is that she may be too adaptable, too willing to put her partners first and to adapt her needs to someone else's. She may compromise too readily to keep the peace.

The majority of her planets—six—lie in cardinal signs. This indicates that she's very good at initiating things, but may not be so good at finishing what she starts. This could explain why her soul or higher self chose the tension inherent in the four Mercury squares and the oppositions to Jupiter. This creates tension and friction that push her to finish what she begins.

The absence of fire in her chart makes it likely that at some point in her life she may have to assume a leadership role. It may be thrust on her by circumstances, by some seemingly external force, and she'll have to deal with it. It may also mean she'll be attracted to people who have a lot of fire in their charts or are "firelike" individuals, aggressive and self-confident.

It's interesting that three mutable planets lie in the sixth house; it indicates she's willing to adapt and to change her approach and understanding of the issues related to that house.

The only fixed planet in the entire chart is Pluto in Scorpio. This emphasizes the importance of getting it right. The cusp of that house, 28♍08, is also in a later degree, which seems to reiterate the whole theme.

Of the planets in critical degrees, only the Moon at 17♍09 qualifies. The critical degrees for any planet in Gemini, Virgo, Sagittarius, or Pisces are four and seventeen, so her Moon is certainly close enough. This strengthens the traits and house placement of her Virgo Moon.

The hemisphere emphasis is definitely to the right, or western side, of the chart, which makes it the classic bowl shape. However, the majority of the planets also lie above the horizon. This makes her sociable and outgoing.

This is the basic overview of the chart. The child is my daughter. Some of the tendencies in her chart showed up rather early; colic as an infant, for instance. She was an early reader. She has a passion for art, writing, and animals of all shapes and sizes. Frustration angers her, especially when she can't get things right. She has lively dreams that she can usually recall in vivid detail. She's compassionate and her feelings are easily hurt.

As a parent, I see her life taking shape. Sometimes it follows the proclivities in her chart and sometimes it doesn't. Like all of us, her free will prevails.

Reading Your chart

In the note section that follows, analyze your own chart. Be objective and logical, but allow your intuition its say. Listen to what the *patterns* tell you and follow the checklist before looking things up in the book. The writing part is important because you have to lay it out in black and white.

Notes on Your Chart

_____

_____

_____

_____

_____

_____

_____

_____

_____

_____

_____

_____

_____

_____

_____

_____

_____

_____

_____

_____

_____

_____

_____

Rectifying a Chart

CHAPTER 14

Your Birth Time

The first time I had my chart drawn up by a professional astrologer, she questioned my 3:00 P.M. birth time because it was exactly on the hour. She'd found that many people who claimed to have been born on the hour were actually born several minutes before or after.

This discrepancy can make a tremendous difference in a natal chart because your exact time of birth personalizes a chart. Your time of birth sets your Ascendant and your Midheaven and their opposites, the Descendant (cusp of the seventh house) and the IC (cusp of the fourth house). You have the four most important angles in a chart.

Nothing is more frustrating to an astrologer than to work up a natal chart based on the wrong time. Imagine it. You sit down with the person's chart in front of you, interpret it, and then the person looks at you as if you've lost your mind. "That's all wrong," he or she exclaims.

Without the time of birth, you can draw up a solar chart, a horoscope based on the date and place of birth. But this means that everyone born on that date, in that place, will have an identical chart. It isn't personalized. You don't have an accurate picture of the houses. You don't have the full picture.

There are ways to rectify or correct a chart if the exact time of birth is unknown. Some astrologers calculate a sunrise chart for the date of birth, which substitutes sunrise as the time of birth. This tells you what the planets were doing on that particular day, but applies to the person only in a general way.

Rectifying a chart takes time even if you have a computer. But it's worth the effort, particularly if the person whose chart you're rectifying plays an important role in your life.

What You Need

You need four to eight important dates in the individual's life. These might include the dates for:

1. Marriage or divorce
2. Death of a parent
3. Birth of a child or sibling
4. Death of a child or sibling
5. A significant move

6. A significant professional achievement or recognition for achievement
7. The onset of an illness
8. Any significant emotional event

In addition to dates, you need your intuition. It's much easier to allow your intuition to do its job if you know the person whose chart you're rectifying. But even if the individual is a stranger, his or her physical appearance should give you a clue about the Ascendant (first house cusp). A quick checklist might include:

1. Round face, with liquid eyes: Cancer
2. Thin or slender body, quick, restless movements: Gemini
3. Pale complexion, oval face, straight nose: Virgo
4. Exceptional height, very thin: Aquarius or Sagittarius
5. Full, compelling, almost mystical eyes; small or beautifully formed hands and feet: Pisces
6. Deep voice, dark hair that is frizzy, curly, and thick: Scorpio
7. Florid complexion, large bones, exuberant personality: Leo
8. Thick or prominent neck, stooped shoulders: Taurus
9. Ruddy complexion, any scar or mark on head or temples, bushy brows: Aries
10. Well-formed body, good looking, youthful appearance: Libra
11. Tendency to stoop, long or oval face, expressive eyes: Sagittarius
12. Body in which bones are prominent, thin neck, long or prominent nose: Capricorn

These attributes are suggested only as guidelines. Quite often, they don't fit at all because of the influence of the chart's ruling planet. Other times, one characteristic will fit but not the others. With experience you'll develop your own sense about individual rising signs.

The Process

If you don't use a computer, chart rectification is a tedious and time-consuming process. Bookstores with computer services generally charge a little more to rectify a chart, but it's worth the expense to have a correct chart.

Even the least expensive software programs usually have the capacity to run transit charts (where the planets are on a given date, time, and place). The computation takes seconds and makes it possible to run dozens of transits for the various dates you have.

How to Rectify a Chart

In my own family, I had birth times for my mother and sister, but not for my father. He was born at home on October 20, 1913, in Quincy, Illinois. His birth time doesn't appear on his birth certificate. His parents are long dead, his siblings don't recall what time he was born, and he doesn't have a clue. Since he is now eighty-four, I had several significant dates in his life that fit the above criteria.

Some astrologers recommend using events that occur before the age of thirty. This is fine if the person is only forty, but when you're dealing with someone older you limit yourself by using only early events.

I began my detective work by first running a solar chart, for the date and place of his birth, using noon as the birth time. The noon chart is in Figure 14-1. His Sun is in Libra; that wasn't going to change. But since it's at more than 26 degrees, the house placement would change. Venus and the Moon were also at late degrees, so their house placements would change as well. It seemed unlikely that the slower-moving planets would change houses.

I felt sure that his Gemini Moon would change into Cancer. Emotionally, his primary focus has been on home and family. He also has excellent intuition and has always loved the water. His Ascendant was never as clear to me.

Physically, he has always been slender, able to eat what he wants without gaining weight. He and my mother have been health conscious most of their lives. They were runners long before Jim Fixx made it fashionable and later gave up running for swimming six days a week. The health part of it smacks of Virgo rising; the thinness sounds like Gemini rising. But mentally, he seems more like an Aquarian rising, with a Uranian mind, highly original, idiosyncratic, and very bright—he was a member of Mensa, the high-IQ society.

Since my dad spent nearly thirty years living and working overseas, I felt sure there would be some indication of this in his ninth house (foreign travel and cultures) or on the cusp of the tenth (Midheaven). He and my mother have been married for fifty-five years, so it seemed logical I would find something in his seventh house or on the cusp to indicate this as well.

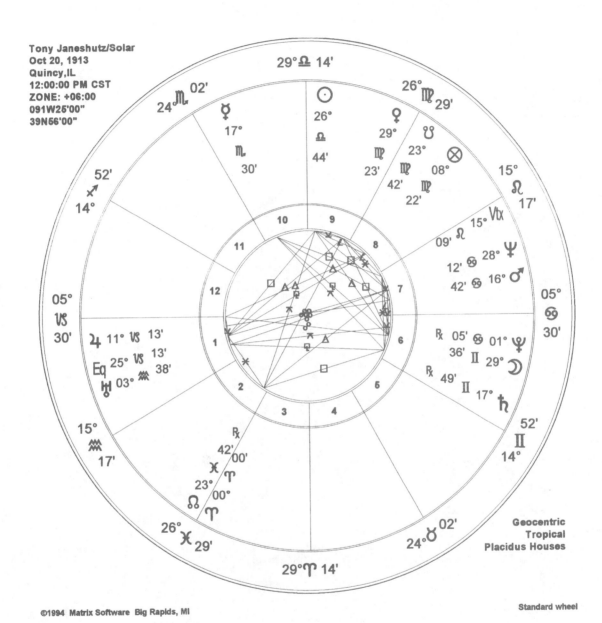

Tony Janeshutz/Solar
Oct 20, 1913
Quincy,IL
12:00:00 PM CST
ZONE: +06:00
091W25'00"
39N56'00"

29° ♎ 14'

26° ♍ 29'

24° ♏ 02'

☿ 17°
♏ 30'

⊙ 26°
♎ 44'

♀ 29°
♍ 23'

☊ 23°
♍ 08'

⊗

15°
♌ 17'

52'
♐ 14°

15° Vtx
09' ♌

♅ 12° ♋ 28°
42' ♋ 16° ♂

05°
♑ 30'

♃ 11° ♑ 13'
Eq 25° ♑ 13'
♅ 03° ♒ 38'

℞ 05' ♋ 01° ♆
36' ♊ 29° ☽

05°
♋ 30'

℞ 49' ♊ 17° ♄

15°
♒ 17'

℞ 42' 00'
♓ ♈
23' 00'
☋ ♈

52'
♊ 14°

26° ♓ 29'

29° ♈ 14'

24° ♉ 02'

Geocentric
Tropical
Placidus Houses

©1994 Matrix Software Big Rapids, MI

Standard wheel

Figure 14-1

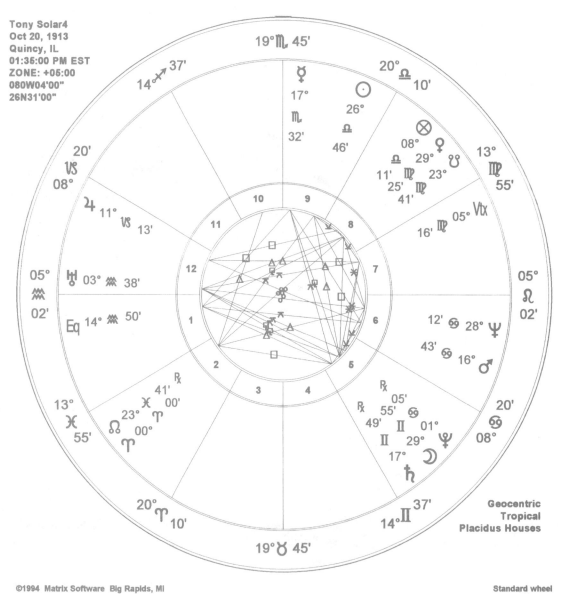

Standard wheel

Figure 14-2

He worked as an accountant until he was fifty, when my parents moved back to the United States, then became a real estate broker. This indicated two major clues that could show up in the Ascendant, the **MC**, or in the tenth or fourth houses. These points were also major transitions in his life, so I suspected they would show up somewhere in the chart, too.

In determining which dates to use in the rectification process, I chose: August 12, 1936, the day my father left Tulsa, Oklahoma for his new job in Caracas, Venezuela; December 12, 1942, the day he married my mother; June 7, 1947, my birth date; January 3, 1953, my sister's birth date; and November 27, 1963, the day he moved back to the U.S. I felt I needed at least one later date, so I chose December 20, 1996, the date my parents moved from Florida to Georgia.

I also knew that his mother was a Cancer (July 3, 1879) who died in February 1931. His father was an Aquarian (February 14, 1877) who died in July of 1929. I intended to use these as backup dates.

He was never particularly close to his parents, but has always been close to his own family. So based on the information I had, I decided to initially set up his chart so that my Sun, at 16♊12, would show up in his fifth house, which governs, among other things, first-born children. I knew from his solar chart that Uranus was in Aquarius that day. Given my father's IQ and the fact that his early childhood was disrupted, I felt fairly sure that Uranus would fall somewhere near the Ascendant.

For this reason, I set his ascendant at Aquarius, then played around with the time until the cusp of his fifth house was at 15♊25, which would put the sun on my birthdate in his fifth house. In Figure 14-2, notice that Uranus (♅) falls within two degrees of his ascendant. His sun in Libra (♎) occupies his ninth house, which would account for his residence and success abroad. His Part of Fortune and Venus fall in Virgo and Libra in the eighth house of other people's resources. This would fit with his profession as an accountant, someone who takes care of other people's money. Taurus on the cusp of the fourth house (**IC**) might also account for his profession as a real estate broker after the age of fifty.

The South Node also falls in the eighth house, with the North Node in the second. This would also fit. His financial gains have been made through his own efforts.

Other Criteria to Consider in Rectifying a Chart

1. What is the person's profession?
2. Does he or she come from a large or small family?
3. What are the parents' birth signs?
4. If married, what is the spouse's birth sign?
5. If the person has children, what is the birth sign of the oldest child?
6. Has the person remained fairly close to the place of birth? If not, were any of the moves to a foreign country?
7. Was the person born with a disability or handicap?
8. Does the individual have any special hobby or passion? What is it?
9. Does the person have any visible scars?
10. How is the individual's general health?
11. What are the individual's personal habits like? Is he or she a neat freak? Disorganized? Sloppy? A controller or manipulator?
12. What is the person's general attitude toward money—his or her own and others'?

After mulling it over for awhile, I realized the Aquarius rising bothered me. My father doesn't have the erratic eccentricity of that sign; he isn't forward thinking in terms of society's ideals the way most Aquarians are. His first profession as an accountant actually fit in better with a Virgo rising. Also, that would put me in his tenth house and my sister in his fifth house. She's not the first born, but I felt at least one of us should show up in the fifth house of children.

I ran the chart using a 2:30 A.M. birth time. In the chart in Figure 14-3, this places the North Node in the seventh house, a tribute to my parents' marriage. Also, his fourth house cusp (**IC**) is Sagittarius, indicating that he might well make his home in another country.

I ran transits to this birth chart for two of the major move dates—November 27, 1963 and December 20, 1996. In the 1963 transit, Uranus was within three degrees of an exact conjunction with his ascendant. This aspect nearly always demands that you re-invent your life and often indicates a move. Pluto formed a wide conjunction of seven degrees to the ascendant and was conjunct Uranus by four degrees. In other words, his personal life underwent upheaval, transformation, and regeneration.

In the transit for 1996, however, Pluto fell in his third house, within three degrees of his fourth house cusp. It was close enough to qualify as a conjunction, but not close enough for the kinds of changes he went through for that move. I changed the birth time to 2:15 A.M., which changed the fourth house cusp to 02♐35 and put the transiting Pluto (03♐39) at slightly more than one degree from an exact conjunction with the **IC**. This felt intuitively correct and once I ran transits to the other dates, everything fit well. The rectified chart is in Figure 14-4.

While this chart illustrates many facets of my father's experiences and the events in his life, it leaves other facets unexplained. This is precisely why rectification is, at best, imperfect.

If you're rectifying a chart for someone you don't know well, whose personal history isn't as well known to you as my father's is to me, then you need to ask questions. Use the checklists given in this chapter. Make up your own checklist. Get as much information about the person as you can. Be nosey. Poke around. Prod. Don't be shy.

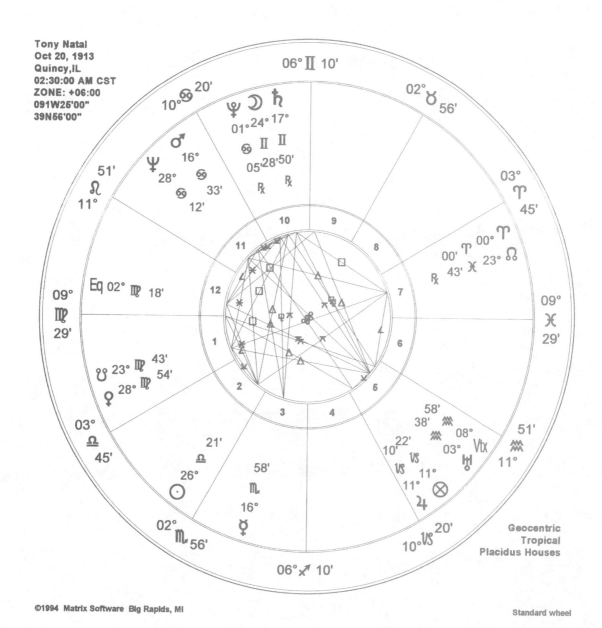

Figure 14-3

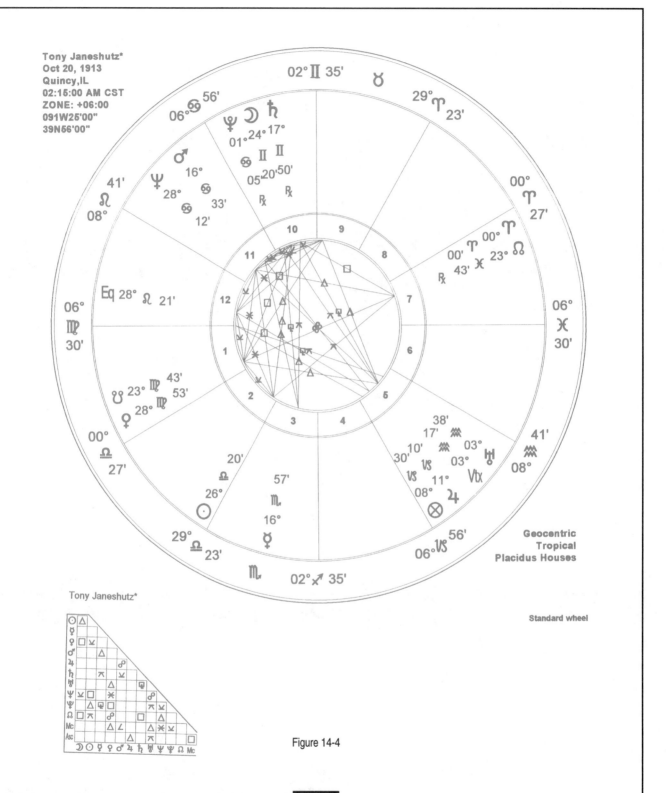

Tony Janeshutz*
Oct 20, 1913
Quincy,IL
02:15:00 AM CST
ZONE: +06:00
091W25'00"
39N56'00"

Geocentric
Tropical
Placidus Houses

Standard wheel

Tony Janeshutz*

Figure 14-4

After Words

There are more complex ways of rectifying a chart than the process I used. Astrologer Llewellyn George, in his tome *A to Z Horoscope Maker and Delineator* goes into quite a bit of detail on the procedure he used. But the bottom line is that no matter what procedure you use or how much intuition you bring to the process, *you'll never know for sure.*

The rectified chart is only an approximation, based on certain *patterns.* If you're a minute or two off, it may change the entire setup of the chart. Yet, in the end, astrology itself is no more or less than this. Just because a particular pattern prevails in a chart doesn't mean that it will manifest the way you see it.

As astrologer Phyllis Vega says, the litmus test with astrology always comes back to the case of identical twins. "If astrologers study identical twins born within one to two minutes of each other, they would have two people with virtually the same chart. Their lives would have marked similarities but major differences." Blame free will. I've never yet found a predictive system that doesn't break down at some point because of it.

Whenever I do a chart for someone—natal, transit, progressed, horary, whatever type of chart it is—I always preface my interpretation by saying that any chart is only a blueprint. It's a visual depiction of the soul's intent for this life. To ever be truly accurate, astrology would have to become multidimensional, somehow depicting the varied and numerous choices each of us faces in a lifetime, and following those many choices from beginning to end, birth to death.

So when you attempt to rectify a chart, remember that your tools are flawed. If your spouse's bout with cancer doesn't show up anywhere in his or her natal, transit, or progressed chart, don't blame astrology. Don't blame yourself. You can't anticipate or divine the way another person will manifest his or her deepest needs. You aren't zipped into that person's skin. You don't live inside them. The best you can do is to look for the broad patterns and interpret them to the best of your ability.

Roundup

CHAPTER 15

Relocating

Let's say you want to move, but aren't sure which area of the country would suit you. One way to gain insight into the issue is to do a relocation chart.

A relocation chart is done by using your date and time of birth with the longitude and latitude for the place you might move. If the city isn't far from your place of birth, the differences between the two charts will be small. But if a considerable distance is involved, the house cusps will change, which will also alter the placement of the planets in the houses.

The value in this is to choose a place where the planet placements emphasize your areas of interest. If you want to make more money, for instance, then you might benefit from a Jupiter placement in the second house. If you want to be more creative, then Jupiter in the fifth house might be better.

Transit Charts

This type of chart shows where the planets are at a particular time, day, and place. It's usually run concurrently with a natal chart and is intended to pinpoint patterns that are happening on a given day and shows how these patterns impact your natal chart.

With a transit chart, it's easy to spot broad patterns that might influence different areas of your family's life. From studying the transits to my daughter's chart, for instance, I know that when transiting Mars is crossing the cusp of her sixth or seventh house, she's more prone to colds, bronchitis, and respiratory problems in general. I know that when a Moon in Cancer transits my fourth house, I'm not in the mood to be away from home. When it's transiting my Midheaven, I usually experience conflicts between my home life and career.

The slower-moving planets exert influence for longer periods of times in transit charts. So if you're running weekly transits to your natal chart, you won't see much change in the areas they affect. But the faster-moving planets can be used for insight into daily events and situations.

Horary Astrology

This type of astrology is geared to answer specific questions. You can ask virtually anything. How's your job interview next week going to go? Where are your lost keys? How soon is your house going to sell? The first house or Ascendant represents the person asking the question and the issue you're asking about is found in the house that rules that issue. You use the ruling planet of each house and look for aspects these planets make to the Moon.

Horary astrology has hundreds of rules and I don't recommend using it until you've mastered the basics of natal astrology.

Election Charts

Are you getting married soon? Staring a business? Planning a vacation? Then an election chart may be just what you need to guide you about timing.

They are similar to horary charts, but with variations on the rules. Again, I recommend using them only after you've grasped the basics of natal astrology.

Progressions

If you want to know the broad patterns you'll be dealing with for the next year, then a progressed chart can shed light on the situation. A progressed chart is an update of your natal horoscope and the two should be read together. There are, however, many ways to do progressions and I recommend a thorough grounding in the basics before you attempt it.

Medical and Mundane Astrology

These two types of astrology are very specialized. Medical astrologers should be thoroughly versed in physiology, nutrition, anatomy, and medicine in general. Unless a medical astrologer is licensed to practice medicine, however, he or she can only diagnose. This type of astrology can be valuable in uncovering hidden factors in illness.

Predictive Astrology

There are a number of excellent books on the market that cover the specific types of astrology.

The classic book on transits is *Planets in Transit: Life Cycle for Living*, by Robert Hand.

Sasha Fenton's book, *Predicting the Future with Astrology*, covers transits, solar and lunar return charts, and progressed charts. Steven Forrest's *The Changing Sky* covers transits and progressions. It's a reader-friendly book and I recommend it for anyone studying predictive astrology.

Nancy Anne Hastings book, *The Practice of Prediction*, covers transits, secondary progressions, and solar arcs. Like Forrest's book, it's user friendly.

The Only Way to... series by Marion D. March and Joan McEvers covers all types of predictive astrology, with ample examples so that even the beginner can grasp the concepts.

Mundane astrology concerns world events—economy, wars, conflicts, elections, weather patterns, current events, anything that impacts a nation.

Parting Words

Millennial fever has arrived. The doom and gloom Nostradamus predicted centuries ago for the year 2000 seems to have taken root and flourished. There are now millennial TV shows, movies, books, and websites. On the web, you can track worldwide disasters—volcanic eruptions, earthquakes, hurricanes, tornadoes—then follow more links to more disasters. All this preoccupation with impending disaster hardly bolsters the optimism of the collective consciousness.

Each of us contributes to the collective consciousness. By doing our part as individuals to create a more humane and caring society and world, we make small changes in the collective sea. These small changes accrue, then earn interest. And eventually, if enough small changes are made, the momentum builds and a new belief system is born. In the end, it all comes back to free will.

INDEX